THE NEW CAMBRIDGE SHAKESPEARE

GENERAL EDITOR
Brian Gibbons

ASSOCIATE GENERAL EDITOR
A. R. Braunmuller

From the publication of the first volumes in 1984 the General Editor of the New Cambridge Shakespeare was Philip Brockbank and the Associate General editors were Brian Gibbons and Robin Hood. From 1990 to 1994 the General Editor was Brian Gibbons and the Associate General Editors were A. R. Braunmuller and Robin Hood.

THE FIRST QUARTO OF ROMEO AND JULIET

Two different versions of *Romeo and Juliet* were published during Shakespeare's lifetime: the first quarto of 1597, and the second quarto of 1599, on which modern editions are usually based. The earlier version was long denigrated as a 'bad' quarto, but recent scholarship sees in it a crucial witness for the theatrical practices of Shakespeare and his company. The shorter of the two versions by about one quarter, the first quarto has high-paced action, fuller stage directions than the second quarto, and fascinating alternatives to the famous speeches in the longer version. The introduction to this edition provides a full discussion of the origins of the first quarto, before analysing its distinguishing features and presenting a concise history of the 1597 version. The text is provided with a detailed collation and commentary which alert the reader to crucial differences between the first and the second quartos.

THE NEW CAMBRIDGE SHAKESPEARE

All's Well That Ends Well, edited by Russell Fraser
Antony and Cleopatra, edited by David Bevington
As You Like It, edited by Michael Hattaway
The Comedy of Errors, edited by T. S. Dorsch
Coriolanus, edited by Lee Bliss
Cymbeline, edited by Martin Butler
Hamlet, edited by Philip Edwards
Julius Caesar, edited by Marvin Spevack
King Edward III, edited by Giorgio Melchiori
The First Part of King Henry IV, edited by Herbert Weil and Judith Weil
The Second Part of King Henry IV, edited by Giorgio Melchiori
King Henry V, edited by Andrew Gurr
The First Part of King Henry VI, edited by Michael Hattaway
The Second Part of King Henry VI, edited by Michael Hattaway
The *Third Part of King Henry VI*, edited by Michael Hattaway
King Henry VIII, edited by John Margeson
King John, edited by L. A. Beaurline
The Tragedy of King Lear, edited by Jay L. Halio
King Richard II, edited by Andrew Gurr
King Richard III, edited by Janis Lull
Macbeth, edited by A. R. Braunmuller
Measure for Measure, edited by Brian Gibbons
The Merchant of Venice, edited by M. M. Mahood
The Merry Wives of Windsor, edited by David Crane
A Midsummer Night's Dream, edited by R. A. Foakes
Much Ado About Nothing, edited by F. H. Mares
Othello, edited by Norman Sanders
Pericles, edited by Doreen DelVecchio and Antony Hammond
The Poems, edited by John Roe
Romeo and Juliet, edited by G. Blakemore Evans
The Sonnets, edited by G. Blakemore Evans
The Taming of the Shrew, edited by Ann Thompson
The Tempest, edited by David Lindley
Timon of Athens, edited by Karl Klein
Titus Andronicus, edited by Alan Hughes
Troilus and Cressida, edited by Anthony B. Dawson
Twelfth Night, edited by Elizabeth Story Donno
The Two Gentlemen of Verona, edited by Kurt Schlueter
The Winter's Tale, edited by Susan Snyder and Deborah T. Curren-Aquino

THE EARLY QUARTOS

The First Quarto of Hamlet, edited by Kathleen O. Irace
The First Quarto of King Henry V, edited by Andrew Gurr
The First Quarto of King Lear, edited by Jay L. Halio
The First Quarto of King Richard III, edited by Peter Davison
The First Quarto of Othello, edited by Scott McMillin
The First Quarto of Romeo and Juliet, edited by Lukas Erne
The Taming of a Shrew: The 1594 Quarto, edited by Stephen Roy Miller

THE FIRST QUARTO OF ROMEO AND JULIET

Edited by
LUKAS ERNE

Professor of English
University of Geneva

CAMBRIDGE
UNIVERSITY PRESS

CAMBRIDGE UNIVERSITY PRESS
Cambridge, New York, Melbourne, Madrid, Cape Town,
Singapore, São Paulo, Delhi, Tokyo, Mexico City

Cambridge University Press
The Edinburgh Building, Cambridge CB2 8RU, UK

Published in the United States of America by Cambridge University Press, New York

www.cambridge.org
Information on this title: www.cambridge.org/9780521178266

First published 2007
First paperback edition 2011

A catalogue record for this publication is available from the British Library

ISBN 978-0-521-82121-6 Hardback
ISBN 978-0-521-17826-6 Paperback

THE NEW CAMBRIDGE SHAKESPEARE
THE EARLY QUARTOS

There is no avoiding edited Shakespeare, the question is only what kind of edit-ing. A Shakespeare play first assumed material form as the author's bundle of manuscript sheets. The company of players required a manuscript fair copy of the play (apart from the individual actors' parts). Into the fair copy were entered play-house changes, and the bookholder used it during each performance. However, none of Shakespeare's plays survives in contemporary manuscript form. There is one pas-sage in the manuscript of *Sir Thomas More* by Hand D which has been ascribed to Shakespeare himself, but this attribution remains in serious dispute. In short, there is no direct access to Shakespeare's play-manuscripts – there is only print, and this implies editing, since the first printed versions of Shakespeare were mediated by compositors and proofreaders at least, and sometimes also by revisers, bookholders, editors, censors, and scribes. The first printers used either the author's or a play-house manuscript or some combination of the two, although for several plays they used a scribal transcript by Ralph Crane, who is known to have habitually effaced and altered his copy.

There are certain quartos which are abbreviated, apparently because they are reported texts or derive from playhouse adaptation. These early quartos are not chosen as copy-texts for modern critical editions and are not readily available, though indispensable to advanced students of Shakespeare and of textual bibliography. Alongside the standard volumes in the New Cambridge Shakespeare, editions of selected quarto texts are to be published in critical, modern-spelling form, including early quartos of *King Lear*, *Hamlet*, *Richard III*, and *Othello*.

While the advanced textual scholar must work either with the rare, actual copies of the earliest printed editions, or with photo-facsimiles of them, there is more general interest in these texts and hence a need to present them in a form that makes them more generally accessible, a form that provides the most up-to-date and expert scholarship and engages with the key issues of how these texts differ from other quarto versions and from the First Folio, and to what effect. These are the precise aims of New Cambridge Shakespeare quartos.

Each volume presents, with the text and collation, an introductory essay about the quarto text, its printing, and the nature of its differences from the other early printed versions. There is discussion of scholarly hypotheses about its nature and provenance, including its theatrical provenance, where that issue is appropriate. The accompanying notes address textual, theatrical, and staging questions, following the spacious and handsome format of the New Cambridge Shakespeare.

BRIAN GIBBONS
General Editor

CONTENTS

ILLUSTRATIONS

PREFACE

In preparing this edition, I have incurred extensive debts to former editors of *Romeo and Juliet*, notably to Brian Gibbons, G. Blakemore Evans, John Jowett, and Jill L. Levenson. My work in progress was much facilitated and accelerated by the time I was allowed to spend at the Folger Shakespeare Library, and I wish to thank the Library for granting me a short-term fellowship and its staff for their assistance. Patrick Cheney, Jeremy Ehrlich, Andrew Gurr, and M. J. Kidnie kindly read the Introduction and helped me with many incisive comments and suggestions. Sarah Stanton offered generous advice and support, while Brian Gibbons's patience and scholarship saved me from many mistakes. My thinking on specific points of this edition was shaped by conversations with David Carnegie, Jeremy Ehrlich, Steven May, Barbara Mowat, William Sherman, James Siemon, and Valerie Wayne, and I am grateful to all of them. I further wish to thank Emma Depledge, who helped me correct the typescript at a late stage, Giorgio Melchiori, who granted me access to an article of his prior to appearance in print, and Barry Kraft of the Oregon Shakespeare Festival, who sent me material about the *Romeo and Juliet* production he directed. For various other kindnesses I am grateful to Pascale Aebischer, Y. S. Bains, Helen Hargest, Jill Levenson, and Michael Suarez, SJ. Finally, I wish to thank Katrin, Rebecca, and Raphael, who have made work on this edition much more pleasurable than it might have been.

ABBREVIATIONS AND CONVENTIONS

Unless otherwise stated, the edition of *Romeo and Juliet* cited is that of the New Cambridge Shakespeare (referred to as 'NCS') of 2003 (2nd edn; 1st edn, 1984), edited by G. Blakemore Evans. Other editions and critical works are cited under the editor's or author's name (Pope, Hoppe). Shakespeare's works are cited in this edition in the abbreviated style of the series, modified slightly from the *Harvard Concordance to Shakespeare*. Quotations from other plays of Shakespeare are taken from the Oxford *Complete Works* (1986), under the general editorship of Stanley Wells and Gary Taylor.

1. Shakespeare's works

Ado	*Much Ado About Nothing*
Ant.	*Antony and Cleopatra*
AWW	*All's Well That Ends Well*
AYLI	*As You Like It*
Cor.	*Coriolanus*
Cym.	*Cymbeline*
Err.	*Comedy of Errors*
Ham.	*Hamlet*
1H4	*The First Part of King Henry the Fourth*
2H4	*The Second Part of King Henry the Fourth*
H5	*King Henry the Fifth*
1H6	*The First Part of King Henry the Sixth*
2H6	*The Second Part of King Henry the Sixth*
3H6	*The Third Part of King Henry the Sixth*
H8	*Henry the Eighth*
JC	*Julius Ceasar*
John	*King John*
LLL	*Love's Labours Lost*
Lear	*The Tragedy of King Lear*
Lucr.	*The Rape of Lucrece*
Mac.	*Macbeth*
MM	*Measure for Measure*
MND	*A Midsummer Night's Dream*
MV	*The Merchant of Venice*
Oth.	*Othello*
Per.	*Pericles*
PP	*The Passionate Pilgrim*
R2	*King Richard the Second*
R3	*King Richard the Third*
Rom.	*Romeo and Juliet*
Shr.	*The Taming of the Shrew*
Son.	*Sonnets*
STM	*Sir Thomas More*

Temp.	*The Tempest*
TGV	*The Two Gentlemen of Verona*
Tim.	*Timon of Athens*
Tit.	*Titus Andronicus*
TN	*Twelfth Night*
TNK	*The Two Noble Kinsmen*
Tro.	*Troilus and Cressida*
Wiv.	*The Merry Wives of Windsor*
WT	*The Winter's Tale*

2. Other works cited, general references, and abbreviations

Works mentioned once in the Introduction, collation, or commentary appear there with full bibliographical information. Those which appear several times are abbreviated to the short form given below.

Abbott	E. A. Abbott, *A Shakespearian Grammar*, 1894
Andrews	*'Romeo and Juliet': Critical Essays*, ed. John F. Andrews, New York, 1993
Blake	N. F. Blake, *A Grammar of Shakespeare's Language*, New York, 2002
Boswell	*The Plays and Poems of William Shakespeare*, ed. James Boswell, 21 vols., 1821
Brooke	Arthur Brooke, *The Tragicall Historye of Romeus and Juliet*, in Bullough, vol. 1, pp. 269–363
Bullough	Geoffrey Bullough, *Narrative and Dramatic Sources of Shakespeare*, 8 vols., London, 1957–75
Cam.	*The Works of William Shakespeare*, ed. W. G. Clark, John Glover, and W. A. Wright, 9 vols., 1863–6 (Cambridge)
Capell	*Shakespeare's Comedies, Histories and Tragedies*, ed. Edward Capell, 10 vols., 1767–8
Collier	*The Works of William Shakespeare*, ed. John Payne Collier, 8 vols., 1842–4
conj.	conjecture
Crystal	David Crystal and Ben Crystal, *Shakespeare's Words: A Glossary and Language Companion*, London, 2002
Daniel, *Parallel Texts*	*'Romeo and Juliet': Parallel Texts of the First Two Quartos*, ed. P. A. Daniel, 1874
Daniel (Q1)	*'Romeo and Juliet': Reprint of Q1 1597*, ed. P. A. Daniel, 1874
Dent	R. W. Dent, *Shakespeare's Proverbial Language: An Index*, Berkeley, 1981
Dessen and Thomson	Alan C. Dessen and Leslie Thomson, *A Dictionary of Stage Directions in English Drama, 1580–1642*, Cambridge, 1999.
Douai MS.	MS. of *Romeo and Juliet* (1694) in Douai Public Library
Dowden	*Romeo and Juliet*, ed. Edward Dowden, 1900 (Arden Shakespeare)
Duncan-Jones	Katherine Duncan-Jones, review of Oxford, in *Review of English Studies* 52 (2001), 446–8

Duthie	G. I. Duthie, 'The text of Shakespeare's *Romeo and Juliet*', *SB* 4 (1951–2), 3–29
Dyce	*The Works of William Shakespeare*, ed. Alexander Dyce, 2nd edn, 9 vols., 1864–7
Eichhoff	Theodor Eichhoff, *Unser Shakespeare: Beiträge zu einer wissenschaftlichen Shakespeare-Kritik, vol. 3, Ein neues Drama von Shakespeare: Der älteste, bisher nicht gewürdigte Text von Romeo and Juliet*, Halle, 1904
Erne	Lukas Erne, *Shakespeare as Literary Dramatist*, Cambridge, 2003
Erne and Kidnie	Lukas Erne and Margaret Jane Kidnie, eds., *Textual Performances: The Modern Reproduction of Shakespeare's Drama*, Cambridge, 2004
F1	Mr William Shakespeares Comedies, Histories, and Tragedies, 1623 (the First Folio)
F2	The Second Folio, 1632
F3	The Third Folio, 1663
F4	The Fourth Folio, 1685
F	F1 to F4
Farley-Hills	David Farley-Hills, 'The "bad" quarto of *Romeo and Juliet*, *S.Sur.* 49 (1996), 27–44
Field	*The Tragedie of Romeo and Juliet: The Players' Text of 1597, with the Heminges and Condell Text of 1623*, ed. B. Rush Field, The Bankside Shakespeare, gen. ed. Appleton Morgan, vol. 5, New York, 1889
Furness	*Romeo and Juliet*, ed. Horace Howard Furness, 1871 (Variorum)
Furness (Q1)	in Furness (see above), pp. 303–64
Gibbons	*Romeo and Juliet*, ed. Brian Gibbons, 1980 (New Arden)
Goldberg	Jonathan Goldberg, '"What? in a names that which we call a rose": the desired texts of *Romeo and Juliet*', in *Crisis in Editing: Texts of the English Renaissance*, ed. Randall McLeod, New York, 1994, pp. 173–202
Gurr, *Shakespeare Company*	Andrew Gurr, *The Shakespeare Company, 1594–1642* Cambridge, 2004
Hanmer	*The Works of Shakespear*, ed. Thomas Hanmer, 6 vols., 1743–4
Hart	Alfred Hart, *Stolne and Surreptitious Copies: A Comparative Study of Shakespeare's Bad Quartos*, Melbourne, 1942
Hoppe	Harry R. Hoppe, *The Bad Quarto of 'Romeo and Juliet': A Bibliographical and Textual Study*, Ithaca, 1948
Hosley	*Romeo and Juliet*, ed. Richard Hosley, 1954 (New Yale)
Hosley, 'Upper stage'	Richard Hosley, 'The use of the upper stage in *Romeo and Juliet*', *SQ* 5 (1954), 371–8
Hubbard	*The First Quarto Edition of Shakespeare's 'Romeo and Juliet'*, ed. Frank G. Hubbard, Madison, WI, 1924
Hudson	*The Work* [sic] *of Shakespeare*, ed. Henry N. Hudson, 11 vols., Boston, 1851–6

Irace	Kathleen O. Irace, *Reforming the 'Bad' Quartos: Performance and Provenance of Six Shakespearean First Editions*, Newark, 1994
JEGP	*Journal of English and Germanic Philology*
Johnson	*The Plays of William Shakespeare*, ed. Samuel Johnson, 8 vols., 1765
Jowett	*Romeo and Juliet*, ed. John Jowett, in *William Shakespeare, The Complete Works*, gen. eds. Stanley Wells and Gary Taylor, Oxford, 1986; with textual notes in *William Shakespeare: A Textual Companion*, ed. Stanley Wells and Gary Taylor with John Jowett and William Montgomery, Oxford, 1987, pp. 288–305
Jowett, 'Chettle'	John Jowett, 'Henry Chettle and the first quarto of *Romeo and Juliet*', *PBSA* 92 (1998), 53–74
Keightley	*The Plays of William Shakespeare*, ed. Thomas Keightley, 6 vols., 1864
Kittredge	*The Complete Works of Shakespeare*, ed. G. L. Kittredge, 1936
Knight	*The Pictorial Edition of the Works of Shakespeare*, ed. Charles Knight, 8 vols., 1838–43
Levenson	in Oxford, pp. 359–429
Levenson and Gaines	*Romeo and Juliet, 1597*, ed. Jill L. Levenson and Barry Gaines, Malone Society Reprints, Oxford, 2000
Loehlin	*Romeo and Juliet*, ed. James N. Loehlin, Shakespeare in Production, Cambridge, 2002.
Malone	*The Plays and Poems of William Shakespeare*, ed. Edmund Malone, 10 vols., 1790
Marlowe	*The Complete Works of Christopher Marlowe*, 5 vols, Oxford, 1987–98
MaRDiE	*Medieval and Renaissance Drama in England*
Melchiori	Giorgio Melchiori, 'The music of words: from madrigal to drama and beyond: Shakespeare foreshadowing an operatic technique', in *Italian Culture in Early Modern English Drama: Rewriting, Remaking, Refashioning*, ed. Michele Marrapodi, Aldershot, 2007, forthcoming
Mommsen	*Shakespeare's Romeo and Julia: Eine kritische Ausgabe des überlieferten Doppeltextes mit vollständiger Varia Lectio bis auf Rowe*, ed. Tycho Mommsen, Oldenburg, 1859
Nashe	*The Works of Thomas Nashe*, ed. Ronald B. McKerrow, corrected reissue ed. F. P. Wilson, 5 vols. Oxford, 1958
OED	*The Oxford English Dictionary*
Onions	C. T. Onions, *A Shakespeare Glossary*, rev. Robert D. Eagleson, Oxford, 1986
Oxford	*Romeo and Juliet*, ed. Jill L. Levenson, 2000 (Oxford Shakespeare)
PBSA	*The Papers of the Bibliographical Society of America*
Pope	*The Works of Shakespear*, ed. Alexander Pope, 6 vols., 1723–5
Q1	The first quarto edition, 1597 (*An Excellent conceited Tragedie of Romeo and Iuliet*)

Q2	The second quarto edition, 1599 (*The Most Excellent and lamentable Tragedie, of Romeo and Iuliet*)
Q3	The third quarto edition, 1609
Q4	The fourth quarto edition, undated (c. 1618–26)
Q5	The fifth quarto edition, 1637
Q	Q1 to Q5
RES	*Review of English Studies*
Ringler	William Ringler, 'The number of actors in Shakespeare's early plays', in *The Seventeenth Century Stage*, ed. G. E. Bentley, Chicago, 1968
Rowe	*The Works of Mr. William Shakespeare*, ed. Nicholas Rowe, 6 vols., 1709
SB	*Studies in Bibliography*
SD	stage direction
SH	speech heading
Singer	*The Dramatic Works of William Shakespeare*, ed. Samuel Weller Singer, 10 vols., 2nd edn 1856
Spencer	*Romeo and Juliet*, ed. T. J. B. Spencer, 1967 (Penguin)
SQ	*Shakespeare Quarterly*
S.St.	*Shakespeare Studies*
S.Sur.	*Shakespeare Survey*
Staunton	*The Plays of Shakespeare*, ed. Howard Staunton, 3 vols., 1858–60
Steevens	*The Plays of William Shakspeare*, ed. Samuel Johnson and George Steevens, 10 vols., 1773
Steevens (1778)	*The Plays of William Shakspeare*, ed. George Steevens, 10 vols., 1778
subst.	substantively
Theobald	*The Works of Shakespeare*, ed. Lewis Theobald, 7 vols., 1733
Thomson	Leslie Thomson, '"With patient ears attend": *Romeo and Juliet* on the Elizabethan stage', *Studies in Philology*, 92 (1995), 230–47
Ulrici	*Romeo and Juliet*, ed. Hermann Ulrici, 1853
Urkowitz	Steven Urkowitz, 'Two versions of *Romeo and Juliet* 2.6 and *Merry Wives of Windsor* 5.5.215–45: an invitation to the pleasure of textual/sexual di(per)versity', in *Elizabethan Theater: Essays in Honor of S. Schoenbaum*, ed. R. B. Parker and S. P. Zitner (London, 1996), pp. 222–38
Warburton	*The Works of Shakespear*, ed. William Warburton, 8 vols., 1747
Watts	*An Excellent Conceited Tragedie of Romeo and Juliet*, ed. Cedric Watts, 1995 (Shakespearean Originals: First Editions)
Wells, *Modernizing*	Stanley Wells, *Modernizing Shakespeare's Spelling*, with Gary Taylor, *Three Studies in the Text of 'Henry V'*, Oxford, 1979
White	*The Works of William Shakespeare*, ed. Richard Grant White, 12 vols., 1857–66

Williams	*The Most Excellent and Lamentable Tragedie of Romeo and Juliet*, ed. George Walton Williams, Durham, NC, 1964
Williams, *Dictionary*	Gordon Williams, *A Dictionary of Sexual Language and Imagery in Shakespearean and Stuart Literature*, 3 vols., London, 1994
Wilson–Duthie	*Romeo and Juliet*, ed. John Dover Wilson and George Ian Duthie, 1955 (New Shakespeare)
Wright	George T. Wright, *Shakespeare's Metrical Art*, Berkeley, 1988

INTRODUCTION

Not too long ago, the 1597 first quarto (Q1) of *Romeo and Juliet* was simply considered a 'bad quarto', and its alleged badness largely disqualified it from critical and editorial circulation. It was referred to and discussed in introductions to editions of *Romeo and Juliet*, and editors ransacked it for what it could tell us about the play. Those who closely engaged with it realised that it was in some ways a text with remarkable qualities, but as long as labels such as 'bad quarto', 'memorial reconstruction' or 'piratical publication' clung to it, it remained in the margins of Shakespeare scholarship and was rarely mentioned in the criticism.

In more recent times, however, the New Bibliographical paradigm which alleged the text's badness has come under attack from various quarters, and, as a result, our view of the 'bad quartos' is about to change. It is becoming more generally recognised that certain of these texts have important things to tell us about early modern drama. Stephen Orgel has pointed out that there is 'very little evidence that will reveal to us the nature of a performing text in Shakespeare's theater; but there is a little. There are the "bad" quartos, whose evidence, in this respect, is not bad, but excellent'.[1] Despite the critical and scholarly turn in Shakespeare studies towards performance since the last decades of the last century, editorial tradition may have prevented us from recognising the true importance of the 'bad' quartos insofar as they reflect, however imperfectly, the plays as they were performed. As Orgel adds, 'If we were less exclusively concerned with establishing texts and more concerned with the nature of plays, these [the 'bad' quartos] would be the good quartos.'[2] Similarly, Gary Taylor has asserted that a 'bad' quarto 'may represent a more finished, dramatic, socialized phase of the text than that preserved in an edition printed from Shakespeare's foul papers'.[3]

Among the 'bad' quartos, Q1 *Romeo and Juliet* is a particularly important publication, with a carefully printed text, exciting stage directions which may well shed light on the play's early modern staging,[4] a shorter, tightened text with considerable pace, and an important number of intelligent alternative readings. Indeed, Q1 *Romeo and Juliet* is in some respects the best witness we have for the dramatic and theatrical practices of Shakespeare and of his company.

Q1 *Romeo and Juliet* is a crucially important witness precisely because of its difference from the longer, better-known version. A writing process is rarely stable,

---

[1] Stephen Orgel, *The Authentic Shakespeare and Other Problems of the Early Modern Stage* (London, 2002), p. 22.

[2] Ibid.

[3] Stanley Wells and Gary Taylor, with John Jowett and William Montgomery, *William Shakespeare: A Textual Companion* (Oxford, 1987), p. 28.

[4] See my discussion of the article by John Jowett, below.

I

and the textual life of a play in the theatre is even less so: early modern play-texts were corrected, revised, abridged, changed.[5] The textual material still extant today is naturally a very imperfect record of the literary and theatrical genesis and transformations of Shakespeare's plays. A printed text preserves only a part, and often a small part, of the history of a play, and its relationship to the words spoken onstage by Shakespeare and his fellow actors is one we cannot hope to guess, on the basis of the extant printed texts. All these problems and limitations granted, *Romeo and Juliet*, by preserving not only the quarto on which modern editions are usually based but also the first quarto, may allow us to glimpse, in the gap that separates one quarto from the other, some of the transformations a Shakespeare play underwent in the first years of its existence.

Accordingly, this edition, even though it is an edition of *The First Quarto of Romeo and Juliet*, does not advocate study of the first quarto for its own sake. Q1 and Q2 throw interesting light on each other, and it is at their peril that students study Q1 without awareness of Q2 – or Q2 without awareness of Q1. Therefore, throughout introduction, collation, and commentary, I propose to study the first quarto by constantly keeping an eye, as it were, on the second quarto. By providing separate critical editions of the first two early quartos, the New Cambridge Shakespeare series invites comparative study of the different versions of *Romeo and Juliet*.

What, broadly, is the difference between the first and the second quartos of *Romeo and Juliet*? The difference in length is conspicuous: with some 700 lines more than Q1, Q2 is almost one third longer than Q1. The two versions have the same characters and dramatise the same events in the same order. Contrast the case of *Hamlet* and *King Henry V*: Q1 *Hamlet* contains a scene unique to it which summarises material present in other scenes in Q2 and the Folio; Q1 *King Henry V* omits a number of notable characters present in the Folio; *Romeo and Juliet* presents a different case. The Chorus at the end of Act 1 (1.5.144–57) is not in Q1, and a short sequence with the Capulet Serving-men (1.5.1–14) is similarly absent from the shorter text, but, apart from these two, all other dramatic movements in Q2 have their equivalents in Q1. Some of these movements are considerably shorter, though, and a number of Q2 speeches disappear entirely from Q1. Q1 also does not include at all or condenses a great many short or very short passages present in Q2. Each Q1 scene is shorter than its equivalent in the longer text, Scene 11 being less than half and Scene 2 being more than 90 per cent of Q2, with the relative length of the other scenes being somewhere in between. In fact, the only part of Q1 that is longer than Q2 is the stage directions, which tend to be more detailed and more numerous in the shorter text.

Length constitutes an important but by no means the only difference between the two versions. Q1's language often departs from Q2's, the difference being at times a matter of isolated words but at others substantial. In general, the relationship between the two texts is relatively close in the first seven scenes (1.1 to 2.4) but becomes less so in the remainder of the play. Here is a representative example of

[5] See the section on 'The mobile text' in Levenson, pp. 103–25.

parallel passages from early on in the play, excerpted from Romeo's conversation
with Benvolio in the first scene:

> Love is a smoke made with the fume of sighs,
> Being purged, a fire sparkling in lovers' eyes,
> Being vexed, a sea nourished with loving tears.
> What is it else? a madness most discreet,
> A choking gall, and a preserving sweet.
>
> (Q2, 1.1.181–5)

> Love is a smoke raised with the fume of sighs,
> Being purged, a fire sparkling in lovers' eyes,
> Being vexed, a sea raging with a lover's tears.
> What is it else? A madness most discreet,
> A choking gall, and a preserving sweet.
>
> (Q1, 1.118–22)

In the first line, Q1 substitutes 'raised' for Q2's 'made', and in third line, the second
quarto has 'nourished' and 'loving tears' where Q1 reads 'raging' and 'a lover's tears'.
Otherwise, the two passages are substantively identical.

Here, by contrast, are parallel passages, also from Romeo's part, more typical of
the latter part of the play:

> I do remember an apothecary,
> And hereabouts 'a dwells, which late I noted
> In tattered weeds, with overwhelming brows,
> Culling of simples; meagre were his looks,
> Sharp misery had worn him to the bones;
> And in his needy shop a tortoise hung,
> An alligator stuffed, and other skins
> Of ill-shaped fishes, and about his shelves
> A beggarly account of empty boxes,
>
> (Q2, 5.1.37–45)

> As I do remember,
> Here dwells a 'pothecary whom oft I noted
> As I passed by, whose needy shop is stuffed
> With beggarly accounts of empty boxes;
> And in the same an alligator hangs,
>
> (Q1, 18.28–32)

Despite its comparative brevity, the passage in Q1 is a recognisable version of that in
Q2: 'I do remember', 'dwells', 'I noted', 'needy shop', 'stuffed', 'beggarly account[s]
of empty boxes', 'an alligator', and forms of the verb 'to hang' are present in both
passages. Nevertheless, the wording of the two passages is altogether different. In
Q2, the alligator is stuffed and a tortoise hangs in the shop, but in Q1 it is the shop that
is stuffed and the alligator hangs, whereas the tortoise has disappeared altogether.
The differences are thus far more substantial than in the first parallel passages I
quoted. The relationship can be looser still, as exemplified by Capulet's lament over
Juliet's seemingly dead body in Scene 17 (4.5):

Despised, distressèd, hated, martyred, killed!
Uncomfortable time, why cam'st thou now
To murder, murder our solemnity?
O child, O child! my soul, and not my child!
Dead art thou. Alack, my child is dead,
And with my child my joys are buried.

                    (Q2, 4.5.59–64)

Cruel, unjust, impartial destinies,
Why to this day have you preserved my life?
To see my hope, my stay, my joy, my life,
Deprived of sense, of life, of all by death?
Cruel, unjust, impartial destinies!

                    (Q1, 17.85–9)

The syntax and the rhetoric of the two passages are in some ways similar, but their wording is not. The two speeches may occur at the same point in the play, but they are linguistically independent of each other.

   All of the above examples are in verse, but parts of Q1 and Q2 are in prose and, at times, one text prints a passage in prose which the other text has as verse. Juliet's mother has several prose speeches in Scene 3 of Q1 which are printed as verse in Q2. The same applies to the Nurse in Scene 4 (1.5). Conversely, Q1 prints the Queen Mab speech (Sc. 4; 1.4) as verse, whereas Q2 has prose. When it comes to the texts' dramatic verse, Q1 and Q2, like Shakespearean drama in general,[6] are predominantly in iambic pentameters but with a share of short and long lines. It is noticeable, however, that Q1's lines, on the whole, are metrically more irregular than Q2's. The parts of Capulet and the Nurse in scene 14 (3.5) might serve as good examples to show the occasional irregularity of the verse in Q1 in comparison with Q2.

   This preliminary survey of differences between Q1 and Q2 of *Romeo and Juliet* has so far concentrated on length and language, but other elements could be added to this. The two versions usually assign the same speeches to the same characters, but on a few occasions they do not. For instance, in the first scene, two Q1 lines given to Montague's Wife are spoken by her husband in Q2, while in Scene 5 (2.1), Mercutio is given a short passage attributed to Benvolio in the longer text. Characters usually enter and exit in the same order and at roughly the same point in the two texts, but here, too, there are exceptions. In the final scene, for example, both Balthasar and Friar Laurence are arrested and brought onstage by the watch, but while Q1's Balthasar precedes the Friar, in Q2 Balthasar follows after him.

   In comparing Q1 to Q2, I have consciously chosen to present a value-neutral comparison, a comparison that refrains from judging the relative merit and explaining the likely reasons for the differences between the two texts. I have done so because responses to the first quarto have too often been marred or at least inflected by a *parti pris* regarding their relative value. If we are predisposed to think of Q2 as a 'good' and of Q1 as a 'bad' text, i.e. a text that has – say – been cobbled together by

<hr />

[6] See Wright, pp. 116–48.

dishonest pirates, then we will be tempted, when the two versions differ, to prefer the presumed 'good' to the 'bad'. The opposite of this prejudiced assumption about Q1 has also happened in the reception history of the texts of *Romeo and Juliet*: in the early twentieth century, Theodor Eichhoff edited the first quarto and went on to write a comparative study of Q1 and Q2 in which he argued for the superiority of the first quarto over the second.[7] Once Eichhoff had convinced himself of the texts' relative merit, he was able to find reasons in virtually every parallel passage why the first quarto is much to be preferred to the second. Eichhoff is an extreme case, but it seems clear that an analysis of the first quarto and its relationship to the second can gain from establishing first *what* there is in the two texts and *what* the differences are between them. Naturally enough, this assessment leads to the question of *why* the first quarto came to take on the form it has, and *why* it differs from the second quarto in the way it does, and it is these complex questions that I now address.

Textual provenance

A CENTURY OF 'BAD QUARTOS'[8]

Scholarly thinking about the provenance of Q1 *Romeo and Juliet* is intimately related to the 'bad quartos' more generally, so I first wish to survey past thinking about this group of texts.[9] It will be well to start by considering two publications that appeared at the end of the first decade of the twentieth century. In *Shakespeare Folios and Quartos*, Alfred W. Pollard invented the textual category which he labelled 'bad quartos'.[10] This invention followed from his revisionary reading of Heminge and Condell's address in the First Folio 'To the Great Variety of Readers'. While earlier commentators had believed that their reference to 'diuerse stolne, and surreptitious copies', with which the readers had previously been 'abus'd', had been to the quarto editions in general, Pollard insisted that only the 'bad quartos' were meant. Since several 'good' quartos had been used as copy when the First Folio was printed, Heminge and Condell, so Pollard argued, could hardly have claimed to have 'cur'd' all the 'surreptitious' and 'maimed' quartos. The texts he identified as 'bad quartos' were Q1 *Romeo and Juliet* (1597), Q1 *King Henry V* (1600), Q1 *The Merry Wives of Windsor* (1602), Q1 *Hamlet* (1603), and Q1 *Pericles* (1609). In the following year, W. W. Greg refined that part of the narrative to which Pollard had paid little attention: the agency behind the manuscript copy of the 'bad quarto' that allows us to account for the text's relationship to the 'good' Folio text. Noting 'the very unusual accuracy with which the part of mine Host is reported' in the 'bad' quarto of *The Merry Wives*

[7] Eichhoff; and Theodor Eichhoff, *Unser Shakespeare: Beiträge zu einer wissenschaftlichen Shakespeare-Kritik*, vol. 4, *Die beiden ältesten Ausgaben von Romeo and Juliet: Eine vergleichende Prüfung ihres Inhalts* (Halle, 1904).

[8] This title is indebted to Paul Westine's 'A century of "bad" Shakespeare quartos', *SQ* 50 (1999), 310–33.

[9] This part of my introduction is indebted to Erne, pp. 196–201.

[10] Alfred W. Pollard, *Shakespeare Folios and Quartos: A Study in the Bibliography of Shakespeare's Plays 1594–1685* (London, 1909). See, in particular, the chapter on 'The good and the bad quartos' (pp. 64–80).

of Windsor and 'the comparative excellence of the reporting of those scenes in which the Host is on the stage', Greg concluded that 'the pirate who procured the copy . . . was none other than the actor of the Host's part'.[11] Even though Greg cannot be credited with having invented the concept of 'memorial reconstruction' (see below), he seems to have provided both the label and the first detailed investigation of it.

The twin theories of 'bad quartos' and 'memorial reconstruction' thus having been put forward in the space of two years by two of the leading scholars of their time, much of the scholarship in the following decades went into consolidating Pollard and Greg's publications of 1909 and 1910 and applying them to other plays. In 1915, H. D. Gray suggested that Q1 *Hamlet* was also a memorial reconstruction, undertaken by the actor who played the role of Marcellus.[12] Once 'memorial reconstruction' had been applied not only to Q1 *Merry Wives* but to all of Pollard's Shakespearean 'bad quartos', the theory spread beyond the bounds of the Shakespeare canon. Comparing the quarto edition of *Orlando Furioso* with Edward Alleyn's extant part of the title character, Greg concluded in 1923 that the quarto is 'a version severely abridged . . . for performance by a reduced cast' and that the text 'is based almost throughout on reconstruction from memory'.[13] By 1930, E. K. Chambers fixed the canon of Shakespeare's 'bad' quartos by endorsing the cases advanced for *1 Contention, Richard Duke of York, Romeo and Juliet, King Henry V, The Merry Wives of Windsor*, and *Hamlet*, while rejecting *The Taming of a Shrew*.[14]

After Chambers's influential pronouncement, the 'bad quarto' and 'memorial reconstruction' theories remained largely unchallenged in their broad outlines for roughly half a century.[15] Summing up in a few sentences a critical territory on which much ink was spilt inevitably results in simplifications. It is certainly true that there was considerable argument as to what exactly was memorially reconstructed, by whom, and to what purpose. A popular reference work such as F. E. Halliday's *Shakespeare Companion* can give a good impression, however, of how orthodox the assumption had become. The six Shakespearean 'bad quartos', Halliday wrote, 'were reconstructed from memory by one or more actors who had played minor parts in a London production, and tried to reproduce the play for a provincial performance. This theory is generally accepted.'[16] With the orthodoxy thus in place, 'memorial reconstruction' became an explanation with which scholars tried to account for textual features of a growing number of early modern play-texts, a number that, by the 1990s, reached a total of more than forty.[17]

---

[11] W. W. Greg, ed., *Shakespeare's 'Merry Wives of Windsor', 1602* (Oxford, 1910), pp. xxxvii, xxxviii, xl.

[12] H. D. Gray, 'The first quarto of *Hamlet*', *Modern Language Review* 10 (1915), 171–80.

[13] W. W. Greg, *Two Elizabethan Stage Abridgements: 'The Battle of Alcazar' and 'Orlando Furioso'* (Oxford), pp. 133–4.

[14] E. K. Chambers, *William Shakespeare: A Study of Facts and Problems*, 2 vols. (Oxford, 1930), vol. 1, pp. 281–5, 324–8, 341–5, 391–4, 415–22, 429–34.

[15] By 1938, Leo Kirschbaum could publish 'A census of bad quartos' (*RES* 14, pp. 20–43) with no fewer than twenty 'bad quartos', including Q1 *Romeo and Juliet*. Ironically, at the same time as the theory Greg had initiated was spreading, Greg had started doubting his original argument about the Host and *Merry Wives*. See Werstine, 'Century', 316.

[16] F. E. Halliday, *A Shakespeare Companion, 1564–1964* (Harmondsworth, 1964), p. 49.

[17] Laurie E. Maguire, *Shakespearean Suspect Texts: The 'Bad' Quartos and Their Contexts* (Cambridge, 1996), pp. 227–322.

PAST THINKING ABOUT Q1 *ROMEO AND JULIET*

Theories about the first quarto of *Romeo and Juliet* started long before the 'bad quartos' came into being as a textual category. Eighteenth-century editors usually considered Q1 as a first draft and Q2, in keeping with its title page ('Newly corrected, augmented, and amended'), an improved and completed text on which they based their editions.[18] Yet there were exceptions: Pope drew eclectically from Q1 and Q2, choosing whichever version he preferred, at times combining the two in the same passage or even line. Warburton, even though he did not base his text on Q1, preferred it to the later version, because the 'trifling and bombast passages are in [the longer text] far more numerous'. He considered the additions in Q2/F to Q1 to be a result of the practice lamented by Hamlet, with actors speaking more than has been set down for them: 'as a proof', Warburton writes, that Shakespeare could not escape this practice, 'in the old editions of *Romeo and Juliet* there is no hint of a great number of the mean conceits and ribaldries now to be found there'.[19]

Prior to the 1840s, editors agreed, however, that Q1 was an authorial version and that it was the earlier of the two. The first editor who opposed this view was John Payne Collier in his edition of 1842–4. He wrote that Q1 had hitherto

been treated as an authorised impression from an authentic manuscript. Such, after the most careful examination, is not our opinion. We think that the manuscript used by the printer or printers . . . was made up, partly from portions of the play as it was acted, but unduly obtained, and partly from notes taken at the theatre during representation. Our principal ground for this notion is, that there is such great inequality in different scenes and speeches, and in some places precisely that degree and kind of imperfectness, which would belong to a manuscript prepared from defective short-hand notes.[20]

While some aspects of Collier's theory are by now generally discredited, it deserves to be pointed out that his thinking is in other respects remarkably astute. He is the first to argue that Q1 basically derives from Q2, he notices the text's uneven quality which makes any monocausal explanation of its genesis problematic, and he also anticipates some modern thinking in arguing that Q1's differences to Q2 can be explained by the theory that Q1 partly reflects 'the play as it was acted'.

For the remainder of the nineteenth century, the traditional 'early draft' theory and Collier's new theory co-existed, some scholars preferring the former (e.g. Knight, Dyce, Staunton, Ulrici, and Hudson) and others the latter (White, Mommsen, Furness, Daniel, and the Cambridge editors). Minor variations of Collier's theory included first and still tentative considerations that the genesis of Q1 might be partly memorial, thus anticipating the 'memorial reconstruction' explanation prevalent in the following century. Writing about Q1 *Hamlet* and *Romeo and Juliet*, Tycho Mommsen, in 1857, held that both texts 'abound with every kind of shallow repetition – now of set phrases, oaths, expletives, then (which is strongly indicative of interpolation) of certain lines and passages of peculiar energy, such as would impress themselves more literally upon *the memory of the hearer*' (my emphasis).[21]

---

[18] See, for instance, Capell vol. 1, pp. 2–3.
[19] Warburton, vol. 1, p. xl.
[20] Collier, vol. 6, pp. 368–9.
[21] Tycho Mommsen, '*Hamlet*, 1603; and *Romeo and Juliet*, 1597', *Athenaeum* 29 (1857), 182.

Four years later, White similarly considered 'the unmitigated failure in the memory' as a possible explanation for parts of Q1.[22] Finally, a few years later still, the Cambridge editors argued for stenographic origins of Q1 but recognised that 'the text of (Q1) is more accurate on the whole than might have been expected from such an origin' and added that 'possibly some of the players may have helped [the short-hand writer] either *from memory*, or by lending their parts in MS' (my emphasis).[23]

The idea that memorial agency had something to do with the genesis of Q1 thus existed prior to the watershed publications by Pollard and Greg in 1909 and 1910, but it was thereafter that the memorial reconstruction theory fully established itself. In 1919, Pollard and J. Dover Wilson co-authored an article about the provenance of Q1 *Romeo and Juliet* which built on Pollard and Greg's publications but was considerably complicated by their belief in the existence of an earlier, non-Shakespearean play. Q1, they thought, 'represents an abridged version of Shakespeare's first revision of an older [non-Shakespearean] play eked out by what a pirate could remember of the later version'.[24] When Chambers reviewed their convoluted narrative in 1930, he soberly concluded: 'I do not find this theory satisfactory.'[25] Nevertheless, Chambers had no doubt that Q1 was 'one of the bad Quartos', held that it is 'certainly a "reported" text', and repeatedly referred to 'the reporter'.[26] The fullest investigation of the provenance of Q1 *Romeo and Juliet*, which was to establish the dominant view for decades to come, was H. R. Hoppe's book-length *The Bad Quarto of 'Romeo and Juliet'* in which he proposed 'to demonstrate that Q1 of *Romeo and Juliet* is a memorial reconstruction of a version that Q2 represents in substantially correct form'.[27] This theory was endorsed by Greg in *The Shakespeare First Folio* and, among recent editors, Brian Gibbons, G. Blakemore Evans, and the editors of the Oxford Shakespeare.[28] The merits of and problems with the 'memorial reconstruction' narrative are explored below, but it seems fair to say that it had a crippling effect on scholarly engagement with Q1. This is exemplified by the following quotations from a 1955 survey of 'Recent Work on the Text of *Romeo and Juliet*' by Wilson: 'it is a pirated edition and . . . exhibits all the stigmata we have learnt to associate with such texts . . . And that is practically all an editor needs to know about this text.'[29]

[22] This is quoted in Furness, p. 420.

[23] Ibid., pp. 422–3. George Ian Duthie's *Elizabethan Shorthand and the First Quarto of 'King Lear'* (Oxford, 1949) effectively demonstrated that no system of stenography known by 1597 would have allowed the transcription of anything as complex as a play.

[24] J. Dover Wilson and A. W. Pollard, 'The "stolne and surreptitious" Shakespearian texts: *Romeo and Juliet*, 1597', *Times Literary Supplement*, 14 August 1919, p. 434.

[25] Chambers, *William Shakespeare*, vol. 1, p. 343. One source of error in Wilson and Pollard's theory is that they took the occasional similarities or even identity between Q1 and Q2 in spelling, capitalisation, and punctuation to be evidence for derivation from the same manuscript. Later scholars established, however, that these closely parallel passages result from Q2 having been partly set up from Q1.

[26] Chambers, *William Shakespeare*, vol. 1, pp. 341–2.

[27] Hoppe, p. 58.

[28] W. W. Greg, *The Shakespeare First Folio: Its Bibliographical and Textual History* (Oxford, 1955), pp. 225–28; Gibbons, pp. 4–13; NCS, pp. 222–4; Jowett, p. 288.

[29] J. Dover Wilson, 'The new way with Shakespeare's texts: II. Recent work on the text of *Romeo and Juliet*', *S. Sur.* 8 (1955), 81–99, 82.

THE EARLY DRAFT/REVISION THEORY

One argument which has recently been revived that conflicts with the memorial reconstruction theory is that Shakespeare revised his own plays, including *Romeo and Juliet*. As pointed out above, the first sketch/authorial revision view had many adherents in the eighteenth and nineteenth centuries. Its modern revival followed in the wake of Ernst Honigmann's *The Stability of Shakespeare's Text* which investigated 'the possibilities of authorial "second thoughts" *before* its delivery to the actors', resulting in 'two copies of a play, each in the author's hand, disagreeing in both substantive and indifferent readings'.[30] In the 1970s and 1980s, the authorial revision debate centred around *King Lear*, which many scholars argued was extant in two substantially different authorial versions. As Greg's argument for memorial reconstruction had created a search for ever more memorially reconstructed plays, so the theory of an authorially revised *King Lear* triggered a reconsideration of Shakespeare's possible revision of several other plays. As part of this reconsideration, the possibility that the 'bad quartos' in fact represented first versions which authorial revision turned into the longer and better-known plays was again examined. Steven Urkowitz supported this theory, arguing that 'each of the multiple texts may represent a different stage in Shakespeare's and his acting company's composing and revising process'.[31] That Q1 *Romeo and Juliet* is an authorial first draft has also been argued by Y. S. Bains: 'Shakespeare composed the First and Second Quartos as two versions for the stage, and the second is superior to the first because he revised it.'[32] An obstacle to belief in this theory resides in the fact that the derivative nature of most of the 'bad quartos' is strongly suggested by passages whose sense only becomes entirely clear after a comparison with the 'good' text. A couple of examples will suffice as illustration.[33] Q1 reads:

> JULIET A blister on that tongue! He was not born to shame.
> Upon his face shame is ashamed to sit.
> But wherefore, villain, didst thou kill my cousin?
> That villain cousin would have killed my husband.
> All this is comfort. (11.41–5)

It is not entirely clear what 'All this' refers to. The second quarto adds a passage between lines 44 and 45 with which Juliet's concluding words make better sense:

> Back, foolish tears, back to your native spring,
> Your tributary drops belong to woe,

---

[30] E. A. J. Honigmann, *The Stability of Shakespeare's Text* (London, 1965), p. 2.

[31] Steven Urkowitz, 'Good news about "bad" quartos', in *"Bad" Shakespeare: Revaluations of the Shakespeare Canon*, ed. Maurice Charney (Rutherford, NJ, 1988), pp. 189–206, 192.

[32] Y. S. Bains, *Making Sense of the First Quartos of Shakespeare's 'Romeo and Juliet', 'Henry V', 'The Merry Wives of Windsor', and 'Hamlet'* (Rashtrapati Nivas: Indian Institute of Advanced Study, 1995), p. 25. See also Donald Foster, 'The webbing of *Romeo and Juliet*', in *Critical Essays on Shakespeare's 'Romeo and Juliet'*, ed. Joseph A. Porter (Boston, 1997), pp. 131–49.

[33] See Chambers, *William Shakespeare*, vol. 1, p. 341 and Hart, pp. 184–90, for further passages which do not make perfect sense in Q1 because of Q2 cuts. It is true that some of these examples have little weight, but the cumulative case remains strong. See also my note at 13.10.

> Which you mistaking offer up to joy.
> My husband lives that Tybalt would have slain,
> And Tybalt's dead that would have slain my husband:
> All this is comfort . . .   (3.2.102–7)

The following passage also requires reference to Q2 to make full sense:

ROMEO I cry you mercy. My business was great, and in such a case as mine a man
      may strain courtesy.
MERCUTIO O, that's as much to say as such a case as yours will constrain a man to
      bow in the hams.
ROMEO A most courteous exposition.   (7.42–6)

As in the previous example, the final words follow from a passage present in Q2 but
absent from Q1:

ROMEO Pardon, good Mercutio, my business was great, and in such a case as mine
      a man may strain courtesy.
MERCUTIO That's as much as to say, such a case as yours constrains a man to bow
      in the hams.
ROMEO Meaning to cur'sy.
MERCUTIO Thou hast most kindly hit it.
ROMEO A most courteous exposition.   (2.4.42–8)

The word 'cur'sy', an early modern variant of and pronounced like 'courtesy', leads
to the pun two lines later. The two omitted lines explain the ambiguity of Mercutio's
'bow in the hams': it refers to the action of bowing, as Romeo says, but it also implies
that Romeo, having 'hit it' in the sense of having had sex, is sexually so exhausted
that he can barely stand up straight. In Q2, one quibble naturally leads to the next
in this densely bawdy passage; in Q1, by contrast, Mercutio's pun is a loose end.

Earlier scholars such as Chambers and Hart have extensively investigated those
passages which provide evidence for Q1's derivative nature (because they require
Q2 to illuminate them), but that this evidence can be considerably strengthened by
an analysis of both texts alongside Shakespeare's acknowledged source text does
not seem to have been fully considered. The close relationship between Brooke's
narrative poem *Romeus and Juliet* (1562) and Shakespeare's play has, of course,
been thoroughly demonstrated. Yet on various occasions, Q2 corresponds closely
to Brooke at moments when Q1 does not. It seems more likely that Shakespeare,
on these occasions, originally echoed Brooke – as he does elsewhere – but that the
echoes subsequently got lost rather than that Shakespeare originally did not follow
Brooke (though he clearly did so elsewhere) and only inserted the echoes to the
narrative poem when revising the play. Here is a first example. Capulet's outrage
at Juliet's opposition to his marriage plans follows Brooke's narrative poem from

which I quote (I highlight significant words here and below):

> Such care thy mother had, so deere thou wert to me,
> That I with long and earnest sute, **provided** have for thee
> One of the greatest lordes, that wonnes about this towne,
> And for his many virtues sake, a man of great renowne.
> Of whom, both thou and I, unworthy are too much,
> So riche ere long he shalbe left, his fathers welth is such.
> Such is the **noblenes**, and honor of the race,
> From whence his father came, and yet thou playest in this case
> The dainty **foole**, and stubberne gyrle; for want of skill,
> Thou dost refuse thy offred weale, and disobey my will.
>   (1961–70)

Q2 adheres to Brooke in general outline and several verbal details:

> CAPULET God's bread, it makes me mad! Day, night, work, play,
>   Alone, in company, still my care hath been
>   To have her matched; and having now **provided**
>   A gentleman of **noble** parentage,
>   Of fair demesnes, youthful and nobly ligned,
>   Stuffed, as they say, with honourable parts,
>   Proportioned as one's thought would wish a man,
>   And then to have a wretched puling **fool**,
>   A whining mammet, in her fortune's tender,
>   To answer 'I'll not wed, I cannot love;
>   I am too young, I pray you pardon me.'   (3.5.176–86)

In Q2 and Brooke, Juliet's father insists on the nobility (or 'noblenes') of the parentage of Juliet's suitor, that he had 'provided' for his daughter, and calls his daughter a 'fool[e]' because of her resistance. Q1 corresponds quite closely to the version in Q2, but two of the differences between them – 'found out' instead of 'provided' and 'princely' for 'noble' – effectively eliminate echoes of Brooke:

> CAPULET God's blessèd mother, wife, it mads me.
>   Day, night, early, late, at home, abroad,
>   Alone, in company, waking, or sleeping,
>   Still my care hath been to see her matched.
>   And having now **found out** a gentleman
>   Of **princely** parentage, youthful, and nobly trained,
>   Stuffed, as they say, with honourable parts,
>   Proportioned as one's heart could wish a man,
>   And then to have a wretched whining **fool**,
>   A puling mammet in her fortune's tender,
>   To say 'I cannot love, I am too young,
>   I pray you pardon me.'   (14.138–49)

A passage close to the end of Act 4 is equally telling:

FRIAR LAWRENCE ...
>   Dry up your tears, and stick your rosemary
>   On this fair corse, and as the **custom** is,
>   And in her best array, **bear her to church**;
>   For though fond nature bids us all lament,
>   Yet nature's tears are reasons's merriment.
CAPULET   All things that we ordainèd festival,
>   Turn from their office to black funeral:
>   Our instruments to melancholy bells,
>   Our wedding cheer to a sad burial feast;
>   Our solemn hymns to sullen dirges change;
>   Our bridal flowers serve for a buried corse;
>   And all things change them to the contrary.
>   (4.5.79–90)

The equivalent passage in Brooke has a similar series of antitheses which oppose the joys of the anticipated wedding to the sorrows of the funeral:

>   Now is the parentes myrth quite chaunged into mone,
>   And now to sorow is retornde the joy of every one.
>   And now the wedding weedes for mourning weedes they chaunge,
>   And Hymene into a Dyrge, alas it seemeth straunge.
>   In steade of mariage gloves, now funerall gloves they have,
>   And whom they should see maried, they follow to the grave.
>   The feast that should have been of pleasure and of joy,
>   Hath every dish, and cup, fild full of sorow and annoye.
>   (2507–14)

In the following eight lines, Brooke explains the Italian custom of the household tomb in which all members of a family are buried. Then he continues with three lines which are echoed in Friar Lawrence's words quoted above:

>   An other **use** there is, that whosoever dyes,
>   **Borne to their church** with open face, upon the beere he lyes
>   In wonted weede attyrde, not wrapt in winding sheete.
>   (2523–5)

Brooke and Shakespeare describe a custom (called 'use' in Brooke), and Shakespeare's 'bear her to church' is verbally close to Brooke's 'Borne to their church'. The passage in Q1 omits not only the echoes in Friar Laurence's speech (instead of 'bear her', Q1 has 'Convey her') but also the series of antitheses in Capulet's following speech which takes up only two lines:

FRIAR LAWRENCE ...
>   Come, stick your rosemary in this dead corpse,
>   And, as the custom of our country is,
>   In all her best and sumptuous ornaments
>   **Convey her** where her ancestors lie tombed.

CAPULET   Let it be so. Come, woeful sorrow-mates,
    Let us together taste this bitter fate.
(17.103–8)

More evidence could be added. Earlier in the same scene, Juliet, in Q2, asks to
be alone in order to pray – 'I have need of many orisons / To move the heavens'
(4.3.3–4) – and, in Brooke, asserts that 'this night, my purpose is to pray (line 2326).
In Q1, by contrast, Juliet says: 'I desire to lie alone, / For I have many things to think
upon' (17.6–7). A few lines later, Q2, in a line with no equivalent in Q1, says, 'Spare
not for cost' (4.4.6) and in Brooke, Juliet's father promises Paris 'a costly feast' (line
2258). It seems plausible to assume that Shakespeare's original adherence to Brooke
in Q2 partly disappeared as the version developed into the text behind Q1.

What further weakens the case for Q1 to Q2 revision is what can be gathered about
the manuscript underlying Q2: its false starts and repetitions strongly suggest that
this version rather than Q1 constituted Shakespeare's earliest version. For instance,
at the end of 2.2, a four-line passage is assigned to Romeo which, in almost identical
form, is assigned to Friar Lawrence at the beginning of 2.3. By the time the version
behind Q1 came into being, the confusion had been cleared up.[34] A more general
reservation about the revision theory is equally powerful. As the Oxford Shakespeare
editors – who find the theory 'fundamentally untenable' – point out, 'the "early
versions" in question [including Q1 *Romeo and Juliet*] differ drastically from the
genuine cases of authorial revision elsewhere in the canon, where both texts exist in
reliable editions . . . the resulting verbal texture cannot be convincingly assigned to
any one period of Shakespeare's career'.[35] One way of verifying this last assertion is
to consult the 'Metrical Tables' in an appendix to Chambers's *William Shakespeare*,
in particular 'Table III': 'Blank Verse: Length and Syllabic Variation': a certain
number of short and long lines are an integral part of Shakespeare's blank verse
throughout his career, but the high percentage of such lines in Q1 *Romeo and Juliet*
and related texts clearly fails to correspond to Shakespeare's practice.[36]

MEMORIAL REPORTERS?
More convincing opposition to the theory of memorial reconstruction has arisen
from other quarters since the 1990s. Some of these challenges have subjected to
close scrutiny the arguments that supported New Bibliographical orthodoxy. Paul
Werstine has shown to what extent the spread of 'memorial reconstruction' has
depended upon scholarly narratives that took on a life of their own in the course of the

---

[34] See Irace, pp. 103–5; chapter 5 on 'Revision' develops a number of obstacles to belief in the theory that
the 'bad quartos' were Shakespearean first versions. Irace concludes that 'for the six short quartos,
differences between the short and the longer versions point to other agents than Shakespeare's revising
hand' (p. 114).

[35] Wells et al., *Textual Companion*, p. 27.

[36] See table XIX in Hart, p. 238, and, more generally, his chapter on 'Verse structure of the bad quartos'
(pp. 222–66). For the 'Metrical tables', see Chambers, *William Shakespeare*, vol. 2, p. 400. See the
section on 'Stage Directions' below for further evidence of Q1's derivative nature.

twentieth century, narratives that at times had no more than a tenuous relationship to what bibliographical methods allow us to ascertain.[37]

A specific target of Westine's attack has been the identity of the reporters. For much of the twentieth century, scholars tried to determine the parts played by the actors who composed the text based on what they remembered from the performances in which they had participated. Greg proposed the Host in *Merry Wives*, Gray suspected 'Marcellus' of being responsible for *Hamlet*, and Hoppe thought he had identified the culprits in *Romeo and Juliet*.[38] In the last chapter of his study of Q1, 'The reporters of *Romeo and Juliet*', he tried to show that the actors playing Romeo and Paris memorially reconstructed the play since their parts tend to be reported with greater accuracy.[39] Jowett has argued that Q1 is 'based on a pirated text' and that 'Hoppe convincingly showed that Q1 was set from a manuscript originally compiled by actors, identifying them as probably those who played Romeo and Paris.'[40] Irace has basically endorsed Hoppe's claims, though she further developed them by adding 'Mercutio' to Hoppe's reporters, pointing out that the parts of Mercutio and Paris could have been doubled.[41] Yet other scholars have been more sceptical. Gibbons refrained from endorsing Hoppe's specific argument, holding instead that 'Presumably the Bad Quarto version was assembled *by a group* who had been involved in the first authentic production' (my emphasis).[42]

Indeed, it seems to me that the theory advanced by Hoppe and developed by Irace is not without problems. For one thing, the figures resulting from Irace's painstaking research arguably belie the conclusions she draws from them. Her 'Charts Indicating Likely Reporters' measure for every character the percentage of lines spoken or overheard in the long text with high correlation in the 'bad' quarto. In *Romeo and Juliet*, the correlation for Mercutio is in the high 70s, for Romeo around 70 and for Paris about 65 per cent.[43] This is virtually identical with Benvolio and Tybalt, whose correlation is also between 60 and 70 per cent, while that of Gregory (the second Capulet serving-man) is even higher than that for Paris. By contrast, in *The Merry Wives of Windsor*, the correlation of lines spoken by the Host is around 80 per cent, with no other character reaching 50 and most of them being below 20. It seems fair to say that one would usually expect actors to be able to recall their own lines with significantly greater accuracy than those of other characters, as is the case in *Merry Wives*. In that play, especially in its early scenes, the differences between the part of the Host and other characters are striking. As long as the Host is offstage, the textual relationship between Q1 and Folio is distant, but as soon as he appears it is close and his own part is very close. In *Romeo and Juliet*, however, no such sharp breaks can be observed that would allow us to relate them to the appearance

---

[37] Werstine, 'Century', 310–33. Maguire concludes that Q1 *Romeo and Juliet* is not memorial reconstruction (*Shakespearean Suspect Texts*, p. 302).

[38] Gray, 'The first quarto of *Hamlet*', 171–80.

[39] Hoppe, pp. 191–222.

[40] Jowett, p. 288.

[41] Irace, pp. 126–31.

[42] Gibbons, p. 4n.

[43] Irace, pp. 180–5.

or exit of certain characters. In Scenes 1 to 7, the relationship is generally close, but it deteriorates in the course of the rest of the play. It seems difficult to account for this development by singling out two or three reporters.

Hoppe's, argument, which Irace tried to develop, has been influential, yet it may be well to recall that his theory arrived late on the scene, was received rather sceptically, and contradicted the views of earlier respectable scholars. In their article of 1919, Pollard and Wilson wrote that 'If the pirate was an actor, it is not so easy to see which parts he took in this play as in the others we have to deal with.' In the absence of any plausible candidate, they venture the guess that, if anyone, there may be 'some evidence that our pirate played the part of Juliet's father'.[44] Chambers, in 1930, thought that 'It does not seem possible to identify the reporter. If he was an actor, Capulet, the Nurse, Benvolio occasionally suggest themselves, but no part is consistently well rendered.'[45] Alfred Hart, in 1942, similarly argued that 'evidence is wanting to justify the selection of any actor of an important part as reporter in preference to the actor of any other'.[46] In the same year, Greg wrote that 'the part of no particular actor appears to stand out as better reported than others'.[47] When reviewing Hoppe's study eight years later, he remained sceptical, pointing out that the theory that the actors playing Romeo and Paris were Q1's memorial reporters 'does not help to explain the breakdown in the reporting of the last two acts, in which the parts in question appear to be no better rendered than the rest'.[48] In *The Shakespeare First Folio* of 1955, he added that Hoppe's 'attempt to identify the [reporters] is less convincing than other portions of his thesis'.[49] It seems to me that the memorial reconstruction theory failed to produce a believable narrative that could account for how the first quarto of *Romeo and Juliet* came about.

STAGE ABRIDGEMENT, NOT MEMORIAL RECONSTRUCTION?

Discontent with New Bibliographical narratives, and in particular with prevailing accounts of the genesis of Q1 *Romeo and Juliet*, may well have facilitated the rise of alternative theories that discard memorial reconstruction altogether. David Farley-Hills has argued that Q1 is 'a shorter version of the text . . . intended for performance by a touring troupe in the provinces'.[50] In contrast to Hoppe and others, Farley-Hills does not ascribe the composition of the text to memorial reporters but to a 'redactor' who was 'at work on a text close to the text represented in Q2'.[51] He believes that 'the copy for both the redactor of Q1 and the compositor of Q2 was the author's "foul papers"'.[52] He thus agrees with Hoppe and others on the derivative nature

---

[44] Wilson and Pollard, 'The "stolne and surreptitious" Shakespearian texts', 434.

[45] Chambers, *William Shakespeare*, vol. 1, p. 342.

[46] Hart, p. 346.

[47] W. W. Greg, *The Editorial Problem in Shakespeare: A Survey of the Foundations of the Text* (Oxford, 1942), p. 64.

[48] W. W. Greg, review of Hoppe, in *RES* n.s. 1 (1950), 64–6, 65.

[49] Greg, *The Shakespeare First Folio*, p. 226, n.4.

[50] Farley-Hills, 28.

[51] Ibid., 31.

[52] Ibid., 33.

of Q1, but he argues that the composition is a matter of non-authorial abridgement which involved a certain amount of rewriting. The real purpose of the writing of Q1 supposedly was the preparation of a text of manageable length: 'the 26 per cent reduction or so [the redactor] is looking for overall'.[53] Farley-Hills imagines the redactor's method as being 'designed to do the job with the minimum of disruption, and as quickly as possible, with the emphasis on producing a text that is effective on stage'.[54] He shows that Hoppe had also believed that Q1 reflects a deliberate abridgement and that it was this abridged text which the reporters tried to reconstruct; yet, Farley-Hills continues, 'what need is there to postulate a memorizer *and* a redactor if the state of the text can be explained in terms of a redactor?'[55] Farley-Hills's confidence in his theory was clearly increased by his understandable view that 'Hoppe's attempt to identify [the reporters] as Paris and Romeo is wholly unconvincing'.[56]

Another article with a related argument appeared at almost the same time as Farley-Hills's. In 'Handy-dandy: Q1/Q2 *Romeo and Juliet*' (1995), Jay L. Halio also argues against memorial reconstruction and in favour of deliberate abridgement, though the agent involved in his narrative is not an anonymous redactor but Shakespeare himself. Shakespeare, Halio believes,

first wrote out a full draft of his play, revising some parts as he went along. Since the draft was too long for a performance lasting two hours or so, a shorter draft was made, with further revisions as and when they were felt necessary or desirable, including numerous tinkerings with what had already been written and found generally acceptable. This became the acting version of the play, from which the promptbook was prepared. This revised, second draft was then printed in 1597 in the first quarto.[57]

The arguments of Farley-Hills and Halio have definite virtues to which I shall return below, but I first need to turn to what is problematic about them. As for Halio, it seems to me that the difference between Q2 and Q1 *Romeo and Juliet* is not fully accounted for by omissions plus 'tinkerings'. If we compare the earliest quarto and the First Folio *Troilus and Cressida*, authorial tinkerings seem indeed likely to account for some of the differences between them: single words differ here and there with rare cases of more extensive variations. Yet the case of *Romeo and Juliet* is far from identical. In the last two acts, in particular, much of the linguistic material in the two quartos and the order in which it is presented is simply different. Also, to recall the Oxford editors' pertinent objection to the early draft theory which applies equally well here, parts of its verbal texture are simply not Shakespearean and 'cannot be convincingly assigned to any one period of Shakespeare's career'.[58]

Regarding Farley-Hills, it seems difficult to understand why a redactor for whom speed and efficiency were an issue, who would have acted 'with the minimum of

---

53 Ibid., 31.
54 Ibid.
55 Ibid., 30.
56 Ibid., 33.
57 Jay L. Halio, 'Handy-dandy: Q1/Q2 *Romeo and Juliet*', in *Shakespeare's 'Romeo and Juliet': Texts, Contexts, and Interpretation*, ed. Halio (Newark, 1995), p. 137.
58 Wells et al., *Textual Companion*, p. 27.

disruption, and as quickly as possible', would have chosen to rewrite substantial portions of the play (especially in Acts 4 and 5) instead of simply cutting enough lines to arrive at the desired reduction in length. Farley-Hills believes that 'any redaction would probably involve the writing of some bridging passages'.[59] However, the extant manuscript playbooks we have, as well as other documents show that abridgement was a standard feature of the preparation of a play text for the stage but that these abridgements generally contained no bridging passages and that no abridgement comes even close to resembling the one Farley-Hills imagines for Q1 *Romeo and Juliet*.[60] Farley-Hills's theory seems particularly difficult to reconcile with all those passages where Q1 is very different from but not shorter, or hardly shorter than Q2 (e.g. the lamentation sequence in Scene 17/4.5 or Friar Laurence's long speech in the last scene). If someone had access to Shakespeare's foul papers and wanted to produce 'as quickly as possible' a shortened performance version, then this could surely be arrived at by simpler means than by composing a version like Q1.

EVIDENCE OF MEMORIAL AGENCY

What renders these theories even more problematic is that – independently of the question of the reporters' identity – there seems to be good evidence suggesting that memorial agency did play a part in the composition of Q1.[61] It is noteworthy that the relationship between Q1 and Q2 is particularly loose at moments of intense stage action.[62] At such moments, the specific wording would have mattered less during the original performances and have been particularly difficult to remember later. In the opening scene, when the conflict between the Capulets and the Montagues gets out of hand, Q2 dramatises the fight in a sequence, in the course of which no fewer than nine characters have short staccato speeches: Sampson, Abram, Benvolio, Tybalt, an officer, Capulet, Montague, and their wives (1.1.52–71). Q1 omits the entire passage and has a lengthy stage direction instead: '*They draw, to them enters* TYBALT, *they fight, to them the* PRINCE, *old* MONTAGUE, *and his* WIFE, *old* CAPULET *and his* WIFE, *and other citizens and part them.*' The Q1 lines preceding this passage all have recognisable equivalents in Q2, and the Q1 lines following it are almost identical with lines present in the longer text, so the lack of textual correspondence during the fight is conspicuous.

It is true that Q1 also omits passages of some length elsewhere, but these cuts usually omit lines that seem theatrically (if not poetically) dispensable. Here, by contrast, the omission requires us to imagine a conflict in the form of a dumb show.

---

[59] Farley-Hills, 28.

[60] 'We have MS evidence of the adaptation of scripts for performance, and there is little in common between the stage adaptation of manuscripts . . . and the process that has in Q1 *Romeo* reduced the Q2 text to about two thirds its original length' (Werstine, 'Century', 333).

[61] Despite his argument, Farley-Hills in fact admits as much, though he holds responsible 'the memory of the actor–redactor' (39) rather than the memorial reporters, thus reintroducing memorial agency through a different channel.

[62] Chambers noted long ago that 'the reporter tends to break down in bustling scenes, with much action and confused speech' (*William Shakespeare*, vol. 1, p. 341).

Something similar may be observed in the fight between Tybalt and Mercutio in Scene 10 / Act 3 Scene 1. An eight-line passage in Q2 with short speeches by Tybalt, Mercutio, and Romeo (3.1.75–82) corresponds to a single short speech by Romeo followed by a stage direction in Q1:

ROMEO Stay, Tybalt! Hold, Mercutio! Benvolio, beat down their weapons.
    Tybalt under Romeo's arm thrusts Mercutio, in and flies

(10.53–4.1 SD)

As in the opening scene, Q1 omits dialogue at the moment when the intensity of the stage action makes verbal language both less important and more difficult to understand for the actors and the audience.

A third passage that needs to be discussed in this context is the lamentation sequence towards the end of Scene 17/Act 4 Scene 5, when the Capulets, the Nurse, and Paris believe that Juliet has died. As the characters proclaim their sorrows in highly wrought language, a Q1 stage direction makes clear that certain lines are to be spoken simultaneously by several characters: '*All at once cry out and wring their hands*' (17.82.1 SD). After this stage direction, two lines, preceded by the speech heading 'ALL', are followed by speeches by Capulet, Paris, and Capulet's Wife, all of equal length and similar in tone, suggesting that they too may have been spoken simultaneously. This is important insofar as this passage, like the ones discussed above, is almost totally independent of Q2. Charles B. Lower has argued that

[T]he Q1 stage direction . . . would make impossible the task of a reporter (on stage, back-stage, or in the audience), and it probably would even negate an actor's responsibility to memorize his own part accurately. The lament speeches in Q1 and Q2 have only minus-cule correspondence in substance, yet are remarkably parallel in tone; this situation seems strange until we see that it may be accounted for by the cacophony of simultaneity in performance.[63]

As in the fight passages in Scenes 1 and 10, memorial agency is suggested by the fact that the relationship between Q1 and Q2 is extremely loose at moments when performance must have made it difficult to understand the words spoken or unnecessary to remember the exact wording of the original script.[64]

ALTERNATIVES TO THE TRADITIONAL NARRATIVE

What the evidence seems to suggest so far is that while the specific memorial recon-struction narrative, involving two or three identifiable actor reporters, seems implau-sible, it would nevertheless be unwise to rule out memorial agency as a component in the making of the 1597 quarto. I thus agree with Werstine who has encouraged scholars to 'avoid concluding that just because . . . it has been impossible for mod-ern criticism to convict actors in specific roles of memorially reconstructing plays,

[63] Charles B. Lower, *Romeo and Juliet*, IV.v: a stage direction and purposeful comedy', *S.St.* 8 (1975), 177–94, 182. See also Melchiori.
[64] Another feature of Q1 which strengthens the case for memorial agency is the presence of Q2 passages which have been transposed in Q1, usually occurring earlier than in the longer version. See the notes at 4.191–2, 6.25, 8.5–6, 8.10–11. For other discussions, see Gibbons, pp. 4–5 and Chambers, *William Shakespeare*, vol. 1, p. 341.

then memorial reconstruction ought no longer be considered as a possible mode of transmission of playtexts into print'.[65] In other words, we may need to allow for other possibilities with which a text like Q1 *Romeo and Juliet* came into being in which memory might also play a role. Peter Blayney, for instance, has come up with a suggestion that goes beyond what Werstine has called the 'twentieth-century critical absorption with arresting a particular actor and charging him with producing a "bad" quarto'.[66] The origin of Blayney's theory is Humphrey Moseley's assertion in the prefatory material to the 1647 'Beaumont and Fletcher' Folio that 'When these *Comedies* and *Tragedies* were presented on the Stage, the *Actours* omitted some *Scenes* and Passages (with the *Authour's* consent) as occasion led them; and when private friends desir'd a Copy, they then (and justly too) transcribed what they *Acted*'.[67] Blayney comments:

As I understand the passage, Moseley is expecting someone to object (because 'everyone knows') that plays were usually and markedly abridged for performance, and that when actors made copies for their friends they wrote down what had been spoken onstage. No texts of that inferior kind, he boasts, will be found in *his* book. What he seems to be referring to, then, – texts of a kind so familiar that someone is bound to bring them up unless he forestalls the objection – are performance texts written down by actors who took part in them. The quality of such texts would vary greatly (both from each other and from scene to scene within a single text), depending on the infinitely variable circumstances of their origins. . . . What Moseley has been trying to tell us since 1647 is, I believe, the commonplace and innocent origin of the kind of text that Pollard called a Bad Quarto – but we have been too busy chasing imaginary pirates to listen.[68]

Blayney's argument for the origin of the 'bad quartos' as 'performance texts written down by actors who took part in them' could easily accommodate the evidence for memorial agency in Q1 *Romeo and Juliet*. Blayney points out that in 1647 'transcribe' was more likely to mean 'to make a copy of' than 'from', suggests that 'Moseley isn't talking about fair copies of promptbooks', and concludes that the actors may well have copied out the text from what they remembered of performances.[69] Blayney's account has other virtues, too. It does not depend upon the ability of two or three actors to remember, at times with great accuracy, the words of characters they did not themselves play (or even witness onstage). The 'infinitely variable circumstances

---

[65] Paul Werstine, 'Narratives about printed Shakespeare texts: "foul papers" and "bad" quartos', *SQ* 41 (1990), 65–86, 84. Werstine makes the same careful distinction in another article published nine years later. Despite his argument that memorial reconstruction cannot 'provide a full account' of traditional 'bad' quartos such as Q1 *Romeo and Juliet*, he adds that 'I believe that Shakespeare quartos could have come into being through a process of memorial reconstruction . . . there is a difference between accepting the possibility of memorial reconstruction in general and accepting it as the established origin of particular printed texts' (Werstine, 'Century', 311).

[66] Werstine, 'Narratives', 80.

[67] I quote from W. W. Greg, *A Bibliography of the English Printed Drama to the Restoration*, 4 vols. (London, 1939–59), vol. 3, p. 1233.

[68] Peter W. M. Blayney, 'The publication of playbooks', in *A New History of Early English Drama*, ed. John D. Cox and David Scott Kastan (New York, 1997), p. 394.

[69] 'Shakespeare's fight with *what* pirates?', Paper presented at the Folger Shakespeare Library, May 1987, quoted and discussed in Maguire, *Shakespearean Suspect Texts*, pp. 104–5.

of their origins' does not preclude the possibility that the players made use of their 'parts', which might account for those portions of Q1 *Romeo and Juliet*, especially early on in the play (especially Scenes 1 to 7) that are close to (albeit quite a bit shorter than) Q2. In fact, the account conforms well to Andrew Gurr's important recent theory about the genesis of the first quarto of *Henry V* (another traditional 'bad quarto'): Q1 *Henry V* is 'a version closely based on the Shakespeare company's own performance script of the play, a text made for or from its first performances in 1599 . . . Most of the manuscript was recorded by dictation, chiefly from the rough playscript, helped in places by the players' memories of their parts.'[70] According to the accounts favoured by Blayney and Gurr, the origins of 'bad quartos' would turn out to be innocuous rather than in some ways surreptitious. Even more importantly, Q1 *Romeo and Juliet* would conform to what Moseley suggests was accepted practice in the case of Fletcher, Shakespeare's direct successor as playwright for the King's Men.[71] It obviously cannot be proven that the practice mentioned by Moseley is at the origin of Q1 *Romeo and Juliet*, but it seems fair to say that it accounts rather better for the evidence than the theories proposed by most twentieth-century scholars.

A VERSION FOR THE PROVINCES?

Two features of past accounts of the provenance of the 'bad quartos' and of Q1 *Romeo and Juliet* in particular remain to be addressed. A recurrent part of the memorial reconstruction narrative had it that the 'bad quartos' were abridgements (which I will address in the next section) designed for provincial touring (the subject of this section).[72] For instance, Jowett considered it 'likely that the actors reproduced a version which had been adapted by Shakespeare's company for provincial performance'.[73] In fact, the 'bad quartos' have been linked to the provinces in one of two ways, depending on whether the texts are believed to be records *of* or *for* provincial performances. The former contention need not detain us long. As has been pertinently asked, 'Are we, then, to believe that all reporters knew only provincial versions?'[74] The latter position has proved longer-lived. A number of scholars have argued that it is 'difficult to imagine why such an abridgement would have been performed anywhere but in the provinces, especially as certain alterations presume a less sophisticated audience'.[75] Yet the denigration of provincial audiences seems to be based on prejudice rather than firm evidence. These allegedly unsophisticated provincial audiences were in fact often the same, as Maguire reminds us, as those

[70] Andrew Gurr, ed., *The First Quarto of King Henry V*, The New Cambridge Shakespeare: The Early Quartos (Cambridge, 2000), pp. ix, 9. See also the following article by Gurr which develops his argument: 'Maximal and minimal texts: Shakespeare v. the Globe', *S.Sur.* 52 (1999), 68–87.

[71] Shakespeare collaborated with Fletcher at the end of his career on *Henry VIII*, *The Two Noble Kinsmen*, and, presumably, the lost *Cardenio*.

[72] This part of my introduction is indebted to Erne, pp. 206–10.

[73] Jowett, p. 289. Similarly, Farley-Hills believes that Q1 *Romeo and Juliet* 'was presumably intended for performance by a touring troupe in the provinces' (28).

[74] Robert E. Burkhart, *Shakespeare's Bad Quartos* (The Hague, 1975), p. 21.

[75] Wells, *Modernizing*, p. 110. To give another example: 'It may well be that all the bad quartos were abridgments for touring purposes' (Michael J. B. Allen and Kenneth Muir, eds., *Shakespeare's Plays in Quarto* (Berkeley, 1981), p. xiv n. 9).

who, not long ago, had performed and watched extremely long and theologically complex mystery cycles. Her point that audiences in provincial towns 'may have been relatively sophisticated' is pertinent, and we can be sure that noble households were even more so.[76]

Another argument with which the 'bad quartos' have occasionally been assigned to the provinces is that they are designed for a reduced cast.[77] As I show in Appendix B, however, the number of actors required to play Q1 *Romeo and Juliet* conforms well to what can be gathered about the cast needed for Shakespeare's plays in the 1590s. Also, in the case of *Hamlet*, Scott McMillin has shown that the 'bad quarto' does not in fact take fewer actors to perform than the 'good', second quarto, an argument which has been endorsed in a recent essay by Ann Thompson and Neil Taylor.[78] Independently of the number of actors required, it has been pointed out by Leslie Thomson that the staging implied by the stage directions in Q1 *Romeo and Juliet* calls for a theatrical space that corresponds to a public playhouse in London: 'While many plays do not require use of the tiring house space above or below, and most of those which do could be performed on a provincial or great-hall stage with neither, *Romeo and Juliet* is not one of these. The source(s) Shakespeare was adapting virtually required the use of both levels.'[79]

Furthermore, it seems worthwhile pointing out how uneconomic the hypothesis is that dramatic scripts were routinely modified and abridged when actors went on tour. Research carried out as part of the Records of Early English Drama (REED) project has unearthed the extent to which touring was an integral part of otherwise London-based companies.[80] Actors, performing many different plays in the same season and with little time for rehearsal, had surely other things to worry about than to try to keep two versions of a role apart. According to Henslowe's diary, Lord Strange's Men performed fifteen different plays in March 1592 and the same number in the following month.[81] Gurr has shown that a professional company in the 1590s performed almost forty plays in a regular season of which about half would be new.[82] Anyone who has performed onstage must be aware of the difficulty of changing a part one has learned by heart and acted. To do so routinely with the number of parts an Elizabethan player had to know would have been an impossible strain on even well-trained memories. It would no doubt have constituted an important source of misrememberings and confusions onstage every time the players were required to switch (as they regularly would have had) from provincial to London versions. This is not to argue for theatrical texts as more fixed entities than they undoubtedly were. There is sufficient evidence suggesting that plays were revived,

[76] Maguire, *Shakespearean Suspect Texts*, p. 6.
[77] See, for instance, Burkhart, *Shakespeare's Bad Quartos*.
[78] Scott McMillin, 'Casting the *Hamlet* quartos: the limit of eleven', in *The 'Hamlet' First Published*, ed. Thomas Clayton (Newark, 1992), pp. 179–94, and Ann Thompson and Neil Taylor, '"Your sum of parts": doubling in *Hamlet*', in Erne and Kidnie, pp. 111–26.
[79] Thomson, 233–4.
[80] See also Siobhan Keenan, *Travelling Players in Shakespeare's England* (London, 2002).
[81] See Neil Carson, *A Companion to Henslowe's Diary* (Cambridge, 1988), p. 85.
[82] See Andrew Gurr, *The Shakespearean Stage 1574–1642*, 3rd edn (Cambridge, 1992), pp. 103–4.

abridged, adapted, revised, and provided with additions or topical insertions. Yet to acknowledge that many play-texts underwent manifold changes in the course of their theatrical history is not the same as to argue that players who were burdened with a great many different parts at any one time would have chosen for no obvious reason to assimilate alternative, abridged parts, too. Adaptation for touring in the provinces is an unconvincing scholarly hypothesis about what would have been an uneconomic theatrical practice.[83]

THEATRICAL ABRIDGEMENT

The argument that Q1 *Romeo and Juliet* is a version for or of the provinces is closely related to the view that it also constitutes a theatrical abridgement. If we think that the much longer Q2 version is what Shakespeare's company performed in London, then the first quarto, even though it is usually recognised to be a stage version, would have to have been staged elsewhere. So if the 'bad quartos' show signs of being deliberate stage abridgements (and, in the case of *Romeo and Juliet*, the evidence for this, as we shall see, is strong), then the argument for the provinces follows naturally unless the basic premise is mistaken, the premise, that is, that the long versions of certain Shakespeare plays, *Romeo and Juliet*, *Hamlet*, and others, were designed to be performed in their entirety.

That the premise is indeed likely to be mistaken has been emerging with increasing clarity in recent times. Stephen Orgel reports that he 'caused a great deal of consternation' when he made the following observation: 'it is a commonplace to remark the discrepancy between the performing time always given for Elizabethan plays – "the two hours' traffic of our stage" – and the actual length of the texts, but . . . no one has ever confronted the implications of the obvious conclusion that the plays Shakespeare's company performed were shorter than the plays Shakespeare wrote for them. The text then, was not the play.'[84] In a different essay, Orgel returns to the subject: 'with very few exceptions, every printed Shakespeare text is far too long for the two to two-and-one-half hours that is universally accepted as the performing time of plays in the period . . . Every play, that is, would normally have been cut for production.'[85] Orgel exaggerates here: even though sixteen of Shakespeare's plays are unusually long (in excess of 2,800 lines), nine of them are shorter than 2,500 and conform well enough to the average length of plays by his contemporaries.[86] Nevertheless, for Shakespeare's long plays Orgel's point remains valid and has recently been reinforced by Gurr who thinks it is likely 'that 2,500 [lines] was close to maximal for a play-script, and that plays of greater length were still

---

[83] In 'Touring and the construction of Shakespeare textual criticism', in *Textual Formations and Reformations*, ed. Laurie Maguire and Thomas L. Berger (Newark, 1998), pp. 45–66, Paul Werstine also challenges the received idea that the 'bad quartos' represent shorted versions of plays for acting companies on provincial tours.

[84] Orgel, *The Authentic Shakespeare*, p. 21.

[85] Ibid., p. 237.

[86] What corroborates this is that the Prologue to *Romeo and Juliet* (in the first and the second quarto) announces 'the two hours' traffic of our stage', a performance time which, if taken literally, is compatible with the first but not with the second quarto. See Erne, pp. 137–41.

routinely cut for performance'.[87] As Orgel points out, habitual theatrical abridgement was 'the situation obtaining in Shakespeare's own company, of which he was
a part owner and director – it was a situation he understood, expected, and helped
to perpetuate. And it implies . . . that his scripts offered the company a range of
possibilities.'[88]

I have recently tried to strengthen Orgel's case by drawing on evidence about
performance times, play-text lengths, manuscript playbooks, Restoration abridgements, and so on, evidence which does not need to be redeployed here.[89] Irace has
produced a valuable study of the nature of the abridgement in Q1 *Romeo and Juliet*.
Having analysed the 'more than eight hundred lines unique to Q2', she shows that the
disappearance of many of them is due to genuine theatrical cuts. This is suggested
by the fact that 'twenty passages are missing in Q1 in sequences that otherwise match
nearly word for word in the two versions',[90] meaning that the failure of memory can
barely account for them. Irace looks at these passages individually and concludes
that 'each of these twenty passages can be defended as a reasonable theatrical cut,
because each one either repeats details in other segments, expands an idea without advancing the action, or contributes to an alternate staging of its sequence'.[91]
Irace confines her analysis to passages which are particularly clear-cut and of some
length, but many other Q1 omissions clearly also resulted from abridgement rather
than from memorial lapses. There are many shorter passages absent from Q1 among
otherwise accurately rendered Q2 material, suggesting that shorter passages were
also excised as the play was prepared for the stage. The same can be observed in
other theatrical abridgements.[92] All in all, it seems likely that somewhere around
two thirds or three quarters of the difference in length between Q1 and Q2 can be
accounted for by the company's theatrical abridgement as part of the company's
preparation of the play for performance (in London and elsewhere). By contrast,
the remaining quarter or so seems more likely to be a matter of actors' condensation
(speeches which basically preserve the contents but reduce the number of words)
and memorial omissions rather than the company's deliberate abridgement.

A word needs to be added about what may have been a collateral effect of the
abridgement, an abridgement that was undertaken, we can assume, by members
of the company and, it seems possible, by Shakespeare among them. Especially in
the early parts of the plays, cuts can be observed amidst otherwise closely parallel
material, material in which, nevertheless, Q1 contains local differences which often
seem to make good sense. The relationship in these passages is in fact similar to
substantial portions of Q1 and F *Othello* or Q and F *Troilus and Cressida*, where
most scholars now agree that Shakespeare may well have made occasional *currente*

[87] Gurr, *Shakespeare Company*, p. 123.
[88] Orgel, *The Authentic Shakespeare*, p. 238; Jonathan Goldberg concurs with Orgel: 'I submit that what
    stands behind Q2 [*Romeo and Juliet*] is a manuscript that offers an anthology of possible performances
    of the play, one of which is captured by Q1' (Goldberg, p. 186).
[89] See Erne, pp. 131–73.
[90] Irace, p. 142.
[91] Ibid.
[92] See Erne, pp. 158–64.

calamo revisions as he revised his foul papers.[93] The following passage may provide a representative example (the Q1 variants are indicated between square brackets):

ROMEO What less than doomsday is the Prince's doom?
FRIAR LAURENCE A gentler judgement vanished from his lips:
  Not body's death, but body's banishment.
ROMEO Ha, banishment [banishèd]? be merciful, say 'death':
  For exile hath more terror in his look, [looks]
  Much more than death [Than death itself]. Do not say 'banishment'!
FRIAR LAURENCE Here [Hence] from Verona art thou banishèd.
  Be patient, for the world is broad and wide.   (3.3.9–16/12.9–16)

Pope adopted the Q1 reading in line 14 and Hanmer preferred Q1's 'Here' to Q2's 'Hence', but the differences are neither significant improvements nor obvious corruptions. It therefore seems possible that some of them are of authorial origin. In other words, the version of *Romeo and Juliet* which was abridged and imperfectly remembered before being published in Q1 quite possibly contained authorial revisions of the kind Shakespeare also made on other occasions. In individual cases where Q1 and Q2 differ but both make sense, it is difficult if not impossible to determine whether Shakespearean revision accounts for the difference, but the sum of such intelligent and closely parallel passages suggests that Shakespeare is responsible for a number of them.[94]

TEXTUAL PROVENANCE: CONCLUSION
In conclusion, it is easier to state what theories do not account, or do not account alone, for the particular textual make-up of Q1 *Romeo and Juliet* than to determine what theories do. The idea that Q1 constitutes a first draft which Shakespeare expanded to Q2 may safely be laid to rest. Nor do I find it possible to believe that Q1 constitutes a version exclusively written for or performed in the provinces. Furthermore, powerful evidence militates against the traditional memorial reconstruction scenario, according to which two or three actors (Romeo, Paris, and possibly Mercutio) reconstituted the play from memory. Nevertheless, certain features of the text are best accounted for by a process of memorisation. Also, it seems unlikely that Q1 constitutes simply an abridgement, undertaken by a redactor or by Shakespeare himself. Shakespeare's original script as reflected by Q2 seems likely to have been abridged before the play reached the stage, but this abridgement accounts only for a portion of the divergences between Q1 and Q2, the omissions, but not the textual differences. While the latter seem partly a matter of memorial agency, it seems possible that small-scale authorial revision also contributed a share towards them.

While some of these conclusions remain naturally no more than tentative, it is nevertheless clear that the first quarto of *Romeo and Juliet* turns out to be a vastly more important text than was commonly believed in the last century. For

---

[93] See Honigmann, *Stability*, pp. 78–120, and Wells et al., *Textual Companion*, pp. 426, 476–7.
[94] See also my note at 10.55–75.

much of the twentieth century, the diagnosis 'memorial reconstruction' suggested an inferior and ultimately unimportant product that could be discarded, not only because of the way the reporters debased the Shakespearean text but also because of the purpose these reconstructions were supposed to serve, such as performance in the provinces. However, much of the difference between Q1 and Q2 is most likely to be a matter of abridgement, and it has become increasingly clear that abridgement, especially of Shakespeare's long, literary texts, must have been a standard feature of the preparation for performance in London. The first quarto of *Romeo and Juliet*, in other words, probably takes us as close as we can get to the play as it would have been performed by Shakespeare and his fellow players in London and elsewhere. In keeping with the recent turn towards performance, the editors of the Oxford Shakespeare *Complete Works* claim to 'have devoted [their] efforts to recovering and presenting texts of Shakespeare's play as they were acted in the London playhouses',[95] and add that they 'have therefore chosen . . . to prefer – where there is a choice – the text closer to the prompt-book of Shakespeare's company'.[96] But in fact, their edition is based on Q2 *Romeo and Juliet* or Folio *Hamlet*, texts which, as Brian Vickers pointed out, are still far too long to have been performed on the early modern stage.[97] If we are interested in getting close to a Shakespeare play as it was performed as well as in the process which turned Shakespeare's original drama into a workable performance script, then there is no better text to turn to than the first quarto of *Romeo and Juliet*.

Dramatic specificities

As long as the first quarto's chief epithet was 'bad', its alleged badness relieved editors and critics of the obligation to pay it the closest attention. Now that awareness of its real importance is increasing, unbiased investigation of its dramatic specificities is called for. Here I can do no more than sketch a few directions such an investigation might take. I will proceed by keeping an eye on Q2, examining how Q1 is simply different from the better-known text.

PACE AND ACTION

Romeo and Juliet is sometimes grouped with plays – *Richard II*, *Love's Labour's Lost*, *A Midsummer Night's Dream* – that were written in the mid-1590s and are characterised by the quality and quantity of their lyrical poetic language.[98] This generic characterisation applies considerably better to Q2 than Q1. By omitting

---

95 Stanley Wells, 'General Introduction', in *The Oxford Shakespeare: The Complete Works*, gen. eds. Wells and Taylor (Oxford, 1986) p. xxxvii.
96 Wells et al., *Textual Companion*, p. 15.
97 Brian Vickers, Review of William Shakespeare, *The Complete Works* and *A Textual Companion*, ed. Stanley Wells and Gary Taylor, with John Jowett and William Montgomery (Oxford, 1986–7), *RES* 40 (1989), 404. For the question of length and for a discussion of the Oxford *Complete Works'* editorial policy, see Erne, chapters 6 and 7. See also Orgel's pertinent comment: 'most editors and critics go to extraordinary lengths to avoid dealing with the notion that our printed texts are not what Shakespeare's actors spoke' (*The Authentic Shakespeare*, p. 22).
98 See Chambers, *William Shakespeare*, vol. 1, p. 267.

more than 700 lines without changing or simplifying the plot, Q1 often abridges those passages in which the action pauses, in which ideas and feelings are developed at some length and with considerable imaginative and verbal artistry. The reason why these passages were abridged is not that theatre audiences would have been unable to follow them – people able to absorb long and complex sermons clearly had considerable aural abilities. Rather, since abridgement was necessary, poetic passages were particularly liable to cutting as their absence did no damage to the plot. Effects of these omissions are a diminution in the play's poetic impact and a condensation of its action.[99] Whereas Q2 amplifies introspection, lyricism, and characterisation, Q1 favours pace and action.

Juliet offers a good example. As Irace has shown, the length of her Q1 part is reduced by almost 40 per cent.[100] Her first soliloquy consists of seventeen lines in Q2 and a mere six in Q1 (2.5.1–17; 8.1–6). The abridgement of her second soliloquy is even more radical: the first four lines are almost identical, but Q1 omits all of the remaining twenty-nine lines in Q2 (3.2.1–33; 11.1–4). Her third soliloquy, before she drinks the vial, takes up forty-five lines in Q2 but is reduced to eighteen in Q1 (4.3.14–58; 17.10–27). Some of her more ingenious speeches are also curtailed or even omitted. In 3.2 Juliet impatiently asks the Nurse for news, but in doing so expresses her impatience, paradoxically, in a lengthy nine-line speech, not present in Q1, in which she extensively puns on 'I', 'ay', and 'eye' (3.2.43–51). In Scene 14 (3.5), Juliet laments Romeo's banishment in terms which make her mother believe that she is mourning her cousin's death, a device she develops over four lines in Q1 (14.76–9), but over an additional seven lines in Q2 (3.5.96–102). When Juliet turns to the Nurse for advice, she asks for it in one straightforward line in Q1 (14.168). In Q2, she describes her plight in nine lines by means of a complex opposition between 'earth' and 'heaven': 'My husband is on earth, my faith in heaven; / How shall that faith return again to earth, / Unless that husband send it me from heaven / By leaving earth?' (3.5.205–8). Similar patterns could be examined by focussing on other characters. This would confirm my point: poetic passages were affected far more than others when Shakespeare's original version was cut.

The other side of the same coin is that these omissions highlight the density of the play's plot. The final scene is a case in point. If we subtract the forty-one lines of the Friar's long speech, the one moment at which the scene's frantic action comes to a standstill, then Q2 totals 269 lines as opposed to 182 in Q1, 182 lines for a scene filled with action and characters, Paris and his page, Romeo and Balthasar, the opening of Juliet's tomb, the fight between Paris and Romeo, Romeo's suicide,

---

[99] In particular, Q1 eliminates a certain amount of repetition (such as part of the conversation between Benvolio and Romeo in 1.1 which continues in 1.2). Repetition can have an important function in performance, and Shakespeare clearly makes much deliberate use of it (especially when he is intent on shaping an audience's attention), so my argument is not that the omitted material must have been thought of as pointless but that, given the constraints imposed by the 'two hours' traffic of our stage', it seemed more easily dispensable than other portions of the text.

[100] Irace, p. 185.

Friar Laurence's arrival, Juliet's awakening, Laurence's escape, Juliet's suicide, the arrival of the watch, the arrest of the Friar and Balthasar, the successive arrivals of the Prince, the Capulets, and Montague, and the final reconciliation. The first quarto compresses action where Q2, by comparison, spreads it out. In other words, Q1 has more pace than Q2; it is a play bustling with action, with characters arriving, acting, fighting, leaving, or dying, at a pace that draws attention to the intensity of the stage action.

STAGE DIRECTIONS

It is in keeping with Q1's emphasis on dramatic action that its stage directions are more numerous and detailed than those in Q2. Following John Jowett, I argue in the section on 'Publication and Printing' below (see pp. 39–41) that the stage directions in Q1 may partly have been composed by Henry Chettle, serving as assistant to the printer John Danter. They have a literary flavour uncommon in Shakespearean playbooks, and it is possible that they contain occasional embellishments which do not correspond to what was performed on the early modern stage. In general, however, it seems more likely that the stage directions reflect what was at least at one stage the performance practice of Shakespeare's company. As pointed out above, they call for the kind of performance space provided by a London playhouse (see p. 21). In any case, the Q1 stage directions seem to record what was performed (or what someone imagined could have been performed) in the theatre.

The stage directions contain information of various kinds: about costume ('*Enter* BALTHASAR, *his man, booted*', 18.9), the delivery of the lines ('*All at once cry out and wring their hands*', 17.82), inaudible speech ('*They whisper in his ear*', 4.188), movement ('*Nurse offers to go in and turns again*', 12.132), and various stage business ('*Tybalt under Romeo's arm thrusts Mercutio, in and flies*', 10.54), sometimes related to the use of props ('*Paris strews the tomb with flowers*', 20.6). Gibbons has described their interest as 'exceptional',[101] and most editors who use Q2 as their copy text adopt many of them from Q1. As far as stage directions are concerned, the modern editions most people read derive in fact at least as much from Q1 as from Q2.

A few stage directions have an important impact on how we imagine the play to have been performed. For instance, at the end of the lamentation sequence, when the Capulets, Paris, and the Nurse believe Juliet to be dead, '*They all but the Nurse go forth, casting rosemary on her* [Juliet] *and shutting the curtains*' (17.108 SD.1–2). These curtains are also mentioned earlier in the scene, when, after drinking the potion, Juliet '*falls upon her bed within the curtains*' (17.27). Neither stage direction has an equivalent in Q2. In the early modern playhouse, Juliet's bed 'probably would have been "thrust out" from the tiring house' (like that in the last scene of *Othello*).[102] In other words, the curtains probably close off not the discovery space but the canopied bed.[103] The effect of this is important. When Juliet falls upon her bed after drinking

---

[101] Gibbons, p. 11.
[102] Thomson, 234.
[103] Ibid., 239.

the potion, she and the bed remain onstage. Throughout what most editions call Act 4 Scene 4, the bed on which spectators know Juliet lies is thus a conspicuous presence of which spectators would have been well aware. The visual juxtaposition is surely significant, the wedding preparations in the bustling Capulet household starkly contrasting with the immobility and quiet of the hidden Juliet on her bed.

Juliet and the bed thus remain onstage throughout Scene 17 (4.3 to 4.5). At the end of this scene, the stage direction asks for the curtains to be shut, raising the intriguing question of whether Juliet and the bed remain onstage even longer, until the bed becomes her tomb in the final scene, where Romeo finds her dead some 170 lines later.[104] As Leslie Thomson points out, 'Not only the conventions of the unlocalized stage, but staging practicality would seem to dictate a verbal – and visual – metamorphosis of bed into bier.'[105] This staging would establish a powerful correspondence, her seeming death in Scene 17 visually foreshadowing her real death in the last scene. While this last point can be no more than speculative, Q1's stage directions in Scene 17 clearly have a significant impact on our interpretation of the stage action.

A stage direction in Scene 14 can also have important repercussions on the staging. The scene begins with Romeo and Juliet on the upper level, 'at the window', as Q1 puts it. After their farewell, Romeo '*goeth down*' (14.37), using the rope ladder. Following Romeo's exit, the Nurse enters '*hastily*' (14.55 SD.2), announcing her mother's arrival. In Q2, the Nurse warns Juliet prior to Romeo's departure, and Juliet is left alone onstage, still above, speaking a short soliloquy. In Q1, by contrast, the Nurse's announcement is followed by a stage direction indicating that Juliet '*goeth down from the window*' (14.57 SD.1). When Juliet's mother enters on the main stage, the actor playing Juliet has thus had time to descend and enters to her mother, the main stage thus becoming Juliet's bedchamber. Q2 omits any mention of Juliet's descent to the main stage and editors, aware that Juliet's confrontation with her parents cannot conceivably be staged on the balcony,[106] insert the stage direction based on Q1 following Juliet's first answer to her mother. This leaves Juliet only half a line to descend, resulting in 'a rather awkward arrangement'.[107] In at least one modern production, the actress playing Juliet's mother, 'took a long pause before and after her short line to allow Juliet time to run down from the balcony to the main stage'.[108] As Jowett points out, 'the staging may not have been fully envisaged when

[104] Thomson, 240–1; this possibility had also been considered by Williams, p. 147. Andrew Gurr ('The date and expected venue of *Romeo and Juliet*', *S. Sur.*, 49 (1996)) recognises the appeal of such 'symbolic symmetry' (22) but ultimately considers it more likely that the tomb was below the trapdoor rather than the former marriage bed (24–5).

[105] Thomson, 241.

[106] See Hosley, 'Upper stage', 371–9. Evans quotes Granville-Barker's point that 'Capulet's outburst could have been effectively played nowhere but on the lower stage' (NCS, p. 31). As Thomson has pointed out, the descent of the action to the main stage is not only a practical matter, but contributes to the 'inexorable downward movement of the action' from above to main stage to bed to tomb (see Thomson, 234).

[107] NCS, p. 31.

[108] Loehlin, p. 197.

Shakespeare first drafted the passage',[109] which, incidentally, could provide further
evidence that Q1 derives from Q2 rather than vice versa (see above, pp. 9–13).

At least one Q1 stage direction even suggests an interpretation that contrasts with
Q2. Bewailing his banishment, Romeo is about to commit suicide, but the Nurse
prevents him from doing so: '*He offers to stab himself, and Nurse snatches the dagger
away*' (12.101). Q2 has no stage direction at this point; the dialogue continues with
Friar Laurence's exclamation 'Hold thy desperate hand!' (3.3.108). Nothing in Q2
suggests that the Nurse takes an active part in stopping Romeo's desperate action,
and several modern productions, including Zeffirelli's and Luhrmann's film versions, have her shrink back in horror while Friar Laurence bravely intervenes. The
contrast between the stage direction in Q1 and standard modern stage practice is
well worth thinking about in the context of a play that questions stereotypical atti-
tudes to gender in a variety of ways, including the protagonists' respective suicides –
poison and stabbing – in an inversion of what traditional gender roles dictate.

THE BETROTHAL SCENE

Scene 9 (2.6), the betrothal scene, is the only scene in Q1 that, textually, is almost
entirely independent of Q2. It dramatises the same events: Romeo and Friar Laurence
expect the arrival of Juliet; she arrives; the Friar leads the young lovers off to their
wedding. As usual, Q1 is somewhat shorter than Q2, twenty-eight lines as opposed
to thirty-seven. What is unusual, however, is that its wording has nothing to do with
that of Q2.

Scholars have come up with different explanations to account for the origins
of the scene. For instance, Gibbons suggested that the reporters 'remembered the
narrative content of the scene, wished to retain it for its dramatic function, but had
to compose it afresh'.[110] Honigmann, having quoted a lengthy passage (9.10–20),
stressed 'the poetic quality of the lines', pointed out that 'many critics think it as
good as, or better than, the definitely Shakespearian text', and thought 'it seems
possible . . . that while one or two phrases stem from the reporter the passage
as a whole, and its splendid lyricism, represents substantially what Shakespeare
himself wrote'.[111] Finally, the scene has also been related to the argument for Henry
Chettle's editorial involvement in the first quarto (see below, pp. 39–41): Sidney
Thomas drew verbal and spelling parallels to argue for Chettle's authorship of the
scene, an argument that has been endorsed and developed by John Jowett.[112]

While the scene's origins and authorship are difficult to determine, it may be
easier to assess its tone and effect. Steven Urkowitz has stressed its 'emotional

---

[109] Jowett, p. 299.
[110] Gibbons, p. 7.
[111] Honigmann, *Stability*, p. 134. As early as 1857, White, who still believed that Shakespeare revised Q1
and turned it into Q2, thought that 'The change made upon the revision was not in all respects for the
better' (quoted in Furness, p. 148). Similarly, Field, in 1889, held that 'It is difficult to comprehend
why Shakespeare should discard such poetical thoughts, and replace them in quarto second with
those so very much inferior' (p. 3).
[112] See Sidney Thomas, 'Henry Chettle and the first quarto of *Romeo and Juliet*', *RES* n.s. 1 (1950),
8–16, 11; Jowett, 'Chettle', 53–74.

exclamations' and 'celebratory dramatic trajectories'.[113] From the beginning, as Romeo and Friar Laurence await Juliet's arrival, the tone is one of joyful anticipation: 'I will do all I may / To make you happy' (9.3–4), the Friar assures Romeo. When Juliet arrives, she enters '*somewhat fast, and embraceth Romeo*' (9.9 SD), as a stage direction puts it; 'embracements' (9.22) seem to continue until Friar Laurence interrupts the young lovers to lead them off for their union to be solemnised. Juliet is entirely focussed on Romeo and expresses her love in simple language. The only words she addresses to Friar Laurence assert her impatience to get married: 'Make haste, make haste, this ling'ring doth us wrong' (9.26).

The lightness and exuberance of the Q1 wedding scene is all the more striking when it is compared to its equivalent in Q2. In contrast to Q1's 'unrelieved cheer',[114] Q2 ominously refers to 'sorrow', 'Death', and 'violent ends' (2.6.2–9). When Juliet enters, no stage direction points out that she does so '*somewhat fast*', nor does she embrace or even address Romeo. Instead, she talks to the Friar with polite restraint and control. This difference has suggested to Urkowitz that Q1's Juliet is an 'innocent victim of Veronese social codes' but Q2's 'a full participant in their subtlety'.[115] Q2's Friar similarly differs from his Q1 counterpart, an authority figure rather than a 'friendly escort to the greater pleasures of marriage'.[116] In Urkowitz's view then, Q1 and Q2 show 'two radically different conceptions of this scene . . . One rings exuberantly, one tolls ominously.'[117]

CHARACTERISATION

While Q1's Juliet and Friar in the betrothal scene can thus be understood as rather different characters from their Q2 counterparts, they are by no means the only characters that differ in the 1597 and the 1599 quartos. I do not argue that Shakespeare or anyone else must have *intended* to change certain characters in a certain way as part of a process of revision. Such arguments have been advanced in the context of the two versions of *King Lear*, but my ambition here is more modestly to view Q1 and Q2 as texts with their own material and historical integrity, independently of the exact origins of specific textual variations.

The Nurse offers a good example: she is an ambivalent character in Q2 as actresses and commentators through the ages have made clear.[118] She is Juliet's confidante and former wet-nurse, a go-between at the service of Juliet and Romeo, but ultimately an unreliable ally whom Juliet decides to leave behind. In the course of the play, Romeo and Juliet meet and speak only four times (the fifth time, one or the other is asleep or dead). It is noteworthy that on three of these occasions, the Nurse intrudes upon them. At the Capulets' feast, she interrupts their first conversation, which takes the form of a sonnet followed by a quatrain, arguably the beginning of a second sonnet

[113] Urkowitz, p. 225.
[114] Ibid., p. 223.
[115] Ibid., p. 230.
[116] Ibid., p. 229.
[117] Ibid.
[118] See Jill L. Levenson, *Shakespeare in Performance: Romeo and Juliet* (Manchester, 1987).

which is stopped by the Nurse (1.5.110). In the course of the 'Balcony Scene', the Nurse repeatedly calls from within, thus interrupting and abridging the lovers' encounter (2.1.135–51). At the end of their wedding night, finally, the Nurse enters as Romeo and Juliet are bidding what will turn out to be their final farewell (3.5.36). This, at least, is how events are dramatised in the play as most people know it. In Q1, however, the Nurse, on two of these three occasions, fails to interrupt the two lovers. In Q1's 'Balcony Scene', Juliet says, 'I hear some coming' (5.158) and momentarily exits as a consequence, but the source of the noise is not identified and nothing suggests that the Nurse has anything to do with it. Nor does she interrupt their final parting. In fact, Q1's Scene 14 starts with a self-contained movement with Romeo and Juliet alone, and the Nurse does not enter until after Romeo has left. Having warned her of her mother's imminent arrival ('Madam, beware, take heed, the day is broke. / Your mother's coming to your chamber, make all sure', 14.56–7), she remains onstage throughout Juliet's confrontation with her mother, whereas her Q2 equivalent does not re-enter until Capulet's appearance later in the scene. So Q2's Nurse, contrary to Q1's, intrudes upon Juliet and Romeo during their amorous encounters but is absent when Juliet might need her.

Other evidence may add to the impression that Q1's Nurse can be understood as a more straightforwardly benevolent character than the Nurse in Q2. In Scene 16 (4.2), Q2's Nurse tells Capulet that Juliet has gone to Friar Laurence and informs him of Juliet's approach (4.2.10–14). Strikingly, Q1's Nurse not only fails to talk to Capulet (her speeches are assigned to Capulet's Wife) but, contrary to her Q2 equivalent, also speaks to Juliet after her arrival, and does so in notably warm terms:

NURSE Come, sweetheart, shall we go?
JULIET   I prithee, let us.
                                             (16.32)

The Nurse's first allegiance in Q2 seems to be to the parents, in Q1 to Juliet, expressed in an iambic pentameter shared between them. Moreover, at the beginning of the following scene, there is a short dialogue between Juliet and the Nurse in which the Nurse shows herself caring (17.1–4), whereas interaction between the two in Q2 is reduced to Juliet asking the Nurse to leave (4.3.1–5). A further difference can be noted in the lamentation passage which, as mentioned above, is a potentially comic moment, not only because the audience knows what the characters do not know, namely that Juliet is alive, but also because the simultaneous delivery of the lines results in utter 'confusions' (4.5.66). It may then be significant that the Nurse participates in the lamentations in Q2 – again aligning her with Juliet's parents – but does not in Q1. If the lamentation passage makes fun of characters who display grief over the supposed death of someone they previously alienated, then Q1 excludes the Nurse from these characters. Whether by accident or design, Q1's Nurse seems repeatedly more benevolent and sympathetic towards Juliet than her counterpart in Q2.

Far less need be said about other characters. A couple of hints may suggest different Tybalts in the two quartos. Prior to the fatal fight in Scene 10 (3.1), Q1's

Tybalt greets Romeo as follows: 'Romeo, the hate I bear to thee can afford / No better words than these: thou art a villain' (10.35–6). Q2's version is very similar except that it has 'love' where Q1 has 'hate' (3.1.53–4). Evans finds Q2's 'love' 'surprisingly ironic coming from the forthright Tybalt' (NCS), a quality Q1's character does not seem to share. In the preceding lines, Tybalt twice addresses Mercutio as 'sir' (3.1.36, 49), mock-polite words which Q1 lacks. When facing his opponents, Q2's Tybalt is thus ironic where Q1's is straightforward. Other local differences may suggest that whereas Q2 highlights the feudal conflict between the houses of the Montagues and the Capulets, Q1, by contrast, plays it down. The two versions run closely parallel at the beginning of the opening scene until Q1 leaves out Q2's 'The quarrel is between our masters, and us their men' (1.1.17). The omission of any mention of the masters' quarrel is intriguing insofar as Capulet and Montague play a different role in Q1 and Q2 when the conflict comes to a head later in the scene. In Q2, they are aggressive towards each other both verbally and physically:

CAPULET My sword, I say! old Montague is come,
  And flourishes his blade in spite of me
      Enter old MONTAGUE *and his wife* [LADY MONTAGUE]
MONTAGUE Thou villain Capulet! – Hold me not, let me go.
                    (1.1.68–70)

Q1 omits this passage, and the stage direction that takes its place does not suggest that they behave as belligerently as their Q2 counterparts: '*They draw, to them enters* TYBALT, *they fight, to them the* PRINCE, *old* MONTAGUE, *and his* WIFE, *old* CAPULET *and his* WIFE, *and other citizens and part them*' (1.48 SD). We cannot expect these words to provide a full and entirely accurate record of what is clearly a moment of intense and disordered stage action. Nevertheless, it is intriguing that the stage direction distinguishes between those who fight (the Serving-men and Tybalt) and those who 'part them' (the Prince, the Montagues, the Capulets, and other citizens). These passages make it seem possible that Q2 emphasises more than Q1 the feudal conflict among the members of the older generation.

I have suggested above that the abridgement strongly affects the play's lyricism and pace, but it also has an impact on characterisation. If a character like Juliet is given far fewer lines to express herself, in particular to express herself by means of soliloquies, then the character will usually display less of what we associate with the complexities and contradictions of human interiority. In our modern times, it may be tempting to equate complex (or 'round') characters with good drama and less complex (or 'flat') characters with poor drama, but it seems in fact more judicious to relate these differences to the media for which the two versions were designed. Q1, as argued above, imperfectly reflects a version abridged for the stage. But what about Q2? As I have argued elsewhere, Shakespeare from quite early on encouraged the publication of his playbooks and was aware that his plays were not only being performed onstage but also read on the page.[119] In other words, Q2 and

---

[119] Erne, pp. 56–100.

similarly long play-texts seem to have been conceived by Shakespeare as reading texts in the knowledge that they would not reach the stage without substantial abridgement. If so, then the greater complexity of characters in the long text may partly be a matter of the medium of literacy for which they were designed. As Walter Ong has pointed out, 'flat' characters derive from 'oral narrative, which can provide characters of no other kind', whereas 'round' characters are a product of 'the private worlds [that writing and reading] generate'.[120] Accordingly, Q1's Nurse, as seen above, may be more straightforwardly benevolent, a relatively 'flat' character, 'fulfilling expectations copiously',[121] compared to Q2's more ambivalent or 'round' figure.

Juliet's father provides another good example. In the second scene, after Paris's question, 'what say you to my suit?', the following dialogue ensues:

CAPULET What should I say more than I said before?
    My daughter is a stranger in the world,
    She hath not yet attained to fourteen years.
    Let two more summers wither in their pride
    Before she can be thought fit for a bride.
PARIS Younger than she are happy mothers made.
CAPULET But too soon marred are these so early married.
    But woo her, gentle Paris, get her heart,
    My word to her consent is but a part.   (2.4–12)

The equivalent Q2 passage is largely identical except for two lines entirely absent from Q1 in Capulet's last speech:

CAPULET And too soon marred are those so early made.
    Earth hath swallowed all my hopes but she;
    She's the hopeful lady of my earth.
    But woo her, gentle Paris, get her heart,
    My will to her consent is but a part;   (1.2.13–17)

The rest of the play does not develop Capulet's allusion to his former loss, and he hardly becomes a 'round' character. Nevertheless, the two lines provide the kind of information – what Ong calls 'deeply interiorized in motivation, powered mysteriously'[122] – from which a character analysis might take off. Even though a loose end in terms of the intrigue, they provide a psychological detail that makes Capulet a somewhat 'rounder' character. It may be significant that it is precisely these lines that Q1, the theatrical version designed for an oral medium, omits, and that Q1's characters, in general, are more 'flat' and less 'round' than Q2's. If Q1 is related to an oral performance and Q2 constitutes a reading version, then this is what we should expect. Here and elsewhere, thinking of Q1 and Q2 as versions designed

---

[120] Walter J. Ong, *Orality and Literacy: The Technologizing of the Word* (London, 1982), pp. 151, 153.
[121] Ibid., p. 151.
[122] Ibid., p. 153.

for two different media can in fact shed light on either text as well as the differences between them.[123]

INCONSISTENT TIME REFERENCES

A final feature of Q1 that deserves special attention is its dramatisation of time. Q1's time scheme is inconsistent, by no means the only Shakespearean instance of such inconsistency, though the case of *Romeo and Juliet* is special owing to the difference between the two early versions.[124] Or rather, the two versions agree at times but differ at others, in particular with regards to Romeo and Juliet's betrothal. When Romeo first visits Friar Laurence in his cell, he tells him about his new love and asks him 'to marry us today' (6.59; 2.3.63–4) in a passage that is substantively identical in Q1 and Q2. Accordingly, when Q2's Romeo speaks to the Nurse later in the day (shortly after noon), he asks her to 'Bid [Juliet] devise / Some means to come to shrift this afternoon, / And there she shall at Friar Lawrence' cell / Be shrived and married' (2.4.148–51). A few lines later, he assures the Nurse that 'Within this hour my man shall be with thee, / And bring thee cords' (2.4.156–7). In Q1, however, these events are planned for the next day: 'Bid her get leave tomorrow morning / To come to shrift to Friar Laurence' cell, / And stay thou, Nurse, behind the abbey wall. / My man shall come to thee and bring along / The cords, made like a tackled stair' (7.145–9). The same discrepancy can be observed in the next scene: in Q1, the Nurse tells Juliet to 'hie you straight to Friar Laurence' cell, / And frame a scuse that you must go to shrift. / There stays a bridegroom to make you a bride' (8.33–5; Q2, 2.5.67–8, is very similar). The words clearly imply that the wedding is to be solemnized later the same day. Nevertheless, the Q1 wedding takes place next morning: 'This morning here she pointed we should meet / And consummate those never-parting bands' (9.5–6), Romeo tells Friar Laurence. In Q2, by contrast, Juliet greets Friar Lawrence with 'Good even' (2.6.21), an expression that is only used after noon.

Another slight inconsistency concerns the Friar's vial scheme. In Q2, Friar Laurence advises the distraught Juliet to 'go home, be merry, give consent / To marry Paris. Wednesday is tomorrow; / Tomorrow night look that thou lie alone' (4.1.89–91). In Q1, however, she is to take action immediately: 'hie thee home, get thee to bed . . . take thou this vial' (15.77–9). In both texts, Scene 13 (3.4) is explicitly set on Monday when Capulet decides that the wedding will take place on Thursday (13.20–4; 3.4.28–30). Scenes 14–16 (3.5 to 4.2) thus dramatize the events of the following day, Tuesday, and in Scene 16, Capulet advances the wedding to Wednesday (16.25–39; 4.2.23–45) so that Juliet, in either version, ends up drinking the potion in the night from Tuesday to Wednesday. Q1's Friar thus temporarily seems to have

---

[123] This paragraph draws on Erne, pp. 242–3 (for a fuller exploration of the impact on Q1 and Q2 of the media for which they were designed, see pp. 220–4).

[124] For an excellent examination of Shakespeare's use of time and, in particular, of the 'double time scheme' in *Othello*, see Emrys Jones, *Scenic Form in Shakespeare* (Oxford, 1971), pp. 41–65. For a concise summary of Shakespeare's efficient use of time in Q2, see NCS, pp. 10–11.

forgotten that the wedding at this point is planned to take place two days later, not the next day.

The reason for the discrepancies in Q1 is difficult to recover. Shakespeare may have revised Q2's time references but inadvertently have done so only in part. Alternatively, when the manuscript behind Q1 was composed, several sources may have been drawn upon (memory, players' parts, an authorial manuscript or a transcript thereof), sources which may have differed with respect to the time scheme. But this, I admit, is no more than speculation. It deserves pointing out that Q1 and Q2 are both inconsistent with regards to the effect of the sleeping potion. Friar Laurence explains to Juliet that she will remain unconscious for 'two-and-forty hours' (15.87; 4.1.105), and after finding out that his letter to Romeo has miscarried, he hastens to the monument because 'Within this three hours will fair Juliet wake' (5.2.25). Juliet drinks the potion in the night from Tuesday to Wednesday and forty-two hours later would thus be Friday evening, yet the final scene takes place at night. Clearly, this and the other inconsistencies present in Q1 are not of a nature to interfere with the pleasure of an audience, and Shakespeare and his fellow actors may have worried little about them.

Publication and printing

THE FIRST QUARTO IN 1597

It is generally assumed that *Romeo and Juliet* was written in or around 1595 and that it was performed by Shakespeare and his fellow actors at the Theatre in the Shoreditch district north-east of the city, the company's regular London playhouse up to 1597. That year or, possibly, the year before, the stationer John Danter must have acquired a manuscript of the play, the manuscript from which the first quarto was set up. How such a transaction might have taken place is illustrated by the anonymous Cambridge play *The Second Part of the Return from Parnassus* (c. 1601) which shows Danter being offered a manuscript. Danter, who claims he lost money on the author's previous book, is at first reluctant to make the purchase but ends up offering '40 shillings and an odde pottle of wine'.[125] Danter must have had the manuscript licensed (meaning that the Stationers' Company granted him the right to print the manuscript), but he did not have it entered in the Stationers' Register as many, though by no means all, stationers did before having a playbook printed. The absence of an entry has sometimes been taken as evidence that the publication of the first quarto was surreptitious and Danter a crook. These theories can safely be laid to rest. He was involved in the publication of several playbooks of good credentials in the years prior to 1597, including Shakespeare's *Titus Andronicus* (1594), Robert Greene's *Orlando Furioso* (1594), and Thomas Lodge's *Wounds of Civil War* (1594), all of which he entered in the Stationers' Register, and Thomas Nashe's *Have With You to Saffron Walden* (1596), which he didn't.[126] Even more importantly, as Peter

---

[125] J. B. Leishman, ed., *The Three Parnassus Plays (1598–1601)* (London, 1949), pp. 247–8.
[126] For the fullest analysis of Danter's dramatic output, see Chiaki Hanabusa's doctoral dissertation, 'John Danter's play-quartos: a bibliographical and textual analysis' (Birmingham, 2002).

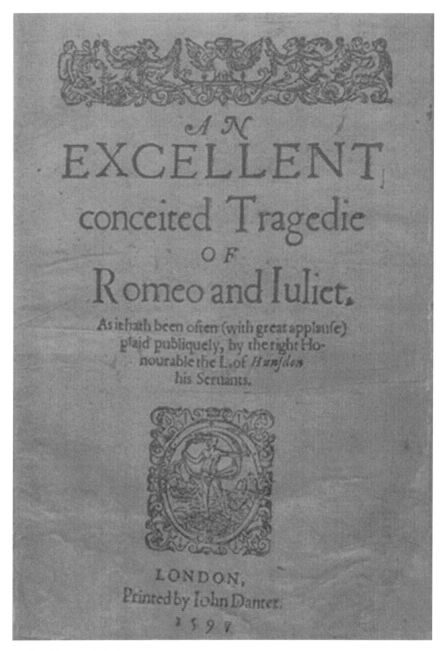

AN

EXCELLENT

conceited Tragedie

OF

Romeo and Iuliet,

As it hath been often (with great applause)
plaid publiquely, by the right Honourable the L. of *Hunsdon*
his Seruants.

LONDON,
Printed by Iohn Danter.
1597.

1   The title page of the first quarto, 1597.

Blayney has pointed out, while licence was mandatory, an entrance in the Register 'was an insurance policy' which 'provided the best possible protection' against anyone else's claim to rights in the play, but it 'was voluntary, and its absence is *never* sufficient reason for suspecting anything furtive, dishonest, or illegal'.[127]

The first quarto of *Romeo and Juliet* was published in 1597 with the following title page (see illustration 1):

AN / EXCELLENT / conceited Tragedie / *OF* / Romeo and Iuliet. / As it hath been often (with great applause) / plaid publiquely, by the right Ho- / nourable the L. of *Hunsdon* / his Seruants. [printer's device][128] LONDON, / Printed by Iohn Danter. / 1597.

Although John Danter is the only printer mentioned on the title page, it has been shown that the printing was in fact shared by two stationers, Danter (sheets A–D) and Edward Allde (sheets E–K).[129] Danter's and Allde's parts can be distinguished readily enough: layout and typeface are different, and the running title in Danter's section reads '*The most excellent Tragedie, / of Romeo and Iuliet*', that in Allde's part reads '*The excellent Tragedie / of Romeo and Iuliet*' (see illustration 2). Hoppe believed that the two printers worked consecutively, with Allde taking over from Danter after the latter got into trouble with the Stationers' Company and had his presses seized some time between 9 February and 27 March 1597.[130] However, it has since been persuasively argued that Danter and Allde printed their portions simultaneously,[131] and bibliographical analysis shows that the book was cast off and set by formes rather than printed seriatim.[132] Shared printing was not unusual and assured maximum speed when the resources of one printing house were limited.[133] Also, even though not only Danter but also Allde had his printing shop raided by the authorities of the Stationers' Company early in 1597, both remained busy printing throughout the year, and it is thus impossible to know whether they printed *Romeo and Juliet* before or after their problems with the Company's authorities early in the year.[134]

The Q1 title page asserts that the play has been performed by Lord Hunsdon's Servants, the name of Shakespeare's company while its patron, George Carey, was Lord Hunsdon. He bore the title from the death of his father, Henry Carey, on

[127] Blayney, 'The publication of playbooks', p. 404.
[128] Device 281 in Ronald B. McKerrow, *Printers' and Publishers' Devices in England and Scotland, 1485–1640* (London, 1913).
[129] See Standish Henning, 'The printer of *Romeo and Juliet*, Q1', *PBSA* 60 (1966), 363–4, and the more thorough and conclusive demonstration by Chiaki Hanabusa, 'Edward Allde's types in sheets E–K of *Romeo and Juliet* Q1 (1597)', *PBSA* 91 (1997), 423–8. On Allde, see R. B. McKerrow, 'Edward Allde as a typical trade printer', *Library* 4th ser. 10 (1929–30), 121–62.
[130] Hoppe, pp. 38–52.
[131] J. A. Lavin, 'John Danter's ornament stock', *SB* 23 (1970), 29–34.
[132] See Frank E. Haggard, 'Type-recurrence evidence and the printing of *Romeo and Juliet* Q1 (1597)', *PBSA* 71 (1977), 66–73, and Hanabusa, 'Edward Allbe's types'.
[133] For Danter and shared printing, see Chiaki Hanabusa, 'Shared printing in Robert Wilson's *The Cobbler's Prophecy*', *PBSA* 97 (2003), 333–49.
[134] See Levenson and Gaines, pp. viii–ix; and *Records of the Stationers' Company, 1576 to 1602, from Register B*, ed. W. W. Greg and E. Boswell (London, 1930), pp. 56–7.

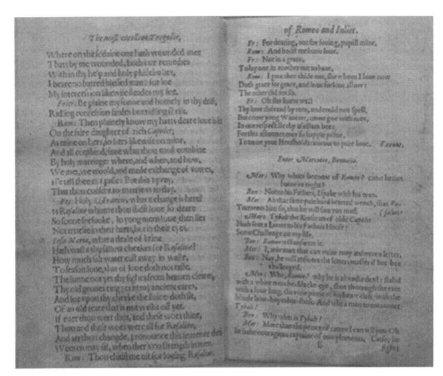

2   A double page from the first quarto, D4v–E1r. On the left is the last page of John Danter's portion; on the right the first page of Edward Allde's portion.

22 July 1596, until his appointment as Lord Chamberlain on 17 April 1597.[135] This has sometimes been taken to imply that the play must have been printed early in 1597 or at the end of 1596. However, the reference to Hunsdon 'may have been up-to-date when written but out-of-date when the book was printed some months later', so neither the title page nor the records of the Stationers' Company allows us to determine when exactly the text was printed.[136]

Danter's and Allde's portions contain certain bibliographical peculiarities. In the former, the Nurse's part in Scenes 3 and 5 is printed in italics. It was conjectured by Greg that 'an actor's part, written in Italian script, had been cut up and pasted into the copy', though he recognised that the differences between Q1 and Q2 make it seem unlikely that the part had been prepared by a book-keeper and suggest that 'an actor may rather have written out his part from memory'.[137] Incidentally, such

[135] See Chiaki Hanabusa, 'A neglected misdate and *Romeo and Juliet* Q1 (1597), *Notes and Queries* 244 n.s. 46 (1999), 229–30.
[136] See Levenson and Gaines, p. ix.
[137] Greg, *Editorial Problem*, p. 62. Things are further complicated by the Serving-man's speech at the end of Scene 3, which is also printed in italics, perhaps owing to a compositor's inattention.

a scenario would support the case for Q1 as a text put together by a group of actors
with the workings of memory accounting for some of the text's features.

The bibliographical peculiarities of the Allde part may have more important
implications. Sheets E–K are set in smaller type, a full page consisting of thirty-two
lines as opposed to thirty-six lines in Danter's portion. The type is more generously
spaced out in the Allde portion, in particular in sheets G–K, by means of blank
lines before and after stage directions. In addition, sheets G–K contain rows of
printer's ornaments inserted between scenes or scenic movements.[138] McKerrow
noticed as early as the 1930s that the extra spacing in sheets E–K compensates for
the additional lines resulting from the smaller type.[139] In other words, it seems that
Allde *accidentally* used smaller type than Danter and needed the extra spacing and
rows of printer's ornaments to stretch his materials so as to fill the six sheets on
which he and Danter had previously agreed.

In an important recent article, John Jowett has argued that not only extra spacing
and ornaments but also additional stage directions were used to waste superfluous
space. Noticing 'the simultaneous appearance in Sheet G of a large number of elabo-
rately literary stage directions and the distinctive rows of ornaments', he argued that
'the stage directions in question, or at least a good number of them, are supplemen-
tary, part and parcel of a redesign'.[140] This provides the basis for his argument that
Q1's stage directions 'often owe their presence and their distinctive quality neither
to the theater nor to Shakespeare as dramatic author. They derive instead from the
printing process.'[141] In a remarkable scholarly *tour de force*, Jowett goes on to identify
tentatively the annotator in the person of 'Danter's former partner and subsequent
assistant, Henry Chettle'.[142] Building on an article by Sidney Thomas,[143] Jowett
provides substantial evidence to suggest that Chettle 'was uniquely well placed to
give Q1 *Romeo* the kind of attention I posit'.[144] He was not only a dramatist (mentioned among the 'Best for Comedy' in Meres's *Palladis Tamia* in 1598) but also had
well attested connections with Danter. For instance, in Anthony Munday's second
part of *Primaleon of Greece*, printed by Danter in 1596, Chettle states in a prefatory
letter that he had done what he could to speed up the text's publication.[145] The case
is bolstered by a wealth of similarities between the 'literary' stage directions in Q1
and those in Chettle's own plays.[146] Jowett's argument is not without its difficulties
as it presupposes that Chettle was involved at two points of the publication process, first writing *some* literary stage directions (as evidenced in Sheets A–F), then

---

[138] This device makes of Q1 *Romeo and Juliet* the earliest Shakespeare play-text that shows any concern
with scene division, the only other example prior to the First Folio being the first quarto of *Othello*
(1622).

[139] See R. B. McKerrow, 'The treatment of Shakespeare's text by his earlier editors, 1709–1768', *Annual
Shakespeare Lecture of the British Academy* (London, 1933), p. 33 n.6; and see Hoppe, p. 44.

[140] Jowett, 'Chettle', 56.

[141] Ibid., 54.

[142] Ibid., 57.

[143] Sidney Thomas, 'Henry Chettle and the first quarto of *Romeo and Juliet*', *RES* n.s. 1 (1950), 8–16.

[144] Jowett, 'Chettle', 58.

[145] Ibid., 57–8.

[146] Ibid., 60–5.

of Romeo and Iuliet.

Nur: I will, and this is wisely done.

She lookes after Nurse.

Iul: Auncient damnation, O most curfed fiend.
Is it more finne to wifh me thus forfworne,
Or to difpraife him with the felfe fame tongue
That thou haft praifde him with aboue compare
So many thoufand times? Goe Counfellor,
Thou and my bofom henceforth fhalbe twaine.
Ile to the Fryer to knowhis remedy,
If all faile els, I haue the power to dye.

Exit.

Enter Fryer and Paris.

Fr: On Thurfday fay ye: the time is very fhort,
Par: My Father *Capolet* will haue it fo,
And I am nothing flacke to flow his haft,
Fr: You fay you doe not know the Ladies minde?
Vneuen is the courfe, I like it not.
Par: Immoderately fhe weepes for *Tybalts* death,
And therefore haue I little talke of loue,
For *Venus* fmiles not in a houfe of teares,
Now Sir, her father thinkes it daungerous:
That fhe doth giue her forrow fo much fway,
And in his wifedome hafts our mariage,
To ftop the inundation of her teares,
Which too much minded by her felfe alone
May be put from her by focietie:
Now doe ye know the reafon of this haft,
Fr: I would I knew not why it fhould be flowd.

H 2

Enter

3 A page from the first quarto, H2r. Notice how the printer's ornament, empty lines, and stage directions reduce the number of dialogue lines printed on the page.

adding quite a few *more* after the printing-house miscalculation. Also, the second phase of Chettle's involvement would have required Chettle's collaboration with members of Allde's printing house, even though the well-documented connection is with Danter, not with Allde. Nevertheless, Jowett's evidence amounts to a good case, suggesting that it is possible, perhaps likely, that many of the stage directions in Q1 were added after the manuscript had been sold to Danter and thus do not derive from the same process as the redaction of the dialogue.[147] Independently of whether the stage directions are 'Chettle's memory of what he saw – or imagined he saw – on stage',[148] or part of a post-performance redaction by the players, the stage directions seem likely to have been composed after the play was first performed rather than being parts of a script designed to help actors prepare a performance.

The first quarto as a whole was carefully printed, in fact more so than the second. Nonetheless, it contains its share of errors produced in the printing, notably a number of inverted letters.[149] There are five extant copies of Q1 *Romeo and Juliet*, at the British Library, the Bodleian Library, Trinity College, Cambridge, the Folger Shakespeare Library, and the Henry E. Huntington Library, though the Folger and the British Library copies are imperfect. Greg lists them in his *Bibliography* and Henrietta C. Bartlett and Pollard's *Census of Shakespeare's Plays in Quarto* provides a full bibliographic description.[150] Collation of the five extant copies has yielded no variants. As Levenson points out, this is unsurprising considering the small number of extant copies.[151]

THE FIRST QUARTO AFTER 1597

The second quarto was published with the following title page:

THE / MOST EX- / cellent and lamentable / Tragedie, of Romeo and Iuliet. / *Newly corrected, augmented, and / amended*: / As it hath bene sundry times publiquely acted, by the / right Honourable the Lord Chamberlaine / his Seruants. LONDON / Printed by Thomas Creede, for Cuthbert Burby, and are to / to sold at his shop neare the Exchange. / 1599.

---

[147] I am less convinced by Jowett's argument for Chettle's authorship of so-called 'non-Shakespearean' portions in the dialogue, including the betrothal scene (Scene 9), and a few other, shorter passages ('Chettle', 65–6). While there seems nothing implausible about the sale of a manuscript which was essentially complete but to which stage directions were added with the aim of 'embellishing the text as a script from the theater' (Jowett, 'Chettle', 57), it seems more difficult to imagine that the manuscript was either incomplete (and thus required Chettle to fill in the holes) or complete but with passages which Chettle felt compelled to revise.

[148] Jowett, 'Chettle', 65. Note that Jowett further pursues his important work on Chettle in 'Henry Chettle: "your old compositor"', *TEXT: An Interdisciplinary Annual of Textual Studies*, 15 (2003), 141–62.

[149] '*Mooutague*' for '*Mountague*' (B1r, 1.59, '*Conntie*' for '*Countie*' (B2r, 2.0.1), 'Nnrce' for 'Nurce' (B4r, 3.14), 'ꓭut' for 'But' (B4v, 3.69), 'hand.' for 'hand·' (inverted period, C3r, 4.123), 'you·' for 'you.' (inverted period, C4r, 4.189), '*uame*' for '*name*' (C4r, 4.202), 'oue' for 'one' (C4r, 4.209), 'speꓭk' for 'speak' (C4v, 5.10), '*Inl*' for '*Iul*' (H1v, 14.160), 'nothiug' for 'nothing' (H2v, 15.46), and '*Rouu*' for '*Rom*' (K1v, 20.57). For the fullest analysis of printing errors in Q1, see Hoppe, pp. 5–9.

[150] Greg, *Bibliography*, vol. 1, p. 234; Henrietta C. Bartlett and Alfred W. Pollard, *A Census of Shakespeare's Plays in Quarto: 1594–1709* (New Haven, 1939), p. 107.

[151] See Oxford, p. 108.

The publication in 1599 suggests that the first edition had been a commercial success and sold out in two years or less. The words '*Newly corrected, augmented, and amended*' indicate that the longer version was conceived of as a selling point. Title pages served publishers as marketing tools in early modern London and were put up on posts and elsewhere. A second or later edition with a longer and different text seems to have been easier to market than a mere reprint, as is suggested by several contemporary title pages, including that of Q3 *Richard III* (1602) which, though advertised as 'Newly augmented', was in fact set up from an earlier quarto.[152]

As Q2 *Romeo and Juliet* presents a longer and in some ways better text, scholars have sometimes believed that Shakespeare and his company released the manuscript in order to have the first, 'bad' quarto superseded, an argument that allegedly found support in the publication history of *Hamlet* ('bad' quarto 1603; 'good' quarto 1604/5) and, more ambiguously, *Love's Labour's Lost* (published 1598 as 'Newly corrected and augmented' and probably following after a lost first edition). However, the 'bad' quarto of *Henry V* was reprinted in 1602, even though it would have been in the publisher's best commercial interest to sell a different, longer text if he could have secured one. So in this case at least, nothing seems to have been undertaken to supersede the 1600 quarto with a longer text. Also, it seems in fact more likely that, despite the announcement on its title page, the lost edition of *Love's Labour's Lost* was a 'good' text from which the first extant edition was set up, and that in the case of *Hamlet* the manuscript from which the second quarto had been set up had been sold before the first quarto was published.[153] The cumulative evidence suggests that the Lord Chamberlain's Men were not unduly troubled by the printing of what modern scholarship has labelled 'bad quartos'.

What strengthens the likelihood that the manuscript from which Q2 was set up had been sold before Q1 appeared in print is that the second quarto was published by Cuthbert Burby, not by John Danter. No entry in the Stationers' Register records a transfer of the rights in the play, even though such an entry would have conformed to usual practice.[154] It thus seems possible that not only Danter but also Burby had their manuscripts of *Romeo and Juliet* licensed but not entered and that Burby had in fact done so first. This would mean that Burby had been the rightful owner of the play all along, but that Danter failed to realise this when he published Q1. Alternatively, it cannot be excluded that Burby acquired the rights in *Romeo and Juliet* after the publication of Q1 but that for some reason the transaction was not recorded in the Stationers' Register. In any case, *Romeo and Juliet* must have been Burby's by 1599 and remained so until 22 January 1607 when he transferred the rights to Nicholas Ling, according to the Stationers' Register.

[152] Wells *et al.*, *Textual Companion*, p. 270.
[153] Erne, pp. 80–1.
[154] Burby is a stationer with whom Shakespeare's company had done business before: he published *Love's Labour's Lost* in 1598 and *Edward III* (which many believe to have been at least co-authored by Shakespeare) in 1596. Other stationers with whom Shakespeare's company seems to have had repeated dealings are Andrew Wise and James Roberts (see Erne, pp. 87–89).

Even though most of the second quarto was 'augmented, and amended', some of it was not but instead set up from the first quarto whose text thus partly survives in the 1599 quarto from where it finds its way into the play's modern editions.[155] The main Q2 passage for which Q1 had served as copy in Scenes 2 and 3 is beyond dispute (c. 2.44 to 3.38).[156] Short passages later in the second quarto also seem to have been based on the first quarto, though the evidence is usually less clear.[157] As Evans has pointed out, a Q2 editor 'is often left with the suspicion that in those many lines and passages where Q1 and Q2 are verbally identical that Creede's compositors . . . allowed themselves to drift from their manuscript copy and followed Q1 for one or more lines . . . but how often . . . must remain uncertain'.[158]

We might assume that Q1 has no importance for seventeenth-century editions of *Romeo and Juliet*, but we would be wrong. Lynette Hunter has recently shown that the third (1609) and the fourth (no date; 1616–26) quartos make remarkable use of the 1597 text. Q3 often agrees with Q1 when it departs from Q2, so much so that 'the sheer overall number of significant agreements . . . between Q3 and Q1 argue for substantial interaction'.[159] As for Q4, Hunter finds a pattern 'allowing Q1 to advise but not dictate . . . throughout the Q4 editorial changes', a pattern that results in many Q1/Q4 agreements 'over significant words or phrases' where Q4 agrees with neither Q3 nor Q2.[160] Hunter's careful article shows that Q4 is 'the result of an editor working just like a modern editor on the text itself', and that 'like Q3, Q4 clearly respects Q1 and treats it as a reliable text'.[161] A similar testimony of early interest and trust in Q1 can also be found in the anthology *Bel-vedére or the Garden of the Muses* of 1600 – see Appendix C.

The first quarto was not reprinted for more than a century and a half. The seventeenth-century Folios made little use of it, and Nicholas Rowe's edition of 1709 was based largely on the fourth Folio. In his edition of 1723–5, however, Alexander Pope broke with this tradition and paid considerable attention to Q1. So did later eighteenth-century editors. At least one editor drew on Q1 with even greater frequency than Pope, and that is Edmond Malone. Appendix D details the Q1 readings in the eighteenth-century editions of Pope, Lewis Theobald, Edward Capell, and Malone. It shows that long before the New Bibliography introduced the label 'bad quarto', eighteenth-century editors from Pope to Malone found that many of Q1's readings are remarkably good, so much so that they preferred them to those in Q2.

---

[155] Earlier scholars had believed that Q2 was set up from an annotated copy of Q1, though an article by Paul L. Cantrell and George Walton Williams, 'The printing of the second quarto of *Romeo and Juliet*', *SB* 9 (1957), 107–28, established conclusively that Q2 was chiefly set up from an independent manuscript.

[156] The precise location of the beginning is not easy to identify. For an attempt, see Richard Hosley, 'Quarto copy for Q2 *Romeo and Juliet*', *SB* 9 (1957), 129–41, 137–41.

[157] Ibid., 134–7.

[158] NCS, p. 225.

[159] Lynette Hunter, 'Why has Q4 *Romeo and Juliet* such an intelligent editor?', *Re-Constructing the Book: Literary Texts in Transmission*, ed. Maureen Bell et al. (Aldershot, 2001), pp. 9–21, 14.

[160] Ibid., p. 15.

[161] Ibid., pp. 19, 15.

The history of modern reprints of Q1 *Romeo and Juliet* begins with George Steevens's original-spelling edition in *Twenty of the Plays of Shakespeare* in 1766 (vol. 4). In 1859, Tycho Mommsen provided the earliest parallel-text edition, in original spelling and with a commentary in German, an edition that is notable for its lack of reliability and disconcerting presentation, the Q1 text appearing alternatingly on the left- and on the right-hand side. Many reproductions have followed since, notably those in W. G. Clark, John Glover, and W. A. Wright's Cambridge edition (1865, 1895), in E. W. Ashbee and J. O. Halliwell-Phillipps's collection of lithographic facsimiles of the early quartos (1866), in H. H. Furness's Variorum edition (1871), by P. A. Daniel (1874), in William Griggs and Charles Prætorius's series of photolithographic facsimiles (1886), and in B. Rush Field's Bankside edition. In 1904, Theodor Eichhoff provided the first edition with modernised spelling which, however, prints the whole play as prose. In 1924, Frank G. Hubbard is the first editor aware of modern bibliographical principles. Photographic facsimiles of Q1 have been provided by M. J. B. Allen and Kenneth Muir, and by Jill L. Levenson and Barry Gaines. Most recently, the text has been edited in original spelling in the 'Shakespearean Originals' series, and in modernised spelling in the back of Levenson's Oxford Shakespeare edition.[162]

With the good news about the 'bad quartos' having spread in recent times, actors and directors are also getting interested in the previously scorned texts, including Q1 *Romeo and Juliet*. The text was performed in a student production, directed by Pascale Aebischer, at Lincoln College, Oxford, in 1998. The 2003 production of *Romeo and Juliet* at the Oregon Shakespeare Festival, directed by Loretta Greco, used 'a thorough conflation of . . . the quartos of 1597 and 1599', with many passages adopted from Q1, including parts of the betrothal scene. As Barry Kraft pointed out in the introduction to the script: 'In all likelihood one can hear more of Q1 *Romeo and Juliet* [in this production] than has been heard on any other stage for centuries!'[163] Considering these recent developments, it would not be surprising if we were to witness the first professional production of the first quarto of *Romeo and Juliet* some time soon.

---

[162] See Mommsen; Cam.; Edmund William Ashbee, ed., *Shakespeare's 'Romeo and Juliet': Facsimiled from the Edition Printed at London in the Year 1597* (London: privately printed, 1866); Furness (Q1) (this edition is based on Ashbee's facsimile); Daniel (*Parallel Texts*), and Daniel (Q1); William Griggs and Charles Prætorius, eds., *'Romeo and Juliet': The First Quarto, 1597*, Shakspere [sic] Quarto Facsimiles, vol. 25 (London: C. Prætorius, 1886); Field; Eichhoff; Hubbard; Allen and Muir, eds., *Shakespeare's Plays in Quarto*; Levenson and Gaines; Watts; and Levenson.

[163] I quote from pp. i–iii. Barry Kraft has kindly provided me with a copy of the production script.

NOTE ON THE TEXT

This is an edition of the first quarto of *Romeo and Juliet* published in 1597, a companion volume to the New Cambridge Shakespeare (NCS) edition of *Romeo and Juliet*, edited by G. Blakemore Evans. In keeping with NCS conventions, spelling and punctuation have been modernised; past participle endings spelt 'ed' are unstressed, whereas stressed endings are spelt 'èd'; and speech headings and names in stage directions have been regularised and abbreviated forms expanded. Inverted letters have not been recorded in the collation, though I provide a list on page 41. Typographic peculiarities such as dialogue text in italics are regularised in the text and discussed in the textual notes. When Q1's lineation has been modified, I indicate the changes in the collation.

Spelling has been modernised thoroughly rather than reluctantly (e.g. 'corse' is modernised to 'corpse'), but distinctive grammatical forms have been preserved (e.g. 'spake'). Difficult decisions are discussed in the textual notes. Punctuation is usually light and grammatical (or logical) rather than rhetorical, though I have aimed at providing punctuation to facilitate understanding where the syntax requires clarification.

Stage directions have been preserved, though I have occasionally complemented the original and added further stage directions between square brackets with the aim of facilitating understanding of the implied stage action. Detailed line-to-line attention as required by editorial work can lead to insights into various aspects of staging that are not always easily accessible to a reader: what actions are being performed, who is being addressed, what properties are visible, or what characters must exit or enter. All these aspects of staging would have contributed in important ways to a spectator's experience of the play in Shakespeare's time, and this experience, while ultimately irrecoverable, can be partly glimpsed by full attention to implied stage action. Occasionally, the implied staging is unclear or offers several possibilities, in which case I discuss it in the textual notes. My decision to add stage directions or to expand some of those present in Q1 is related to my argument, presented in the Introduction, that the first quarto, contrary to the second, is the closest we get to a performance version of the play.

In the collation, the authority for the text adopted in this edition is indicated immediately after the lemma. Other significant readings follow in chronological order. When I follow a reading that is in none of the early quartos or folios, I indicate the earliest editor of any version of *Romeo and Juliet* – and thus not necessarily the earliest editor of the first quarto of *Romeo and Juliet* – who adopted this reading as my authority.

This edition is interested throughout in the relationship of first and second quartos, and the collation and commentary reflect this interest. However, as the relationship between the two texts is closer in the early parts of the play than in the later, I only attempt an exhaustive record of substantive differences between them in Scenes 1 to 7 (including Q2 passages absent from Q1). In the remaining scenes, the relationship between the two versions is such that it would have been impossible to record all differences, and so I only retain what seems of particular interest.

Q1 indicates neither scene nor act breaks (though the section set up in Allde's printing house separates scenic movements by rows of ornaments). I follow the text's sequence of scenes by numbering them consecutively without reference to the act division which editorial tradition since Rowe has imposed upon the play. To facilitate cross-reference to the NCS edition of *Romeo and Juliet*, I indicate the corresponding act and scene numbers in the textual notes.

LIST OF CHARACTERS

THE TRAGEDY OF ROMEO AND JULIET

The Prologue

[*Enter* PROLOGUE]

[PROLOGUE]   Two household friends alike in dignity,
        In fair Verona, where we lay our scene,
    From civil broils broke into enmity,
        Whose civil war makes civil hands unclean.
    From forth the fatal loins of these two foes   5
        A pair of star-crossed lovers took their life,
    Whose misadventures, piteous overthrows,
        Through the continuing of their fathers' strife
    And death-marked passage of their parents' rage,
    Is now the two hours' traffic of our stage.   10
    The which if you with patient ears attend,
    What here we want we'll study to amend.   [*Exit*]

Title] F; *AN / EXCELLENT / conceited Tragedie / OF /* Romeo and Iuliet, / As it hath been often (with great applause) / plaid publiquely, by the right Ho- / nourable the L. of *Hunsdon* / his Seruants. Q1 *(title page);* The most excellent Tragedie of / *Romeo and Iuliet.* Q1 *(head title preceding Scene 1);* The most excellent Tragedie, / of *Romeo and Iuliet.* Q1 *(running title, sigs.* A4v–D*);* The excellent Tragedie / of *Romeo and Juliet.* Q1 *(running title, sigs.* E–K4r)   **0** SD] *Levenson; not in* Q, F   **1** SH] *Levenson; not in* Q1; Corus. Q2   **1** Two] Q1 *(TVVo)*   **1** friends] Q1 *(Frends); both* Q2   **3** civil . . . enmity] Q1 *(subst.); auncient grudge, breake to new mutinie* Q2   **4** Whose] Q1; *where* Q2   **4** war] Q1 *(warre); bloud* Q2   **6** took] Q1 *(tooke); take* Q2   **7** misadventures] Q1 *(misaduentures); misaduentur'd* Q2   **8–9** Through . . . rage,] Q1 *((Through the continuing of their Fathers strife, / And death-markt passage of their Parents rage)); Doth with their death burie their Parents strife. / The fearfull passage of their death-markt loue, / And the continuance of their Parents rage:* Q2   **12** we want . . . amend] Q1 *(subst.); shall misse, our toyle shall striue to mend* Q2   **12** SD] *Capell; not in* Q, F

Prologue

The Prologue consists of twelve lines, two quatrains and two couplets, whereas that in Q2 (spoken by 'Corus') is a Shakespearean sonnet. The Prologue is not included in the Folio editions. In comparison with Q2, Q1's main omission is the idea of a reconciliatory function served by the lovers' death. In Q1 and Q2, the text of the Prologue is printed in italics.

1 Two household friends Contrary to Q2's Prologue, Q1's tells us about Capulet and Montague's former friendship. Duthie (18) considered these words 'nonsense', but Elizabethans did not adhere to the stricter rules of modern compound-word formation (Abbott 428–35).

3–6 broke . . . took Q1's Prologue relates the play's events in the past tense, Q2's in the present tense.

4 civil war makes Q1 magnifies the conflict between the Capulets and the Montagues by calling it a 'civil war', whereas the conflict in Q2 only results in 'ciuill bloud'. The present tense suggests a general comment or warning: enmity can lead to civil war.

8–9 These two lines transpose and condense material of three successive lines (8–10) in Q2's Prologue (see collation).

9–10 Between these two lines, Q2 prints a verse absent from Q1: 'which but their childrens end nought could remoue' (line 11).

10 two hours' . . . stage This duration seems to correspond better to a performance of a text of the length of Q1 than of Q2. See Introduction, p. 22.

[1]   *Enter two* SERVING-MEN *of the Capulets*

[1 CAPULET SERVING-MAN] Gregory, of my word, I'll carry no
   coals.
2 CAPULET SERVING-MAN No, for if you do, you should be a collier.
1 CAPULET SERVING-MAN If I be in choler, I'll draw.
2 CAPULET SERVING-MAN Ever while you live, draw your neck out   5
   of the collar.
1 CAPULET SERVING-MAN I strike quickly being moved.
2 CAPULET SERVING-MAN Ay, but you are not quickly moved to
   strike.
1 CAPULET SERVING-MAN A dog of the house of the Montagues   10
   moves me.
2 CAPULET SERVING-MAN To move is to stir, and to be valiant is
   to stand to it. Therefore, of my word, if thou be moved thou't
   run away.
1 CAPULET SERVING-MAN There's not a man of them I meet but   15
   I'll take the wall of.
2 CAPULET SERVING-MAN That shows thee a weakling, for
   the weakest goes to the wall.

---

0 SD] *Levenson; Enter 2. Seruing-men of the* Capolets. Q1; *Enter* Sampson *and* Gregorie, *with Swords and Bucklers, of the house of* Capulet. Q2   1 SH] *Levenson (*FIRST CAPULET SERVING-MAN*); not in* Q1   1 of] Q1; on Q2   1 I'll] Q1; weele Q2   3 SH] *Levenson (*SECOND CAPULET SERVING-MAN*); 2* Q1 *(throughout scene)*   3 if . . . a] Q1 *(*if you doo, you should be a*); then we should be Q2   4 SH] *Levenson (*FIRST CAPULET SERVING-MAN*); 1* Q1 *(throughout scene)*   4 If I be] Q1; and we be Q2   4 I'll] Q1 *(*Ile*);* weele Q2   5–6 out . . . collar] Q5; out of the the collar Q1; out of choller Q2   8 Ay] Q1 *(*I*)*   8 you] Q1; thou Q2   10 the Montagues] Q1 *(subst.); Mountague* Q2   13 stand to it] Q1; stand Q2   13 of my word] Q1; *not in* Q2   17 weakling] Q1; weake slaue Q2

Scene 1
Act 1, Scene 1 in the NCS edition.
Much of this scene corresponds closely to the
equivalent scene in Q2. Larger cuts occur as the
brawl gets out of hand, in the Prince's speech calling his subjects to order, in Benvolio's account of
the brawl, in Montague's description of his son's
love-sickness, and in the dialogue between Romeo
and Benvolio. While these cuts total some seventy-
five lines, other local omissions amount to less than
ten.
  0 SD Q1's stage directions and speech headings
do not specify the Serving-men's names ('Sampson', 'Gregorie', and 'Abram' in Q2), though
Gregory is named in the dialogue. Later in the

play, the Prince is called 'Escalus' in Q2 but not
in Q1. Similar instances in other plays include
Mountjoy and Williams in Folio *Henry V*, who are
simply called 'Herauld' and '2. Souldier' in Q1,
and Claudius (Q2) and Bernardo and Francisco
(Q2 and F) in *Hamlet*, who are referred to as 'King'
and 'two Centinels' in Q1. This suggests that
Shakespeare occasionally gave personal names to
characters where the players or the redactors of
the short quartos were content with generic des-
ignations.
  15 The beginning of this speech in Q2 has no
equivalent in Q1: 'A dog of that house shall moue
me to stand' (1.1.10).

1 CAPULET SERVING-MAN That's true. Therefore I'll thrust the
    men from the wall, and thrust the maids to the walls. Nay, thou   20
    shalt see I am a tall piece of flesh.
2 CAPULET SERVING-MAN 'Tis well thou art not fish, for if thou
    wert thou wouldst be but poor John.
1 CAPULET SERVING-MAN I'll play the tyrant: I'll first begin with
    the maids, and off with their heads.   25
2 CAPULET SERVING-MAN The heads of the maids?
1 CAPULET SERVING-MAN Ay, the heads of their maids, or the
    maidenheads, take it in what sense thou wilt.
2 CAPULET SERVING-MAN Nay, let them take it in sense that feel it.
    But here comes two of the Montagues.   30

        Enter two SERVING-MEN *of the Montagues*

1 CAPULET SERVING-MAN Nay, fear not me, I warrant thee.
2 CAPULET SERVING-MAN I fear them no more than thee, but draw.
1 CAPULET SERVING-MAN Nay, let us have the law on our side, let
    them begin first. I'll tell thee what I'll do: as I go by I'll bite my
    thumb which is disgrace enough if they suffer it.   35
2 CAPULET SERVING-MAN Content! Go thou by and bite thy
    thumb, and I'll come after and frown.
1 MONTAGUE SERVING-MAN Do you bite your thumb at us?
1 CAPULET SERVING-MAN I bite my thumb.

---

19 thrust] Q1; push Q2   20 the maids] Q1; his maides Q2   21 tall] Q1; pretie Q2   27 their] Q1; the
Q2   30 comes two] Q1; comes Q2   30 SD] Q1 *(Enter two Seruingmen of the* Mountagues.*); Enter two
other seruing men.* Q2   33 have] Q1 *(haue); take* Q2   35 thumb] Q1 *(thumbe); thumb at them* Q2
38 SH] Levenson (FIRST MONTAGUE SERVING-MAN*); 1Moun:* Q1 *(throughout scene)*

20 It may be significant that Q1 here omits Q2's
'The quarel is betweene our maisters, and vs their
men' (1.1.17), as an omission later in the scene
(see note at 1.48 SD) suggests that Q1 may put less
emphasis on the conflict among the older generation. See Introduction, p. 32.
    21–3 The 'flesh'/'fish' joke constitutes the only
notable instance of a transposition in this scene;
the equivalent passage occurs a few lines later in
Q2, immediately preceding the arrival of the Montague Serving-men. Unlike Q1, Q2 extends this
passage to include further bawdy puns on 'thy
toole' and a 'naked weapon'.
    27 their maids Q1's 'their' may be a mistake

for 'the' ('their' occurs two lines earlier), though
it seems equally possible that the First Capulet
Serving-man, contrary to Q2's Sampson, is still
specifically thinking of the Montagues' maids.
    32 I fear . . . thee Q1's Serving-man displays
macho bravery where Q2's Gregory reacts with
mock cowardice ('No marrie, I feare thee').
    34–7 Q1 inverses Q2's order of projected provo-
cations.
    38–46 In both Q1 and Q2, the staccato dialogue
is partly shaped by repetition, but the two texts
repeat different sentences: Q2, 'Do you bite your
thumbe at vs sir?' (1.1.37–9); Q1, 'Ay, but is't at
us?' and 'I bite my thumb'.

2 MONTAGUE SERVING-MAN Ay, but is't at us?   40

1 CAPULET SERVING-MAN I bite my thumb. [*To 2 Capulet
Serving-man*] Is the law on our side?

2 CAPULET SERVING-MAN No.

1 CAPULET SERVING-MAN [*To the Montague Serving-men*] I bite
my thumb.   45

1 MONTAGUE SERVING-MAN Ay, but is't at us?

Enter BENVOLIO

2 CAPULET SERVING-MAN Say 'Ay', here comes my master's
kinsman.

They draw, to them enters TYBALT, *they fight, to them the* PRINCE,
old MONTAGUE *and his* WIFE, *old* CAPULET *and his* WIFE,
and other citizens and part them

PRINCE Rebellious subjects, enemies to peace,
On pain of torture, from those bloody hands   50
Throw your mistempered weapons to the ground.
Three civil brawls bred of an airy word,
By thee, old Capulet, and Montague,
Have thrice disturbed the quiet of our streets.
If ever you disturb our streets again,   55
Your lives shall pay the ransom of your fault.
For this time every man depart in peace.

---

40 SH] *Levenson (*SECOND MONTAGUE SERVING-MAN*); 2 Moun:* Q1   40 Ay] Q1 *(I)*   41 SD] *This edn (after
Capell); not in* Q, F   44 SD] *This edn (after Capell); not in* Q, F   46 SD] Q1 *(Beneuolio)*   47 my] Q1; *one of my* Q2
53 thee] Q2; *the* Q1   56 ransom . . . fault] Q1 *(ransome);* forfeit of the peace Q2   57 in peace] Q1; away Q2

46–8 The onset of the fight is considerably
shorter in Q1 than in Q2, with only two as opposed
to nine short speeches.

48 SD This lengthy stage direction simplifies and
rearranges stage action which takes place in Q2
where no fewer than nine characters speak (Sampson, Abram, Benvolio, Tybalt, an officer, Capulet,
Montague, and their wives). In the theatre, the
specific words used during a fight may be difficult for an audience to hear and at times do not
greatly matter. The probably theatrical Q1 – as
opposed to the more literary Q2 – registers this by

not specifying the words accompanying the fight.
See Introduction, p. 17. The wording of the stage
direction may suggest that Capulet and Montague
help '*part them*' and do not participate in the brawl
as they do in Q2. See Introduction, p. 32. The
Prince, called 'Escalus' in Q2, is nowhere given
a first name. He arrives '*with his train*' in Q2 but
with no train in Q1.

49–62 The Prince's fourteen-line speech corresponds with very few differences to the equivalent
lines in Q2 but omits nine additional lines present
in the longer text.

Come, Capulet, come you along with me,
And Montague, come you this afternoon,
To know our farther pleasure in this case,   60
To old Freetown, our common judgement place.
Once more: on pain of death, each man depart.
                Exeunt [all but Montague, his Wife, and Benvolio]

MONTAGUE'S WIFE Who set this ancient quarrel first abroach?
        Speak, nephew, were you by when it began?
BENVOLIO Here were the servants of your adversaries   65
        And yours close fighting ere I did approach.
MONTAGUE'S WIFE Ah, where is Romeo, saw you him today?
        Right glad I am he was not at this fray.
BENVOLIO Madam, an hour before the worshipped sun
        Peeped through the golden window of the east,   70
        A troubled thought drew me from company,
        Where underneath the grove Sycamore
        That westward rooteth from the city's side,
        So early walking might I see your son.
        I drew towards him, but he was ware of me,   75
        And drew into the thicket of the wood.
        I, noting his affections by mine own,
        That most are busied when th'are most alone,
        Pursued my honour, not pursuing his.

---

61 Freetown] Q1 *(Free Towne)*   62 SD] *Hudson; Exeunt.* Q1, Q2   63 SH] Q1 *(M: wife)*   63 first] Q1; new
Q2   67 SH] Q1 *(VVife)*   70 Peeped through] Q1 *(Peept)*; Peerde forth Q2   71 thought drew] Q1; minde driue Q2;
mind draue Q3   71 from company] Q1 *(companie)*; to walke abroad Q2   72 grove Sycamore] Q1 *(groue Sicamoure)*;
groue of Syramour Q2; groue of sycamour F1   73 the city's side] Q1 *(Cities)*; this Citie side Q2   74 might] Q1;
did Q2   76 drew] Q1; stole Q2   76 thicket] Q1; couert Q2   77 noting] Q1; measuring Q2   78] Q1; Which then
most sought, where most might not be found Q2   79 honour] Q1 *(honor)*; humor Q2

63–4 Q2 assigns this speech to Montague rather
than to his wife. Rowe and other eighteenth-
century editors followed the SH in Q1.

65–6 Benvolio's two-line speech corresponds
closely to the initial lines of the equivalent passage
in Q2 which goes on, however, for another eight
lines summarising the brawl – Tybalt's arrival, the
fight, and the Prince's arrival. In Q1, Romeo's parents may well arrive at nearly the same time as
Tybalt and the Prince, which is why these lines
may have seemed dispensable when the text was
abridged for performance. The present and other

differences between Q1 and Q2 suggest that a feature of the longer text is the delivery, at salient
points, of long messenger-type speeches describing action the audience have already seen performed onstage.

72 grove Sycamore The line in Q1 is a syllable
short, but the fact that '*Sicamore*', as the original
spelling has it, is printed in italics argues against
an accidental compositor's slip. Benvolio is referring to a grove named 'Sycamore' rather than to a
grove of sycamore, as Q2 has it.

MONTAGUE Black and portentous must this honour prove,   80
  Unless good counsel do the cause remove.
BENVOLIO Why tell me, uncle, do you know the cause?

     Enter ROMEO

MONTAGUE I neither know it nor can learn of him.
BENVOLIO See where he is. But stand you both aside;
  I'll know his grievance or be much denied.   85
MONTAGUE I would thou wert so happy by thy stay
  To hear true shrift. Come, madam, let's away.
       [Exeunt Montague and his Wife]

BENVOLIO Good morrow, cousin.
ROMEO   Is the day so young?
BENVOLIO But new stroke nine.
ROMEO   Ay me, sad hopes seem long.
  Was that my father that went hence so fast?   90
BENVOLIO It was. What sorrow lengthens Romeo's hours?
ROMEO Not having that which, having, makes them short.
BENVOLIO In love?
ROMEO Out.
BENVOLIO Of love?   95
ROMEO Out of her favour where I am in love.
BENVOLIO Alas that love, so gentle in her view,
  Should be so tyrannous and rough in proof.

---

80 portentous] F2; portentious Q1; portendous Q2   82 SD] Q1 *(Enter Romeo.); before line 80* Q2   84 is] Q1;
comes Q2   87 SD] *Capell; not in* Q1; *Exeunt.* Q2   89 hopes] Q1; houres Q2   91 sorrow] Q1; sadnesse Q2   93 love?]
Q1 *(loue.)*   95 love?] Q1 *(loue.)*   96 her] Q1; his Q2

80–3 These four lines are all that survives of a twenty-six line passage in Q2. In particular, two speeches by Montague have been much abridged. They describe the symptoms of Romeo's love-sickness, each speech containing an elaborate simile. One of the poetic 'flowers' which William Drummond of Hawthornden overscored in his copy of *Romeo and Juliet* stems from this omitted passage (see Erne, 228).

89 stroke A variant form of 'struck' in use from the fourteenth to the seventeenth centuries (*OED* Strike *v.*).

97 Benvolio's personified love is masculine in Q2 ('his') but feminine in Q1 ('her'). As the *OED* (Love *n* 5a) points out, the personification, though usually masculine, was 'formerly sometimes feminine, and capable of being identified with Venus'. See also *LLL*, 'Forerun fair love, strewing her way with flowers' (4.3.356).

ROMEO Alas that love, whose view is muffled still,
   Should without laws give pathways to our will.   100
   Where shall we dine? [*Seeing blood*] Gods me, what fray
    was here?
   Yet tell me not, for I have heard it all.
   Here's much to do with hate, but more with love.
   Why then, O brawling love, O loving hate,
   O anything of nothing first create,   105
   O heavy lightness, serious vanity,
   Misshapen chaos of best-seeming things,
   Feather of lead, bright smoke, cold fire, sick health,
   Still-waking sleep, that is not what it is –
   This love feel I, which feel no love in this.   110
   Dost thou not laugh?
BENVOLIO   No coz, I rather weep.
ROMEO Good heart, at what?
BENVOLIO   At thy good heart's oppression.
ROMEO Why, such is love's transgression.
   Griefs of mine own lie heavy at my heart,
   Which thou wouldst propagate to have them pressed   115
   With more of thine. This grief that thou hast shown
   Doth add more grief to too much of mine own.
   Love is a smoke raised with the fume of sighs,
   Being purged, a fire sparkling in lovers' eyes,
   Being vexed, a sea raging with a lover's tears.   120
   What is it else? A madness most discreet,
   A choking gall, and a preserving sweet.
   Farewell, coz.

---

100 laws give] Q1 *(lawes giue)*; eyes, see Q2 100 our] Q1; his Q2 101 SD] *Jowett; not in* Q, F 101 Gods me,] Q1;
ô me! Q2 105 create] Q1; created Q2; create F2 107 best-seeming things] Q1 *(best seeming thinges)*; welseeing
formes Q2; welseeming formes Q4 112 heart] Q1 *(hart)*; breast Q2 115 wouldst] Q1; wilt Q2 115 them] Q1;
it Q2 116 grief] Q1 *(griefe)*; loue Q2 117 grief to too] Q1 *(griefe)*; griefe, too too Q2 118 raised] Q1 *(raisde)*;
made Q2 120 raging . . . lover's] Q1 *(louers)*; nourisht with louing Q2 122–3 A . . . coz.] *Arranged as in Hubbard;
as one line* Q1

100 Q2's 'Should, without eyes, see pathwaies
to his will' (1.1.163) draws on the image of blind
Cupid to construct a paradox: Cupid is blindfold
yet sees. By contrast, Q1's line relies on causality
rather than paradox, suggesting that since Cupid
is blindfold, he is blind in the sense of heedless or
reckless (*OED* Blind *a.* 3a).

101 **Gods me** A contracted form of 'God save
me' (*OED* God, 8b).

105 **create** Editors usually prefer Q1's 'create'
to Q2's 'created'. The former is also a participle
(see Abbott 342).

BENVOLIO   Nay, I'll go along,
              And if you hinder me, you do me wrong.
ROMEO Tut, I have lost myself, I am not here,   125
              This is not Romeo, he's some other where.
BENVOLIO Tell me in sadness whom she is you love.
ROMEO What shall I groan and tell thee?
BENVOLIO Why no, but sadly tell me who.
ROMEO Bid a sick man in sadness make his will.   130
              Ah, word ill-urged to one that is so ill.
              In sadness, cousin, I do love a woman.
BENVOLIO I aimed so right whenas you said you loved.
ROMEO A right good mark-man, and she's fair I love.
BENVOLIO A right fair mark, fair coz, is soonest hit.   135
ROMEO But in that hit you miss: she'll not be hit
              With Cupid's arrow. She hath Diana's wit,
              And in strong proof of chastity well armed
              'Gainst Cupid's childish bow she lives unharmed.
              She'll not abide the siege of loving terms,   140
              Nor ope her lap to saint-seducing gold.
              Ah, she is rich in beauty, only poor,
              That when she dies, with beauty dies her store.
                                                          Exeu[nt].

---

124 hinder me] Q1; leaue me so Q2   127 whom she is] Q1 *(whome)*; who is that Q2   129 Why no] Q1; Grone,
why no Q2   130 Bid a] Q1; A Q2   130 make] Q1; makes Q2   131 Ah] Q1; A Q2; O, F2   133 right] Q1; neare
Q2   133 whenas you said] Q1 *(when as you said)*; when I supposde Q2   136 But] Q1; Well Q2   137 Diana's]
Q1 *(Dianaes)*; Dians Q2   139 'Gainst Cupid's] Q1 *(Gainst Cupids)*; From loues weak Q2   139 unharmed] Q1
(vnharm'd); vncharmd Q2   140 She'll not abide] Q1 *(Shee'le)*; Shee will not stay Q2   143 SD] Q1 *(Exeu.)*

124 And if Q1 and Q2 spell 'And if', which existed alongside 'An if' (both meaning simply 'if' in modern English). 'And' or 'an' by itself could also mean 'if' (e.g. *Lear* 1.4.162); the repetition is probably an intensifier, not a redundancy.
129 Why no The omission of Q2's 'Grone' at the beginning of this line turns a headless pentameter into an iambic tetrameter.
130 Q1's line is metrically smoother than Q2's 'A sicke man in sadnesse makes his will.' As a result, a number of editions have adopted the Q1 reading, beginning with Q4.
140–1 Between these two lines, Q2 adds: 'Nor bide th'incounter of assailing eies' (1.1.204). The

preceding fifty-six and the following three Q1 lines all have a counterpart in Q2, so the omission may be accidental, perhaps occasioned by the repetition of 'Nor' at the beginning of two successive lines.
143 At the point where the Q1 scene ends, Q2 has another twenty-two lines with Romeo describing his love-sickness in Petrarchan terms and Benvolio urging him to 'Examine other bewties' (1.1.219) and to 'forget to thinke' (1.1.216) of Rosaline, advice which may have been omitted because Benvolio more or less repeats it in the following scene.

[2]   *Enter County* PARIS, *old* CAPULET

[PARIS] Of honourable reckoning are they both,
          And pity 'tis they live at odds so long.
          But leaving that, what say you to my suit?
CAPULET What should I say more than I said before?
          My daughter is a stranger in the world,   5
          She hath not yet attained to fourteen years.
          Let two more summers wither in their pride
          Before she can be thought fit for a bride.
PARIS Younger than she are happy mothers made.
CAPULET But too soon marred are these so early married.   10
          But woo her, gentle Paris, get her heart,
          My word to her consent is but a part.
          This night I hold an old-accustomed feast
          Whereto I have invited many a guest,
          Such as I love; yet you among the store,   15
          One more, most welcome, makes the number more.
          At my poor house you shall behold this night
          Earth-treading stars that make dark heaven light.
          Such comfort as do lusty young men feel
          When well-apparelled April on the heel   20
          Of lumping winter treads, even such delights

---

0 SD] Q1 *(subst.)*; Enter Capulet, *Countie* Paris, *and the Clowne.* Q2   1 SH] Q2 *(Par.)*; *not in* Q1   1 they] Q1; you Q2   5 daughter is] Q1; child is yet Q2   6 yet . . . to] Q1 *(subst.)*; seene the chaunge of Q2   10 married] Q1 *(maried)*; made Q2   12 word] Q1; will Q2   16 the] Q1; my Q2   17 you shall] Q1; looke to Q2   19 young men] Q2; youngmen Q1   21 lumping] Q1; limping Q2

Scene 2
Act 1, Scene 2 in the NCS edition.
This scene corresponds closely to its Q2 equivalent and contains few cuts: it omits three lines at the beginning, four lines in one of Capulet's speeches and eight words in the Serving-man's soliloquy. The relationship between Q1 and Q2 is particularly close from line 44 as the rest of the Q2 scene was set up from Q1 (see note at 44–95 below).
   0 SD Q2 has a 'Clowne', later identified as a Serving-man, who enters with Capulet and Paris. In Q1, the servant does not enter until line 27.
   1–2 Q1 omits a three-line speech by Capulet at the beginning of this scene in which he explains that the Prince is enforcing the same obligations on him and Montague. In Q1, the scene begins *in medias res*, and we overhear the end of a conversa-

tion of which we do not know the context and in which no referent for 'they' is provided.
   6 **attained to** lived on to a certain time or age (*OED* Attain *v.* 11).
   8 The line in Q1, with its passive construction, is more general and impersonal than Q2's 'Ere we may thinke her ripe to be a bride'.
   10 **married** Q2's 'made' allows for wordplay on 'maid', while Q1's 'married' draws on the proverb 'Marrying is marring' (Dent M701).
   10 Q1 here cuts two lines. Q2's 'Earth hath swallowed all my hopes but she' provides the kind of loose end with which 'round' characters typical of literary texts are constructed. See Introduction, p. 33.
   12 Following these words, Q1 omits another two Q2 verses in which Capulet reiterates that he will not impose a husband on Juliet.

Amongst fresh female buds shall you this night
Inherit at my house. Hear all, all see,
And like her most, whose merit most shall be.
Such amongst view of many, mine being one,   25
May stand in number, though in reckoning none.
Where are you, sirrah?

Enter SERVING-MAN

Go, trudge about
Through fair Verona streets, and seek them out
Whose names are written here [*Gives a paper*], and to them
    say
My house and welcome at their pleasure stay.   30
                           Exeunt [Capulet and Paris]

SERVING-MAN 'Seek them out whose names are written here', and
    yet I know not who are written here. I must to the learned to
    learn of them. That's as much to say, as the tailor must meddle
    with his last, the shoemaker with his needle, the painter with
    his nets, and the fisher with his pencil, I must to the learned.   35

Enter BENVOLIO *and* ROMEO

BENVOLIO [*To Romeo*] Tut, man, one fire burns out another's
                burning;
    One pain is lessened with another's anguish.
    Turn backward, and be holp with backward turning.
    One desperate grief cures with another's languish.
    Take thou some new infection to thy eye,   40
    And the rank poison of the old will die.
ROMEO Your plantain leaf is excellent for that.

---

22 female] Q1; fennell Q2   25 Such amongst] Q1; Which one more view, Q2   27 SD] Q1 *(subst.; following line 26)*   29 here] Q1; there Q2   29 SD] *Staunton (after Capell); not in* Q, F   30 SD] *Rowe; Exeunt* Q1; *Exit* Q2   31 Seek] Q1 *(Seeke); Find Q2   34 needle] Q1; yard Q2   36 SD] *Jowett (to Romeo); not in* Q, F   37 with] Q1; by Q2   38 backward] Q1; giddie Q2   42 plantain] Q1 *(Planton)*

22 **female** Some editors (e.g. Gibbons) here adopt the Q1 reading instead of Q2's 'fennell' (a plant associated with love and brides). As Jowett points out, the common spelling 'femelle' which may have stood in the MS. might have resulted in a misreading of minims.

27 SD In Q1, this stage direction occurs after line 26, but Capulet's words, 'Where are you, sirrah?', suggest that he has not entered yet.

31–5 The Serving-man's prose speech follows its Q2 equivalent less closely than most of the scene's verse. In Q1, he declares his inability to read at the beginning of the speech, in Q2 at the end; the professions he mentions are the same, but they occur in a different order; and only Q1 repeats the words 'I must to the learned'.

36–41 In Q1 and in Q2, these lines form a sestet.

BENVOLIO For what?

ROMEO For your broken shin.

BENVOLIO Why, Romeo, art thou mad?   45

ROMEO Not mad, but bound more than a madman is.
        Shut up in prison, kept without my food,
        Whipped and tormented, and – [*To Serving-man*] Good
        e'en, good fellow.

SERVING-MAN God gi' good e'en. I pray, sir, can you read?   50

ROMEO Ay, mine own fortune in my misery.

SERVING-MAN Perhaps you have learned it without book. But I
        pray, can you read any thing you see?

ROMEO Ay, if I know the letters and the language.

SERVING-MAN Ye say honestly, rest you merry.   55

ROMEO Stay, fellow, I can read.

He reads the letter

'Signor Martino and his wife and daughters,
County Anselm and his beauteous sisters,
The lady widow of Vitruvio,
Signor Placentio and his lovely nieces,   60
Mercutio and his brother Valentine,
Mine uncle Capulet his wife and daughters,
My fair niece Rosaline, and Livia,
Signor Valentio and his cousin Tybalt,

---

48 SD] *This edn (following Jowett); not in* Q, F   50 God gi' good e'en] Q1 *(Godgigoden),* Q2   50 read?] Q1 *(read,)*   57–66 *Arranged as in Dyce (conj. Capell); as prose* Q, F   57 Signor] Q1 *(SEigneur)*   59 Vitruvio] F3 *(Vitruuio);* Vtruuio Q1, Q2   60 Signor] Q1 *(Seigneur)*   63 and Livia] Q1 *(and Liuia);* Liuia Q2   64 Signor] Q1 *(Seigneur)*

44–95 and 3.1–38 These lines correspond very closely to Q2 – including features of layout, typography – probably because Q2 was here set up from a copy of Q1. Perhaps a passage of the manuscript from which Q2 was printed had gone missing or was unreadable (Jowett, 289). The precise beginning and end of the Q1 passage used by the Q2 compositors is difficult to define, but line 44 seems the likeliest starting point (see Richard Hosley, 'Quarto copy for Q2 *Romeo and Juliet*', *SB* 9 (1957), 137–41). The ninety lines from 2.44–3.38 contain only four significant differences between the two texts: Q1 accidentally omits 'the' at 3.34, whereas Q2 lacks 'and' in line 63 below, substitutes 'you' for 'thee' in line 72 below, and accidentally prints 'stal' where Q1 has 'shall' (3.19).

52–3 Q2 prints the Serving-man's speech as verse, Q1 as prose. Since the rhythm does not easily conform to an identifiable pattern, I follow Q1 (and Pope) in printing it as prose.

57–66 Q1 and Q2 print these words as prose, but the passage conforms well to blank verse, and recent editors usually print the lines as verse. With the exception of some of the names (which are in roman type), the letter is printed in italics.

59 Vitruvio The Italianised name of the famous classical architect Vitruvius.

63 and Livia The Q2 omission of 'and' in a passage where Q2 was clearly set up from Q1 may be due to the fact that it is the last word on page B3r.

Lucio and the lively Helena.'   65
A fair assembly, whither should they come?
SERVING-MAN Up.
ROMEO Whither to supper?
SERVING-MAN To our house.
ROMEO Whose house?   70
SERVING-MAN My master's.
ROMEO Indeed, I should have asked thee that before.
SERVING-MAN Now I'll tell you without asking. My master is the
    great rich Capulet, and if you be not of the house of Montagues,
    I pray come and crush a cup of wine. Rest you merry.   [*Exit*]   75
BENVOLIO At this same ancient feast of Capulet's
          Sups the fair Rosaline, whom thou so loves,
          With all the admirèd beauties of Verona.
          Go thither, and with unattainted eye
          Compare her face with some that I shall show,   80
          And I will make thee think thy swan a crow.
ROMEO When the devout religion of mine eye
          Maintains such falsehood, then turn tears to fire,
          And these who, often drowned, could never die,
          Transparent heretics, be burnt for liars.   85
          One fairer than my love! The all-seeing sun
          Ne'er saw her match since first the world begun.
BENVOLIO Tut, you saw her fair none else being by,
          Herself poised with herself in either eye.
          But in that crystal scales let there be weighed   90
          Your lady's love against some other maid
          That I will show you shining at this feast,
          And she shall scant show well that now seems best.
ROMEO I'll go along no such sight to be shown,
          But to rejoice in splendour of mine own.   95

                                                    [*Exeunt*]

---

68 Whither to supper?] Q1 *(Whether)*, Q2; Whither? to supper? F; Whither? / *Ser.* To Supper *Theobald (conj.*
Warburton)   72 thee] Q1; you Q2   75 SD] F1; *not in* Q   95 SD] Pope; *not in* Q, F

66 **fair assembly** According to this list, at
least twenty-three guests are invited. Of these,
only Mercutio, Tybalt, and probably Capulet's
'cousin' – meaning 'kinsman' – are among those
present at the feast. Petruchio and the son and heir
of old Tiberio, who are named at 4.195 and 4.197,
are not on the list.

72 **thee** Some editors find Q1's 'thee' a more
appropriate form of address to a servant than Q2's
'you', but, as Abbott (232) explains, 'a master finding fault often resorts to the unfamiliar *you*'.

82–7 In Q1 and in Q2, these lines form a sestet.

[3] *Enter* CAPULET'S WIFE *and* NURSE

CAPULET'S WIFE Nurse, where's my daughter? Call her forth to
  me.
NURSE Now by my maidenhead at twelve year old,
  I bade her come. What lamb, what ladybird,
  God forbid! Where's this girl? What Juliet!

Enter JULIET

JULIET How now, who calls?   5
NURSE Your mother.
JULIET Madam, I am here. What is your will?
CAPULET'S WIFE This is the matter: – Nurse, give leave a while,
  We must talk in secret. – Nurse, come back again,
  I have remembered me, thou's hear our counsel.   10
  Thou knowest my daughter's of a pretty age.
NURSE Faith, I can tell her age unto an hour.
CAPULET'S WIFE She's not fourteen.
NURSE I'll lay fourteen of my teeth, and yet to my teen be it spoken,
  I have but four, she's not fourteen. How long is it now to   15
  Lammas-tide?
CAPULET'S WIFE A fortnight and odd days.
NURSE Even or odd, of all days in the year,
  Come Lammas Eve at night shall she be fourteen.
  Susan and she – God rest all Christian souls –   20
  Were of an age. Well, Susan is with God;

2–4] *Arranged as in Johnson; as prose* Q, F   8–11] *Arranged as in Capell; as prose* Q, F   10 counsel] Q1 *(counsaile);* Q2
counsel   12 an] Q1 *(a)*   18–50] *Arranged as in Levenson (following Capell); as prose* Q, F

Scene 3
Act 1, Scene 3 in the NCS edition.
Slightly more than the first half of this scene in
Q1 served as copy for, and is therefore very close
to, Q2. The rest of the scene in Q1 has a few local
differences from Q2, but in general corresponds
closely to it, except for three significant cuts of
nine, five, and seventeen lines.
  1–38 For these lines' close correspondence to
Q2, see note above at 2.44–95.
  1 CAPULET'S WIFE The speech headings for
this character change in the course of the play.
Whereas she is called '*Wife*' (or '*W*') in Scenes 1,
3, and 4 (the Danter portion), she is referred to
as '*Moth*', '*Mo*', or '*M*' for mother in later scenes

(the Allde portion). Because of the speech heading '*La*' (probably short for 'Lady of the House'),
which occurs on a number of occasions in Q2, editors since Rowe often call her 'Lady Capulet' in
speech headings and stage directions. In fact, in
Q1 (and Q2) Juliet's mother is nowhere referred to
as 'Lady Capulet'.
  2–66 Throughout this and the next scene, Q1
prints the Nurse's part in italics, a feature Q2 takes
over in this scene. The Serving-man's speech at
3.71–3 is similarly in italics. See Introduction,
p. 38. Q1 and Q2 print all the Nurse's speeches
as prose, and various editors have followed the
quartos.

She was too good for me. But as I said,
On Lammas Eve at night shall she be fourteen,
That shall she, marry, I remember it well.
'Tis since the earthquake now eleven years,   25
And she was weaned – I never shall forget it –
Of all the days of the year upon that day.
For I had then laid wormwood to my dug,
Sitting in the sun under the dovehouse wall.
My lord and you were then at Mantua,   30
Nay, I do bear a brain. But, as I said,
When it did taste the wormwood on the nipple
Of my dug, and felt it bitter, pretty fool,
To see it tetchy and fall out wi'th' dug.
'Shake', quoth the dovehouse, 'twas no need, I trow,   35
To bid me trudge.
And since that time it is eleven year,
For then could Juliet stand high-lone, nay, by the rood,
She could have waddled up and down,
For even the day before she brake her brow,   40
And then my husband (God be with his soul,
He was a merry man):
'Dost thou fall forward, Juliet?
Thou wilt fall backward when thou hast more wit,
Wilt thou not Juliet?' And by my holidam,   45
The pretty fool left crying and said 'Ay'.
To see how a jest shall come about!
I warrant you, if I should live a hundred year,

---

34 wi'th' dug] Q2 *(with the Dugge)*; *with Dugge* Q1   37 year] Q1 *(yeare)*; *yeares* Q2   39 waddled] Q1 *(wadled)*; *run and wadled* Q2   39 up and down] Q1 *(vp and downe)*; *all about* Q2   40 brake] Q1 *(brake)*; *broke* Q2   43 forward, Juliet] Q1 *(forward* Iuliet*)*; *vpon thy face* Q2   45 Juliet] Q1 *(*Iuliet*)*; *Iule* Q2   46 fool] Q1 *(foole)*; *wretch* Q2   47 how] Q1 *(how)*; *now how* Q2   48 year] Q1 *(yeare)*; *yeares* Q2

36 For short lines in Shakespeare's plays, see Wright, 116–42.

37 year Contrary to Q2 ('yeares'), Q1 has an uninflected plural, which was not uncommon in nouns that indicate mass, weight, or time (see Blake, 3.2.1.1[e]).

40 brake For irregular participial formations, see Abbott 344. The analogous form 'spake' occurs on four occasion later in the play.

41–2 my husband (God . . . man) In Q1, the Nurse introduces her husband's reported sentence elliptically. Q2, by contrast, reads: 'a merrie man, tooke vp the child, yea quoth he, doest thou'.

47 To see how a jest Contrary to the equivalent line in Q2, this verse is one foot short.

48 year See note at 3.37 above.

I never should forget it, 'Wilt thou not Juliet?'
And by my troth, she stinted and cried 'Ay'.   50
JULIET And stint thou too, I prithee, Nurse, say I.
NURSE Well, go thy ways. God mark thee for his grace,
    Thou wert the prettiest babe that ever I nursed.
    Might I but live to see thee married once,
    I have my wish.   55
CAPULET'S WIFE And that same marriage, Nurse, is the theme
    I meant to talk of. Tell me, Juliet,
    How stand you affected to be married?
JULIET It is an honour that I dream not of.
NURSE An honour! Were not I thy only nurse,   60
    I would say thou hadst sucked wisdom from thy teat.
CAPULET'S WIFE Well, girl, the noble County Paris seeks thee for
    his wife.
NURSE A man, young lady, lady, such a man
    As all the world. Why, he is a man of wax.
CAPULET'S WIFE Verona's summer hath not such a flower.   65
NURSE Nay, he is a flower, in faith, a very flower.
CAPULET'S WIFE Well, Juliet, how like you of Paris' love?

---

50 cried] Q1 *(cried); said* Q2   51 prithee] Q1 *(prethee); pray thee* Q2   52–5] *Arranged as in Pope; as prose* Q, F   52 Well . . . ways] Q1 *(VVell goe thy waies); Peace I haue done* Q2   52 for] Q1 *(for); too* Q2   53 wert] Q1 *(wert); wast* Q2   56 And . . . marriage] Q1; *Marrie, that marrie* Q2   57 meant] Q1; *came* Q2   57 Juliet] Q1 *(Iuliet); daughter Iuliet* Q2   58 stand you affected] Q1; *stands your dispositions* Q2; *stands your disposition* F   59 honour] Q1; *houre* Q2   60–1] *Arranged as in Pope; as prose* Q, F   60 honour] Q1 *(honor); houre* Q2   62 noble] Q1 *(Noble); valiant* Q2   62 thee] Q1; *you* Q2   62 wife] Q1 *(Wife); loue* Q2   63–4] *Arranged as in Pope; as prose* Q, F

50–1 Between these two lines, Q1 omits a nine-line passage in which Capulet's Wife tries to interrupt the Nurse and the Nurse recalls her husband's interaction with Juliet.

52 God mark thee for his grace In Shakespeare's time, Q2's 'to' as well as Q1's 'for' were possible prepositions; 'to' has since become obsolete (see *OED* Mark *v.* 6a).

55 See note at 3.36 above.

58 affected to disposed, inclined (*OED* Affected *ppl. a.,* 1).

59–60 honour . . . honour Modern editors

usually follow Pope in emending Q2's 'houre' by adopting Q1's 'honour'.

62 Capulet's Wife's six-line speech in Q2 is greatly reduced. In Q1, Juliet's mother therefore does not exert pressure on her daughter by telling her that Veronese 'Ladies of esteeme' have got married at Juliet's age, and that she herself did so too.

66 Following this line, Q2 has seventeen lines absent from Q1, all but one of which taken up by a long, poetic speech by Juliet's mother in which she likens Paris's face to a book.

JULIET I'll look to like if looking liking move,
    But no more deep will I engage mine eye
    Than your consent gives strength to make it fly.   70

Enter SERVING-MAN

SERVING-MAN Madam, you are called for, supper is ready, the
    Nurse cursed in the pantry, all things in extremity.
    Make haste, for I must be gone to wait.

                                                        [*Exeunt*]

[4]   *Enter masquers [bearing torches,* BENVOLIO, MERCUTIO,] *with*
      ROMEO, *and a page*

ROMEO What, shall this speech be spoke for our excuse,
    Or shall we on without apology?
BENVOLIO The date is out of such prolixity,
    We'll have no Cupid hoodwinked with a scarf,

---

69 engage] Q1; endart Q2   70 it fly] Q1 *(it flie);* flie Q2   70 SD] Q2 *(Enter Seruing.); not in* Q1 *(Enter Clowne. catchword)*   71 SH] Q2 *(Ser.);* Clowne: Q1   71 SD] Q2; *not in* Q1
    0 SD] *This edn; Enter Maskers with* Romeo *and a Page* Q1; *Enter* Romeo, Mercutio, Benuolio, *with fiue or sixe other Maskers, torchbearers.* Q2

69 engage mine eye Whereas Q2's 'endart' calls up the piercing eyes of the Petrarchan mistress, Q1's 'engage' implies a reluctance to entangle or commit herself (*OED* Engage *v.* 11a, 13a). See also *Ham.*, 'O limèd soul that, struggling to be free, / Art more engaged' (3.3.68–9).

70 SD, 71 SH SERVING-MAN In SD and SH, Q1's Serving-man is referred to as 'Clowne'. Q2 similarly has a 'Clowne' enter at the beginning of the preceding scene, and a stage direction in what corresponds to 4.5 calls for 'Will Kemp', an actor in the company famous for his comic parts (see notes at 2.0 SD and 17.41). It seems likely that Will Kemp doubled as Peter and the Capulet Serving-man. See Appendix B, p. 64.

71–3 Like the Nurse's speeches in this and the following scene, the Serving-man's words are printed in italics (see note at 2–66 above). The Serving-man's speech in Q1 is nine words shorter than that in Q2 and is less close to its equivalent in the longer text than much of the rest in this scene. In Q2, the speech is followed by two one-line speeches by Capulet's Wife and the Nurse at the very end of the scene urging Juliet to seek happiness with Paris.

Scene 4
Act 1, Scenes 4 and 5 in the NCS edition.
Scene 4 corresponds quite closely to Q2 with a few notable exceptions. In the dialogue between Mercutio and Romeo preceding the Queen Mab speech, a passage of eighteen lines is reduced to three in Q1. Q2's transitory passage with four Capulet Serving-men leading up to the feast, totalling some fifteen lines, is absent from Q1. And five and a half lines have been omitted from Capulet's speech at the beginning of the feast. Apart from that, Q1 differs from Q2 only in a few minor cuts and local transpositions and changes.

    0 SD The original stage direction does not mention Benvolio and Mercutio, who are thus subsumed among the masquers. How many mute masquers enter at this point is left open by the stage direction, but the number of actors needed later in the scene suggests there were few if any in early performances (see Hoppe, 95–7). The stage direction in Q2 reads '*Enter* Romeo, Mercutio, Benuolio, *with fiue or sixe other Maskers, torchbearers.*' This is what editors used to call a permissive SD. Pressures on casting make it seem unlikely that this scene would ever have been performed with as many extras in Shakespeare's time (see Appendix B, p. 165).

Bearing a Tartar's painted bow of lath,   5
Scaring the ladies like a crow-keeper;
Nor no without-book prologue faintly spoke,
After the prompter, for our entrance.
But let them measure us by what they will,
We'll measure them a measure and be gone.   10
ROMEO A torch for me, I am not for this ambling,
Being but heavy I will bear the light.
MERCUTIO Believe me, Romeo, I must have you dance.
ROMEO Not I, believe me. You have dancing shoes
With nimble soles, I have a soul of lead   15
So stakes me to the ground I cannot stir.
MERCUTIO Give me a case to put my visage in,
A visor for a visor. What care I
What curious eye doth quote deformity?
ROMEO Give me a torch. Let wantons, light of heart,   20
Tickle the senseless rushes with their heels.
For I am proverbed with a grandsire phrase:
I'll be a candleholder and look on;
The game was ne'er so fair, and I am done.
MERCUTIO Tut, dun's the mouse, the constable's old word.   25
If thou beest dun, we'll draw thee from the mire

---

16 stir] Q1 *(stirre)*; moue Q2   **19** quote] Q1 *(coate)*; cote Q2   **19** deformity] Q1 *(deformitie)*; deformities Q2   **25** old] Q1; own Q2

7–8 These lines do not appear in Q2 for reasons which, despite various conjectures, remain unclear. They constitute an autonomous unit that could have been added at a later stage of composition than that reflected by Q2. It is not impossible that their absence in Q2 is due to a compositor's oversight, though accidental omissions of two lines are rare. Pope was the first to include the lines in his edition. Many have followed since, including NCS, Gibbons, and Jowett (though not Oxford). It may be by pure accident that one of the few passages in the theatrical Q1 with no equivalent in the more literary Q2 makes explicit reference to theatrical practice. 'To speak (etc.) without book' is proverbial (Dent B 532).

8 entrance Probably trisyllabic. Pope added a tenth syllable to the line by changing the word to 'enterance'.

15 I have a soul of lead Q1's spelling, 'soule', maintains the sole/soul ambiguity.

16–17 Between these lines, Q2 prints a passage of twelve lines with short speeches by Romeo and Mercutio, the former still indulging in his love-sickness, the latter in bawdy puns. Pope follows the Q1 omission.

19 quote observe, notice. Q1's 'coate' and Q2's 'cote' were common variant spellings of 'quote' in Shakespeare's time (see Wells, *Modernizing*, 11).

19–20 Between these lines, Q2 adds one verse to Mercutio's speech ('Here are the beetle browes shall blush for me') followed by a two-line speech by Benvolio ('Come knock and enter, and no sooner in, / But euery man betake him to his legs').

24 done With a pun on 'dun' (dull, dark, grey), as the following line makes clear. The spelling in the first three quartos differs: Q1, 'done'; Q2, 'dum', and Q3, 'dun'. Q2 is probably a minim misreading corrected in Q3. Recent editions (NCS, Gibbons, Jowett, Oxford) adopt Q1's spelling.

25 the constable's old word As Mercutio is drawing on a proverb (Dent D 644), Q1's 'old' seems no less appropriate than Q2's 'own'. It is of course easy to misremember or mishear 'old' as 'own'.

Of this sir-reverence love wherein thou stick'st.
Leave this talk, we burn daylight here.

ROMEO   Nay, that's not so.

MERCUTIO   I mean, sir, in delay
We burn our lights by night, like lamps by day.   30
Take our good meaning, for our judgement sits
Three times a day ere once in her right wits.

ROMEO   So we mean well by going to this masque,
But 'tis no wit to go.

MERCUTIO   Why, Romeo, may one ask?

ROMEO   I dreamt a dream tonight.

MERCUTIO   And so did I.   35

ROMEO   Why, what was yours?

MERCUTIO   That dreamers often lie.

ROMEO   In bed asleep while they do dream things true.

MERCUTIO   Ah, then I see Queen Mab hath been with you.

BENVOLIO   Queen Mab? What's she?

[MERCUTIO]   She is the fairies' midwife and doth come   40
In shape no bigger than an agate stone
On the forefinger of a burgomaster,
Drawn with a team of little atomi

---

27 Of this sir-reverence love] Q1 *(Of this surreuerence loue)*; Or saue you reuerence loue Q2; Or, saue your reverence, Love F4   30 burn] Q1 *(burne)*; waste Q2   30 by night] Q1; in vaine Q2   30 like lamps by day] Q1 *(Lampes)*; lights lights by day Q2   32 Three] Q1; Fiue Q2   32 a day] Q1; in that Q2   32 her right] Q1; our fine Q2; our five *Malone*   33 So] Q1; And Q2   34 Why, Romeo,] Q1 *(Why Romeo)*; Why, Q2   36 Why] Q1; Well Q2   38 Ah] Q1; O Q2   40 SH] Q2; *not in* Q1   40 doth come] Q1; she comes Q2   42 burgomaster] Q1 *(Burgomaster)*; Alderman Q2   43 atomi] Q1 *(Atomi)*; ottamie Q2; atomies Q3

27 **Of this sir-reverence love** Q2's 'Or saue you reuerence loue' (emended to and modernised as 'Of – save your reverence – love' in NCS and Jowett) inserts a mock-apology that puns on 'sir-reverence'. 'Sir-reverence' meant 'with all respect for' or 'with apologies to' but could also designate human excrement (*OED n.* 1, 2). See also Dent, 'Saving your (Sir) reverence' (B93).

31–2 Mercutio is asking Romeo to infer the correct meaning instead of misconstruing him, human judgement being fallible enough (erring three times out of four), even when it willingly co-operates.

39 **Queen Mab? What's she?** Benvolio's question is not in any other early edition. Editors from Keightley to Jowett have occasionally integrated Benvolio's questions into their text, arguing that the words 'This is she' with which the Q2 speech ends make sense as a reply to Benvolio's question. The remaining text on the same page in

Q2 is extremely crammed, and Jowett believes that the omission may have been occasioned by pressures of space on a compositor who was working rigorously to a casting-off mark.

40 As the speech heading is missing in Q1, the edition mistakenly assigns the whole Queen Mab speech to Benvolio.

40–73 The Queen Mab speech is printed in verse in Q1, but in prose in Q2. Modern editors usually follow Q1 and Pope in setting the speech in verse. Sidney Thomas ('The Queen Mab Speech in *Romeo and Juliet*', *S.Sur.* 25 (1972), 73–80) has argued for 'The superiority of Q1 to Q2' (78) throughout Mercutio's speech.

42 **burgomaster** Q1's word for Q2's 'Alderman'; Shakespeare also uses the word in *1H4*, 2.1.76.

43 **atomi** Plural of Latin *atomus*, atom; modern editors usually adopt this word from Q1.

Athwart men's noses when they lie asleep.
Her wagon-spokes are made of spinners' webs,   45
The cover of the wings of grasshoppers;
The traces are the moonshine-watery beams,
The collars, crickets' bones, the lash of films.
Her wagoner is a small grey-coated fly,
Not half so big as is a little worm,   50
Picked from the lazy finger of a maid.
And in this sort she gallops up and down
Through lovers' brains, and then they dream of love;
O'er courtiers' knees, who straight on curtsies dream;
O'er ladies' lips, who dream on kisses straight,   55
Which oft the angry Mab with blisters plagues,
Because their breaths with sweetmeats tainted are.
Sometimes she gallops o'er a lawyer's lip,
And then dreams he of smelling out a suit,
And sometime comes she with a tithe-pig's tail,   60
Tickling a parson's nose that lies asleep,
And then dreams he of another benefice.
Sometime she gallops o'er a soldier's nose,
And then dreams he of cutting foreign throats,
Of breaches, ambuscados, countermines,   65
Of healths five fathom deep, and then anon
Drums in his ear, at which he starts and wakes,
And swears a prayer or two, and sleeps again.

---

44 Athwart] Q1; ouer Q2   45 are made of spinners' webs] Q1 *(spinners); made of log spinners legs Q2   47 The]* Q1; her Q2   47 moonshine-watery] Q1 *(Moone-shine watrie); moonshines watry Q2   48 The collars] Q1 (collers);* her whip Q2   49 fly] Q1 *(flie); Gnat Q2   51 Picked] Q1 (Pickt); prickt Q2   51 maid] Q1 (maide); man Q2; woman* F2   52 sort] Q1; state Q2   52 up and down] Q1 *(subst.); night by night Q2   54 O'er] Q1 (O're); On Q2   54* curtsies] Q1 *(cursies)   58 lawyer's lip] Jowett; Lawers lap Q1; Courtiers nose Q2   62 dreams he] Q1; he dreams Q2* 63 gallops] Q1; driueth Q2   63 nose] Q1; neck Q2   65 countermines] Q1; spanish blades Q2   68 And swears] Q1 *(sweares); and being thus frighted, sweares Q2*

---

47 Q1 condenses a slightly longer Q2 passage: 'her traces of the smallest spider web, her collors of the moonshines watry beams'.

51 **maid** Many editors since Pope have adopted the Q1 reading 'maid' instead of Q2's 'man'. Hoppe believed that 'maid' goes back to a MS. reading 'maie' (= maiden).

51–2 Between these two lines, Q2 adds a short passage in which Queen Mab's chariot is described.

54 **curtsies** Q1 has 'cursies', Q2 'Cursies'. In Shakespeare's time, the word could mean either 'curtsies' or 'courtesies', an ambivalence an edi-

tion with modernised spelling cannot maintain (see Wells, *Modernizing*, 10–11).

54–5 Between these two lines, Q2 adds: 'ore Lawyers fingers who strait dreame on fees'. Thomas (see note at 4.40–73) argued that 'The effective . . . chiasmus of [lines 54–5] in Q1 is considerably weakened in Q2 . . . by the insertion of an additional line' (78).

58 Q1's 'lap' is likely to be wrong as it fails to establish the connection to smelling presupposed in the next line, a problem for which the emendation 'lip' may provide a plausible solution.

       This is that Mab that makes maids lie on their backs,
       And proves them women of good carriage.   70
       This is the very Mab that plaits the manes of horses in the
          night,
       And plaits the elf-locks in foul sluttish hair,
       Which once untangled much misfortune breeds.
ROMEO Peace, peace, thou talk'st of nothing.
MERCUTIO True, I talk of dreams,   75
       Which are the children of an idle brain,
       Begot of nothing but vain fantasy,
       Which is as thin a substance as the air,
       And more inconstant than the wind which woos
       Even now the frozen bowels of the north,   80
       And being angered puffs away in haste,
       Turning his face to the dew-dropping south.
BENVOLIO Come, come, this wind doth blow us from ourselves.
       Supper is done, and we shall come too late.
ROMEO I fear too early, for my mind misgives   85
       Some consequence is hanging in the stars,
       Which bitterly begins his fearful date
       With this night's revels, and expires the term
       Of a despisèd life closed in this breast
       By some untimely forfeit of vile death.   90
       But he that hath the steerage of my course
       Directs my sail. On, lusty gentlemen.

---

69 that . . . makes] Q1; the hag, when maides Q2   70 And proves] Q1 *(proues)*; Making Q2   71 plaits] Q1 *(plats)*; bakes Q2   73 breeds] Q1 *(breedes)*; bodes Q2   79] *Arranged as in* Q2; . . . winde, / . . . north, Q1   81 in haste] Q1; from thence Q2   82 face] Q1; side Q2   84 is] Q1; and Q2   87 Which . . . begins] Q1; Shall bitterly begin Q2   88 expires] Q1 *(expiers)*; expire Q2   92 Directs] Q1; Direct Q2   92 sail] Q1 *(saile)*; sute Q2   92 SD] Q1 *(Enter old* Capulet *with the Ladies.)*; / Enter all the guests and gentlewomen to the Maskers Q2

69–73 These five lines appear in Q2 in a different order: the last three are followed by the first, then by a line missing in Q1 ('That presses them and learnes them first to beare'), and finally by the second. At the very end of the speech, Q2 concludes 'This is she.'

92 Directs my sail The extended nautical metaphor is completed by reference not to a canvas but to 'An act of sailing; a voyage or excursion in a sailing vessel' (*OED n.*² 1). Shakespeare uses the word in a similar context in *Oth.* 5.2.275. Recent editors are divided over whether or not to adopt Q1's 'sail'.

92–3 Between these two lines, Q2 prints a short passage with four Capulet servants. Most editors since Steevens begin a new scene before this passage, even though the stage does not seem to have been cleared. The Q2 SD reads: '*They* [the masquers] *march about the Stage, and Seruingmen come forth with Napkins.*' Yet on the next line follows the contradictory '*Enter* Romeo', suggesting that Shakespeare may at one point have intended the masquers to exit and re-enter later on. While a case for a scene break in Q2 can thus be made, the same is not true for Q1, where the servants passage is omitted and the masquers are immediately welcomed as the Capulets and their other guests enter. See Appendix A, p. 157.

92 SD The scene moves to a different location, a hall in Capulet's house, the feast thus

Enter old CAPULET, [CAPULET'S COUSIN, TYBALT, *and his page,*]
  with the ladies, [CAPULET'S WIFE, JULIET, *the* NURSE, *and*
                    serving-men]

CAPULET Welcome gentlemen, welcome gentlemen!
        Ladies that have their toes unplagued with corns
        Will have a bout with you. Aha, my mistresses,   95
        Which of you all will now refuse to dance?
        She that makes dainty, she, I'll swear, hath corns.
        Am I come near you now? – Welcome gentlemen, welcome!

                          [*They dance*]

        [*To serving-men*] More lights, you knaves, and turn these
            tables up,
        And quench the fire, the room is grown too hot. –   100
        Ah, sirrah, this unlooked-for sport comes well. –
        Nay sit, nay sit, good cousin Capulet,
        For you and I are past our standing days.
        How long is it since you and I were in a masque?
CAPULET'S COUSIN By Lady, sir, 'tis thirty years at least.   105
CAPULET 'Tis not so much, 'tis not so much,
        'Tis since the marriage of Lucentio,
        Come Pentecost as quickly as it will,
        Some five-and-twenty years, and then we masqued.
CAPULET'S COUSIN 'Tis more, 'tis more, his son is elder far.   110

---

94 have] Q1 *(haue);* walke Q2   95 a bout] *Pope;* about Q1   95 Aha] Q1 *(ah ha);* Ah Q2   96 refuse] Q1; denie Q2   98 SD] *This edn; not in* Q1; *Musick playes and they dance* Q2   99 SD] *Jowett; not in* Q, F   103 standing] Q1; dauncing Q2   105 years at least] Q1 *(yeares);* yeares Q2   107 marriage] Q1 *(mariage);* nuptiall Q2

coming to the masquers rather than the reverse. The Q1 SD, '*Enter old* CAPULET *with the ladies*', is vague and fails to provide an entrance for some of the characters (e.g. Capulet's Cousin, Tybalt, Juliet), leaving questions about early staging unanswered. Capulet's Wife remains mute throughout the scene, though we may assume that she is onstage. The Nurse does not speak until line 179. As pressure on casting is high in this scene, it cannot be excluded that the Nurse doubled as Tybalt's page, thus reducing by one the number of actors required for this scene. Paris was invited to the feast by Capulet in Scene 2, but no reference is made to him. Again, pressure on casting makes it seem possible that Paris was not necessarily present at Capulet's feast in early performances

(see Appendix B, p. 164).

98–9 Between these two lines, Q2 adds a SD and a line and a half to Capulet's speech: 'Musitions play. / *Musick playes and they dance.* / A hall, a hall, giue roome, and foote it gyrles.' Hoppe (95–7) has argued that the omission of any mention of music is bound up with pressures on casting.

101 **Ah, sirrah . . . well** It is not clear to whom Capulet addresses these words. 'Sirrah' would be an unusual form of address for his cousin, so it seems more likely that Capulet is talking to either a Serving-man or a young male guest. A further possibility is that he is speaking to himself (see Onions, entry for 'sirrah').

105 **By Lady** A contracted form of 'By our Lady' (Q2 reads 'Berlady').

CAPULET Will you tell me that it cannot be so?
            His son was but a ward three years ago.
            Good youths, i'faith, O, youth's a jolly thing.
ROMEO [*Aside*] What lady is that that doth enrich the hand
            Of yonder knight?   115
            O, she doth teach the torches to burn bright!
            It seems she hangs upon the cheek of night
            Like a rich jewel in an Ethiop's ear,
            Beauty too rich for use, for earth too dear.
            So shines a snow-white swan trouping with crows,   120
            As this fair lady over her fellows shows.
            The measure done, I'll watch her place of stand,
            And touching hers make happy my rude hand.
            Did my heart love till now? Forswear it, sight,
            I never saw true beauty till this night.   125
TYBALT This by his voice should be a Montague.
            Fetch me my rapier, boy.

                                               [*Exit page*]

                        What, dares the slave
            Come hither, covered with an antic face,
            To scorn and jeer at our solemnity?
            Now by the stock and honour of my kin,   130
            To strike him dead I hold it for no sin.
CAPULET Why, how now, cousin, wherefore storm you so?
TYBALT Uncle, this is a Montague, our foe,
            A villain that is hither come in spite
            To mock at our solemnity this night.   135

---

112 three] Q1; 2. Q2   114 SD] *This edn; not in* Q, F   115–16] *Arranged as in Hubbard; as one line* Q1   120 shines . . . swan] Q1 *(Swan);* showes a snowie Doue Q2   121 this fair] Q1 *(faire);* yonder Q2   123 happy] Q1 *(happie);* blessed Q2   127 SD] *Collier (Exit Boye.); not in* Q, F   129 scorn and jeer] Q1 *(subst.);* fleere and scorne Q2   132 cousin] Q1 *(Cosen);* kinsman Q2   135 mock] Q1 *(mocke);* scorne Q2

113 This line is not in Q2. It provides a reso-
nant transition to the youthful Romeo falling in
love with Juliet.
114 In Q2, Romeo's question is directed at a
Capulet Serving-man who cannot identify Juliet:
'I know not sir.' By thus raising the question yet
delaying the answer, Shakespeare is clearly achiev-
ing a calculated dramatic effect, though it may
seem odd that he does so by means of a Capulet
Serving-man who, unaccountably, is unable to
identify Juliet. In Q1, Romeo seems to be speaking
to himself.

115 See note at 3.36.
120 Q1 has 'snow-white swan' where Q2 reads
'snowie Doue'. The line recalls Benvolio's earlier
'And I will make thee think thy swan a crow' (2.81;
the line is identical in Q2), and Jowett believes the
Q1 version may be a reporter's recollection. Note,
though, that Shakespeare also wrote 'snow-white
swan' in *Lucr.* (line 1011).
127 SD Q1 and Q2 provide no SD for the page's
exit, nor is there a later SD indicating whether, and
if so when, the page returns.

CAPULET Young Romeo, is it not?

TYBALT   It is that villain Romeo.

CAPULET Let him alone.
          He bears him like a portly gentleman,
          And, to speak truth, Verona brags of him
          As of a virtuous and well-governed youth.   140
          I would not for the wealth of all this town
          Here in my house do him disparagement.
          Therefore be quiet, take no note of him;
          Bear a fair presence, and put off these frowns,
          An ill-beseeming semblance for a feast.   145

TYBALT It fits when such a villain is a guest,
          I'll not endure him.

CAPULET He shall be endured. Go to, I say he shall!
          Am I the master of the house or you?
          You'll not endure him? God shall mend my soul,   150
          You'll make a mutiny amongst my guests,
          You'll set cock-a-hoop, you'll be the man!

TYBALT Uncle, 'tis a shame.

CAPULET   Go to, you are a saucy knave.
          This trick will scathe you one day, I know what.
          [*To the dancers*] Well said, my hearts. [*To Tybalt*] Be quiet!   155
          [*To serving-man*] More light, ye knave, or I will make you
            quiet.

TYBALT Patience perforce with wilful choler meeting
          Makes my flesh tremble in their different greetings.
          I will withdraw, but this intrusion shall,
          Now seeming sweet, convert to bitter gall.   [*Exit*]   160

137–8] *Arranged as in Hubbard; as one line* Q1   138 He] Q1 *(he)*; A Q2   143 quiet] Q1; patient Q2   144 Bear] Q1 *(Beare)*; Shew Q2   150 him?] Q1; him, Q2   153 knave] Q1 *(knaue)*; boy Q2   155 SD.1] *Oxford; not in* Q, F   155 SD.2] *Jowett; not in* Q, F   156 SD] *This edn (after Jowett); not in* Q, F   158 greetings] Q1; greeting Q2   160 bitter] Q1; bittrest Q2; bitter Q3   160 SD] Q2; *not in* Q1

143–4 Between these lines, Q2 prints an additional verse: 'It is my will, the which if thou respect'.

152 Q1's 'You'll' as opposed to Q2's 'You wil' makes for a headless line. As Wright (175) points out, Shakespeare occasionally uses such lines to convey a speaker's anger as in Mercutio's 'Where the deule should this *Romeo* be?' (2.4.1; no metri-cal equivalent in Q1).

153–6 Capulet's speech totals thirty-three words in Q1 as opposed to fifty-five in Q2. The difference is due to the omission of one full line ("You must contrarie me, marrie tis time', between lines 154 and 155) and a few repetitions and interjections present in Q2 but not in Q1.

ROMEO [*To Juliet, touching her hand*] If I profane with my unworthy
　　　　hand
　　　　This holy shrine, the gentle sin is this:
　　　　My lips, two blushing pilgrims, ready stand
　　　　To smooth the rough touch with a gentle kiss.
JULIET Good pilgrim, you do wrong your hand too much,　　　　　165
　　　　Which mannerly devotion shows in this;
　　　　For saints have hands which holy palmers touch,
　　　　And palm to palm is holy palmer's kiss.
ROMEO Have not saints lips, and holy palmers too?
JULIET Yes, pilgrim, lips that they must use in prayer.　　　　　170
ROMEO Why then, fair saint, let lips do what hands do:
　　　　They pray; yield thou, lest faith turn to despair.
JULIET Saints do not move, though grant, nor prayer forsake.
ROMEO Then move not till my prayer's effect I take.
　　　　　　　　　　[*He kisses her*]
　　　　Thus from my lips, by yours, my sin is purged.　　　　　175
JULIET Then have my lips the sin that they have took.
ROMEO Sin from my lips? O trespass sweetly urged.
　　　　Give me my sin again!
　　　　　　　　[*He kisses her again*]
JULIET　　　　　　　　　　You kiss by the book.
NURSE Madam, your mother calls.

---

161 SD] *Jowett; not in* Q, F　　161 unworthy] Q1 *(vnworthie);* vnworthiest Q2　　162 gentle] Q, F; gentler *Jowett*
(conj. Dowden)　　162 sin] Q, F *(subst.);* fine *Theobalt (conj. Warburton);* pain *Wilson–Duthie*　　163 ready] Q1; did
readie Q2　　164 the] Q1; that Q2　　164 gentle] Q1; tender Q2　　167 holy palmers] Q1 *(Palmers);* Pilgrims hands
Q2　　170 Yes] Q1; I Q2　　171 fair] Q1 *(faire);* deare Q2　　172 yield] Q1 *(yeeld);* grant Q2　　173 move, . . . forsake]
Hubbard; mooue though: grant nor praier forsake Q1; moue, thogh grant for praiers sake Q2　　174 till] Q1; while
Q2　　174 prayer's] *Capell;* praiers Q; prayers F; prayers' *Warburton*　　174 SD] *Rowe (Kissing her, after line 175); not in*
Q, F　　175 yours] Q1; thine Q2　　178 SD] *Capell (kissing her again); not in* Q, F　　179 calls] Q1 *(calles);* craues a word with
you Q2　　179 SD] *Jowett; not in* Q, F

162 **gentle sin** Various emendations have been
proposed for either word in attempts to make the
sentence logical. However, the identity of all early
readings argues against local corruption, and the
phrase makes good enough poetic (if not logical)
sense. The integrity of 'sin' is further supported
by Romeo's later comment on Juliet's lips which
'blush, as thinking their owne kisses sin' (3.3.39;
no Q1 equivalent).

163 Recent editors agree that Q1's reading is
correct and omit the extra-metrical 'did' in Q2's
'did readie stand'.

173 **forsake** decline, refuse (*OED v.* 2). Juliet
is saying that while it is Romeo who must take the
initiative, she will not refuse if he offers to kiss
her.

[*Juliet moves towards her mother*]

ROMEO What is her mother?

NURSE   Marry, bachelor,   180
Her mother is the lady of the house,
And a good lady, and a wise, and a virtuous.
I nursed her daughter that you talked withal.
I tell you, he that can lay hold of her
Shall have the chinks.

ROMEO   [*Aside*] Is she a Capulet?   185
O dear account! My life is my foe's thrall.

CAPULET Nay, gentlemen, prepare not to be gone,
We have a trifling foolish banquet towards.
                    They whisper in his ear
I pray you, let me entreat you. Is it so?
Well then, I thank you honest gentlemen.   190
I promise you, but for your company,
I would have been abed an hour ago.
[*To serving-man*] Light to my chamber, ho!
                    Exeunt [*all but Juliet and Nurse*]

JULIET Nurse, what is yonder gentleman?
NURSE The son and heir of old Tiberio.   195

180–5 Marry . . . chinks] *Arranged as in* Q2; *as prose* Q1   185 SD] *Jowett; not in* Q, F   185–6 Is she . . . thrall.] *Arranged as in* Q2; Is . . . account, / My . . . thrall. Q1   185 Capulet] Q2; *Mountague* Q1   186 thrall] Q1; debt Q2   189 I . . . entreat you] Q1 *(subst.); not in* Q2   190 honest gentlemen] Q1 *(subst.); all* Q2   193 SD.1] *Levenson; not in* Q1   193 SD.2] *Malone; Exeunt.* Q1   194 yonder] Q1; yond Q2

179–210 As in the preceding scene, the Nurse's part is printed in italics and, where distinguishable, in prose (see note at 3.2–66). My relineation follows Q2.

186–7 Between these two lines, Q2 prints two one-line speeches by Benvolio and Romeo: '*Ben.* Away begon, the sport is at the best. / *Ro.* I so I feare, the more is my vnrest.' The lines form a necessary transition for a reader to understand to whom Capulet's ensuing speech is referring, but they are easily replaced by stage action in the theatre.

188 SD This is one of Q1's descriptive stage directions, with no equivalent in Q2, believed by some to have originated in John Danter's printing house and thus to have been added for readers, as part of a 'literary' presentation. Jowett ('Chettle', 73) compares the present stage direction to 'he whispers Lectorius' in *The Wounds of Civil War* (1594), another Danter play quarto.

191–2 These two lines are entirely different from those in Q2 but correspond to a passage in Capulet's speech in Q2 at 3.4.6–7. While the passage in Q2 thus appears over an act later than in Q1, it occurs in what is in fact Capulet's very next speech, as Juliet's father makes no appearance between Scene 4 (1.5) and Scene 13 (3.4). In other words, in the 'part' on which Capulet's lines would have been written out and from which the player would have learned them by heart, the lines appeared close to the speech to which they have been transposed in Q1, and perhaps this proximity occasioned (or facilitated) the transposition.

193 Like the preceding two lines, these words find their equivalent not in the corresponding Q2 scene but in 3.4.33. Hoppe (146) interpreted this and the preceding transpositions as the result of faulty memory of actors reconstructing the text.

JULIET What's he that now is going out of door?
NURSE That, as I think, is young Petruchio.
JULIET What's he that follows there that would not dance?
NURSE I know not.
JULIET Go learn his name.

                                                    [*The Nurse goes*]

              If he be married,   200
    My grave is like to be my wedding bed.
NURSE [*Returning*] His name is Romeo, and a Montague,
    The only son of your great enemy.
JULIET My only love sprung from my only hate,
    Too early seen unknown and known too late.   205
    Prodigious birth of love is this to me,
    That I should love a loathèd enemy.
NURSE What's this? What's that?
JULIET Nothing, Nurse, but a rhyme I learnt even now of one
    I danced with.
NURSE Come, your mother stays for you. I'll go along with you.   210
                                                    Exeunt

[5]   *Enter* ROMEO *alone*

ROMEO Shall I go forward and my heart is here?
    Turn back, dull earth, and find thy centre out.
    [*He withdraws.*]

---

197 That . . . is] Q1 *(subst.)*; Marrie that I thinke be Q2   **198** there] Q1; here Q2   **200** learn] Q1 *(learne)*; aske Q2   **200** SD] *Jowett; not in* Q, F   **202** SD] *Jowett; not in* Q, F   **202–3**] *Arranged as in* Q2; *as prose* Q1   **206** is this] Q1; it is Q2   **207** should] Q1; must Q2   **208** this? What's that] Q1 *(this? what's that)*; tis? whats tis Q2; this? whats this F   **209** with] Q1; withall Q2   **210**] Q1 *(subst.)*; Anon, anon: / Come lets away, the strangers all are gone. Q2   **1** Shall] Q1; Can Q2   **1** and] Q1; when Q2   **2** SD.1] *Gibbons; not in* Q, F   **2** SD.2] Q1 *(Enter Benuolio Mercutio.)*; Enter Benuolio *with* Mercutio. Q2

208 The Nurse adopts a dialectal form in Q2 ('Whats tis? whats tis') but does not in Q1.

Scene 5
Act 2, Scenes 1 and 2 in the NCS edition.
Scene 5 corresponds in general closely to the equivalent part of Q2. The lovers' protracted leave-taking is shortened by the omission of two passages of fifteen and seven lines, and a four-line passage in Q2 at the end of the scene which immediately reappears at the beginning of the next is absent from Q1. Other than that, divergences are minor: the substitution or addition of single words or short phrases, a handful of very short passages absent from Q1, and the attribution to Mercutio of two lines in Q1 that are spoken by Benvolio in Q2.

1 Q1 omits the sonnet ('Now old desire doth in his deathbed lie') spoken by Q2's Chorus before this scene. Note that the first, short quarto of *H5* omits the Chorus present at the beginning of each of the five acts. Q2 *Rom.*, by contrast, only has a chorus at the beginning of Acts 1 and 2; Q1 provides a slightly shorter version of that in Act 1 and omits the one in Act 2.

Enter BENVOLIO, MERCUTIO

BENVOLIO Romeo, my cousin Romeo!
MERCUTIO Dost thou hear, he is wise.
    Upon my life, he hath stol'n him home to bed.   5
BENVOLIO He came this way and leapt this orchard wall.
    Call, good Mercutio.
MERCUTIO   Call? Nay, I'll conjure too:
    Romeo! Madman! Humours! Passion! Liver!
    Appear thou in likeness of a sigh,
    Speak but one rhyme, and I am satisfied.   10
    Cry but 'Ay me!', pronounce but 'love' and 'dove',
    Speak to my gossip Venus one fair word,
    One nickname for her purblind son and heir,
    Young Abraham Cupid, he that shot so trim
    When young King Cophetua loved the beggar wench.   15
    He hears me not.
    I conjure thee by Rosalind's bright eye,
    High forehead, and scarlet lip,
    Her pretty foot, straight leg, and quivering thigh,
    And the demesnes that there adjacent lie,   20
    That in thy likeness thou appear to us.
BENVOLIO If he do hear thee, thou wilt anger him.

---

3 my cousin Romeo] Q1 *(my cosen Romeo)*; my Cosen *Romeo, Romeo* Q2   4 Dost . . . he] Q1 *(subst.);* He Q2   5 Upon] Q1 *(Vpon);* and on Q2   6 came] Q1; ran Q2   7 Call? Nay,] *Hubbard;* Call, nay Q1; Nay Q2   8–21] *Arranged as in* Q2; *as prose* Q1   8 Liver] Q1 *(liuer);* louer Q2   9 in likeness] Q1 *(likenes);* in the likenesse Q2   10 one] Q1; on Q2   11 pronounce] Q1 *(Pronounce);* prouaunt Q2; pronounce Q4   11 'dove'] Q1 *(Doue);* day Q2; die Q4   13 heir] Q1 *(heire);* her Q2; heire Q4   14 trim] Q1; true Q2   15 wench] Q1; mayd Q2   16 hears me not] Q1 *(heares);* heareth not Q2   17 Rosalind's] Q1 *(Rosalindes);* Rosalines Q2   18 High] Q1 *(high);* By her high Q2   19 Her pretty] Q1 *(subst.);* By her fine Q2   20 demesnes] Q1 *(demaines);* demeanes Q2   22 If he do] Q1 *(doe);* And if he Q2

7–29 Call? . . . him This and the following speech by Mercutio are printed as prose in Q1 but as verse in Q2.

8 Liver! Hubbard and Levenson amend this to 'lover', following Q2; but 'liver' has its own logic here. The word was 'Formerly often mentioned fig[uratively] with allusion to its importance as a vital organ of the body . . . ; also with allusion to the ancient notion that it was the seat of love and of violent passion generally' (*OED*); see *Lucr.*, 'To quench the coal which in his liver glows' (line 47). Gibbons points out that W. W. Greg considered the Q1 reading 'plausible'.

11 'dove' Editors since Pope usually adopt Q1's 'dove' rather than Q2's 'day'.

14 trim Reading 'trim' where Q2 has 'true', Q1 accurately quotes the ballad of King Cophetua and the Beggar Maid alluded to in the following line and preserved in Richard Johnson's *Crown Garland of Golden Roses* (1612). Shakespeare also refers to the ballad on a number of other occasions, *LLL* 1.2.94–101, 4.1.60–79; *R2* 5.3.78; *2H4* 5.3.103. Most modern editors (including Gibbons, NCS, and Jowett, but not Oxford) follow Steevens in adopting Q1's 'trim'.

16 Following this sentence, Q1 lacks a short passage present in Q2: 'he stirreth not, he moueth not, / The Ape is dead, and I must conjure him.'

17 Rosalind's The name is spelt 'Rosaline' on all other occasions.

MERCUTIO   Tut, this cannot anger him. Marry, if one
　　　　Should raise a spirit in his mistress' circle
　　　　Of some strange fashion, making it there to stand   25
　　　　Till she had laid it and conjured it down:
　　　　That were some spite. My invocation
　　　　Is fair and honest, and in his mistress' name
　　　　I conjure only but to raise up him.
BENVOLIO   Well, he hath hid himself amongst those trees   30
　　　　To be consorted with the humorous night.
　　　　Blind is his love, and best befits the dark.
MERCUTIO   If love be blind, love will not hit the mark.
　　　　Now will he sit under a medlar tree
　　　　And wish his mistress were that kind of fruit   35
　　　　As maids call medlars when they laugh alone.
　　　　Ah Romeo, that she were, ah that she were
　　　　An open et cetera, thou a popp'rin' pear.
　　　　Romeo, good night. I'll to my trundle-bed.
　　　　This field-bed is too cold for me.   40
　　　　Come, let's away, for 'tis but vain
　　　　To seek him here that means not to be found.
　　　　　　　　　　[*Exeunt* BENVOLIO *and* MERCUTIO]
　　　　　　　　[*Romeo comes forward*]
ROMEO   He jests at scars that never felt a wound.

23–6] *Arranged as in* Q2; *as prose* Q1   23 Tut, this] Q1 *(*Tut this*)*; This Q2   23–4 Marry . . . Should] Q1 *(subst.)*;
twould anger him / To Q2   25 fashion, making] Q1; nature, letting Q2   25 to stand] Q1; stand Q2   27–8] *Arranged
as in Capell; as prose* Q1; . . . spight. / . . . name, Q2   28 and in] Q1; in Q2   29] *Arranged as in* Q2; *as prose*
Q1   30 Well] Q1; Come Q2   30 those] Q1; these Q2   31 with] Q1 *(*wlth*)*   32 is] Q2; in Q1   33 will not] Q1; cannot
Q2   37 Ah . . . ah] Q1 *(subst.)*; O . . . ô Q2   38 open et cetera] Q1 *(*open *Et cætera)*; open, or Q2; open & catera,
and Q4; open-arse or *Hosley;* open-arse and *Wilson–Duthie*   39 good] Q1 *(*God*)*   39 trundle-bed] Q1 *(*trundle bed*)*;
truckle bed Q2   40 for me] Q1 *(*mee*)*; for me to sleepe Q2   41 let's . . . vain] Q1 *(subst.)*; shall we go? / *Ben.* Go then,
for tis in vaine Q2   42 SD.1] Q4, F *(Exeunt.); Exit.* Q2; *not in* Q1   42 SD.2] *Spencer; not in* Q, F

38 open et cetera Instead of Q1's euphemism
(which was adopted by Malone and many editors
in the nineteenth century), modern editors basing
their text on Q2 usually adopt Hosley's emendation, 'open-arse', which is an old name for the
medlar, both fruit and tree (*OED*). Q2 actually
reads 'An open, or', perhaps a compositor's error
for 'open ars' or even 'openers' (as in Chaucer's
Reeve's Prologue, 17).
　　39 trundle-bed A low bed running on castors

usually beneath another bed when not in use. Q2's
'truckle bed' is a synonym.
　　41–2 for 'tis . . . found. Q2 attributes the final
words before their exit to Benvolio, not to Mercutio.
　　43 Editors since the eighteenth century usually start a new scene here (Jowett and Oxford
are recent exceptions), but Romeo has not left the
stage and the action is continuous. See Appendix
A, p. 157.

[*Enter* JULIET *above*]

But soft, what light forth yonder window breaks?
It is the east, and Juliet is the sun.   45
Arise, fair sun, and kill the envious moon
That is already sick and pale with grief
That thou, her maid, art far more fair than she.
Be not her maid, since she is envious;
Her vestal livery is but pale and green,   50
And none but fools do wear it. Cast it off.
She speaks, but she says nothing. What of that?
Her eye discourseth; I will answer it.
I am too bold, 'tis not to me she speaks;
Two of the fairest stars in all the skies,   55
Having some business, do entreat her eyes
To twinkle in their spheres till they return.
What if her eyes were there, they in her head?
The brightness of her cheeks would shame those stars
As daylight doth a lamp. Her eyes in heaven   60
Would through the airy region stream so bright
That birds would sing and think it were not night.
O, now she leans her cheek upon her hand.
I would I were the glove to that same hand,
That I might kiss that cheek.

---

43 SD] Capell; *not in* Q, F   44 forth] Q1; *through* Q2   47 That] Q1; *Who* Q2   50 pale] Q1; *sicke* Q2   52 but] Q1; *yet* Q2   55 skies] Q1; *heauen* Q2   56 do] Q1 *(doe)*; *to* Q2; *do* Q3   59 cheeks] Q1 *(cheekes)*; *cheek* Q2   60 eyes] Q1; *eye* Q2   63 O, now] Q1 *(Oh now)*; *See how* Q2   63 cheek] Q2 *(cheeke)*; *cheekes* Q1   64 I would] Q1; *O that* Q2   64 the] Q1; *a* Q2   64 to that same] Q1; *vpon that* Q2

44 window Here and in two stage directions in Scene 14, reference is made to a 'window'. Leslie Thomson ('Window scenes in Renaissance plays: a survey and some conclusions', *MaRDiE* 5 (1991), 225–43) has argued that in Renaissance plays, 'window' can usually be taken to refer 'to the all-purpose gallery openings' (229). Opposing the view of W. J. Lawrence who believed, in the early twentieth century, that there were real windows on the Elizabethan stage, Thomson suggests that 'the more description – verbal window dressing – we are given the less there was to see' (237). Thomson may be right, but it deserves pointing out that the evidence about gallery openings is by no means abundant or conclusive. Note that the two 'windows' in stage directions in Scene 14 occur on sheet G where space had to be wasted (see Introduction, pp. 39–41).

50 pale and green Q1 omits Q2's reference to green-sickness ('sicke and greene'). The disease was believed to affect girls of marriageable age.

51 Following this verse, Q1 omits a line present in Q2: 'It is my Lady, ô it is my loue, ô that she knew she wer.'

63 her cheek upon her hand The physiological difficulties involved in leaning both cheeks upon one hand as well as the recurrence of 'cheek' two lines further down argue against Q1's 'cheeks' and in favour of 'cheek' as in Q2.

JULIET   Ay me.

ROMEO [*Aside*]   She speaks.   65
          O speak again, bright angel, for thou art
          As glorious to this night, being over my head,
          As is a wingèd messenger of heaven
          Unto the white upturnèd wond'ring eyes
          Of mortals that fall back to gaze on him,   70
          When he bestrides the lazy-pacing clouds
          And sails upon the bosom of the air.

JULIET   Ah Romeo, Romeo, wherefore art thou Romeo?
          Deny thy father and refuse thy name,
          Or if thou wilt not, be but sworn my love,   75
          And I'll no longer be a Capulet.

ROMEO [*Aside*] Shall I hear more, or shall I speak to this?

JULIET   'Tis but thy name that is mine enemy.
          What's Montague? It is nor hand, nor foot,
          Nor arm, nor face, nor any other part.   80
          What's in a name? That which we call a rose
          By any other name would smell as sweet.
          So Romeo would, were he not Romeo called,
          Retain the divine perfection he owes
          Without that title. Romeo, part thy name,   85
          And for that name, which is no part of thee,
          Take all I have.

ROMEO   I take thee at thy word.
          Call me but love, and I'll be new baptised,
          Henceforth I never will be Romeo.

65–7 She . . . head] *Arranged as in* Q2; *Rom*: She speakes, . . . Angell: / For . . . head, Q1   65 kiss] Q1; touch Q2   65 SD] *Wilson–Duthie; not in* Q, F   71 lazy-pacing] Q1 *(lasie pacing)*; lazie puffing Q2; lazy-passing *Ulrici (conj. Collier)*   73 Ah] Q1; O Q2   77 SD] *Rowe; not in* Q, F   77 to] Q1; at Q2   80 nor . . . part] Q1; ô be some other name / Belonging to a man Q2   82 name] Q1; word Q2   83 were] Q1; wene Q2   84 the divine] Q1 *(diuine)*; that deare Q2   84 he] Q1; which he Q2   84–5 owes / Without] Q2 *(owes, / Without)*; owes: / Without Q1   85 title. Romeo] Q5 *(title: Romeo)*; title Romeo Q1; tytle, *Romeo* Q2; title *Romeo*, F1   85 part] Q1; doffe Q2   86 that] Q1; thy Q2   87 I have] Q1 *(haue)*; my selfe Q2

---

71 lazy-pacing This may be a variant form of 'lazy-passing', 'pace' being a sixteenth-century spelling of 'pass' (*OED*). Q2's 'puffing' seems likely to describe the movement of the clouds 'floating as puffs or perhaps swaggering across the sky' (Oxford).

78 Following this line, Q2 prints a line absent from Q1: 'Thou art thy selfe, though not a *Mountague.*'

80 The arrangement most editors have adopted since Malone – 'nor any other part / Belonging to a man. O be some other name!' – in fact conflates words present in Q1 or Q2, but not in both. Q1 makes better sense than Q2: 'Whats Mountague? it is nor hand nor foote, / Nor arme nor face, ô be some other name / Belonging to a man.' Shakespeare may have accidentally deleted the phrase 'nor any other part' when revising the passage. See also Goldberg.

JULIET What man art thou that thus bescreened in night   90
         Dost stumble on my counsel?
ROMEO By a name I know not how to tell thee.
         My name, dear saint, is hateful to myself,
         Because it is an enemy to thee.
         Had I it written, I would tear the word.   95
JULIET My ears have not yet drunk a hundred words
         Of that tongue's utterance, yet I know the sound.
         Art thou not Romeo, and a Montague?
ROMEO Neither, fair saint, if either thee displease.
JULIET How cam'st thou hither, tell me, and wherefore?   100
         The orchard walls are high and hard to climb,
         And the place death, considering who thou art,
         If any of my kinsmen find thee here.
ROMEO By love's light wings did I o'erperch these walls,
         For stony limits cannot hold love out,   105
         And what love can do, that dares love attempt.
         Therefore thy kinsmen are no let to me.
JULIET If they do find thee, they will murder thee.
ROMEO Alas, there lies more peril in thine eyes
         Than twenty of their swords. Look thou but sweet,   110
         And I am proof against their enmity.
JULIET I would not for the world they should find thee here.
ROMEO I have night's cloak to hide me from their sight,
         And but thou love me, let them find me here.
         For life were better ended by their hate,   115
         Than death proroguèd, wanting of thy love.
JULIET By whose directions found'st thou out this place?
ROMEO By love, who first did prompt me to enquire.
         Ay, he gave me counsel, and I lent him eyes.
         I am no pilot, yet wert thou as far   120

---

90 bescreened] Q3 *(bescreend)*; beskrind Q1; beschreend Q2   91 Dost stumble] Q1 *(Doest)*; So stumblest Q2   92 thee] Q1; thee who I am Q2   96 not yet] Q1; yet not Q2   97 that] Q1; thy Q2   97 utterance] Q1 *(vtterance)*; vttering Q2   99 saint] Q1 *(Saint)*; maide Q2   99 displease] Q1; dislike Q2   100 cam'st] Q1 *(camst)*; camest Q2; cam'st F   103 kinsmen] Q1; kismen Q2; kinsmen Q3   104 By] Q1; With Q2   107 let] Q1; stop Q2   108 find] Q1 *(finde)*; see Q2   112 should find] Q1 *(shuld)*; saw Q2   113 me] Q2; thee Q1   113 sight] Q1; eies Q2   115 For] Q1; My Q2   118 who] Q1; that Q2   119 Ay, he] Q1 *(I he)*; He Q2, *Levenson*

112 Q1 introduces an extra syllable, 'should', that does not easily conform to a metrical pattern.   to what would otherwise be a metrically regular line.
     119 **Ay, he** Q1 adds an eleventh syllable ('Ay')

As that vast shore washed with the furthest sea,
I would adventure for such merchandise.
JULIET Thou know'st the mask of night is on my face,
Else would a maiden blush bepaint my cheeks
For that which thou hast heard me speak tonight.   125
Fain would I dwell on form; fain, fain deny
What I have spoke. But farewell, compliments.
Dost thou love me? Nay, I know thou wilt say 'Ay',
And I will take thy word. But if thou swear'st,
Thou mayst prove false. At lovers' perjuries,   130
They say, Jove smiles. Ah gentle Romeo,
If thou love, pronounce it faithfully.
Or if thou think I am too easily won,
I'll frown and say thee nay and be perverse,
So thou wilt woo, but else not for the world.   135
In truth, fair Montague, I am too fond,
And therefore thou mayst think my haviour light.
But trust me, gentleman, I'll prove more true
Than they that have more cunning to be strange.
I should have been strange, I must confess,   140
But that thou overheard'st ere I was ware
My true love's passion. Therefore pardon me,
And not impute this yielding to light love,
Which the dark night hath so discoverèd.
ROMEO By yonder blessed moon I swear,   145
That tips with silver all these fruit-trees' tops –

---

121 washed] Q1 *(washt)*; washeth Q2; washet Q3   121 furthest] Q1; farthest Q2   122 would] Q1; should Q2   124
cheeks] Q1; cheeke Q2   127 compliments] Q1 *(complements)*; complement Q2   128 Nay, I] Q1 *(Nay I)*; I Q2   129
But] Q1 *(but)*; yet Q2   130–2] *Arranged as in* Q2; . . . false: / . . . smiles. / . . . faithfully: Q1   130 false . . . perjuries,]
Q1 *(false: / At Louers periuries)*; false at louers Periurires. Q2   131 smiles] Q1; laughes Q2   131 Ah] Q1; oh
Q2   132 love] Q1 *(loue)*; dost loue Q2   133 think] Q1 *(thinke)*; thinkest Q2   133 easily] Q1
(easely); quickly Q2   134 say . . . perverse] Q1 *(peruerse)*; be peruerse, and say thee nay
Q2   137 haviour] Q1 *(hauiour)*; behauior Q2; haviour F2   139 they] Q1; those Q2   139 more cunning] Q1; coying
Q2   140 been strange] Q1 *(bin)*; bene more strange Q2   142 true love's] Q1 *(true loues)*; truloue Q2; trueloue Q3;
true loue Q4; true Loues F1   145 By] Q1; Lady, by Q2   145 swear] Q1 *(sweare)*; vow Q2   146 fruit-trees'] Q1 *(fruit
trees)*; frute tree Q2

131 **smiles** In Ovid's *Ars Amatoria*, Jove laughs
('Iuppiter ex alto periuria ridet amantum', I, 633),
as in Q2.

139 **cunning** Some editors since Pope (including Capell and Malone) have adopted Q1's 'more
cunning', partly because the line in Q2 is metrically irregular. Yet Q2's 'coying' seems possible. See, for instance, Thomas Lodge, *Scillaes*

Metamorphosis (1589): 'But she unkind rewarded
me with mockes, / Such are the fruites that spring
from Ladies coying, / Who smile at teares, and are
intrapt with toying' (sig. B2v).

140 Q2 is metrically more regular, the absence
of Q2's 'more' in 'more strange' leaving the Q1 line
one syllable short.

JULIET O swear not by the moon, the unconstant moon,
That monthly changeth in her circled orb,
Lest that thy love prove likewise variable.

ROMEO Now by –

JULIET   Nay, do not swear at all,   150
Or if thou swear, swear by thy glorious self,
Which art the god of my idolatry,
And I'll believe thee.

ROMEO   If my true heart's love –

JULIET Swear not at all. Though I do joy in thee,
I have small joy in this contract tonight.   155
It is too rash, too sudden, too unadvised,
Too like the lightning that doth cease to be
Ere one can say 'It lightens.' [*Noise within*] I hear some
coming.
Dear love, adieu. Sweet Montague, be true.
Stay but a little, and I'll come again.   [*Exit*] 160

ROMEO O blessèd, blessèd night! I fear, being night,
All this is but a dream I hear and see,
Too flattering true to be substantial.

[*Enter* JULIET *above*]

JULIET Three words, good Romeo, and good night indeed.
If that thy bent of love be honourable,   165
Thy purpose marriage, send me word tomorrow
By one that I'll procure to come to thee,

---

147 the unconstant] Q1 *(vnconstant)*; th'inconstant Q2   148 circled] Q1; circle Q2; circled Q3   150 Nay, do] Q1 *(Nay doo)*; Do Q2   151 swear, swear] Q1 *(sweare, sweare)*; wilt, sweare Q2   151 glorious] Q1; gracious Q2   152 art] Q1; is Q2   153 true heart's love] Q1 *(subst.)*; hearts deare loue Q2   154 Swear . . . Though] Q1 *(subst.)*; Well do not sweare, although Q2   154 do joy] Q1 *(doo ioy)*; ioy Q2   155 small] Q1; no Q2   155 in] Q1; of Q2   156 too sudden, too unadvised] Q1 *(subst.)*; too vnaduisd, too sudden Q2   157 that] Q1; which Q2   158 coming] Q1 *(comming)*; noyse within Q2   158 SD] *This edn; not in* Q1, Q2; One calls within *Levenson*   160 and I'll] Q1 *(il'e)*; I will Q2   160 SD] *Rowe; not in* Q, F   161 I . . . night] Q1 *(subst.)*; I am afeard / Being in night Q2   163 true] Q1; sweete Q2   163 SD] *Rowe;* Enter. F2; *not in* Q, F1   164 good Romeo] Q1 *(Romeo)*; deare *Romeo* Q2

150 Now by – Whereas Q2's Romeo asks Juliet 'What shall I swear by?', Q1's starts another oath only to be interrupted by Juliet.
158 'It lightens.' Following these words, Q1 lacks sixteen lines present in Q2 which mark the beginning of the lovers' protracted farewell.
159 adieu Q1 here omits Q2's 'Anon good

nurse'. It is notable that Q1 lacks all dialogue between Juliet and the Nurse which punctuates the passage in Q2. As the identity of the person who threatens to break in upon Romeo and Juliet remains undisclosed, the sense of danger evoked earlier in the scene is thus arguably reactivated.

> Where and what time thou wilt perform that rite,
> And all my fortunes at thy foot I'll lay,
> And follow thee, my lord, throughout the world.   [*Exit*]   170

ROMEO Love goes toward love like schoolboys from their books,
    But love from love, to school with heavy looks.

                     [*Retiring slowly*]

              [*Enter* JULIET *above*]

JULIET Romeo, Romeo! O for a falc'ner's voice
    To lure this tassel-gentle back again.
    Bondage is hoarse and may not cry aloud,   175
    Else would I tear the cave where Echo lies,
    And make her airy voice as hoarse as mine
    With repetition of my Romeo's name.
    Romeo!
ROMEO It is my soul that calls upon my name.   180
    How silver-sweet sound lovers' tongues in night.
JULIET Romeo.
ROMEO Madam.
JULIET At what o'clock tomorrow shall I send?
ROMEO At the hour of nine.   185
JULIET I will not fail; 'tis twenty years till then.

---

168 that] Q1; the Q2   168 rite] F3; right Q1, Q2; rights Q4; rites Q5   170 lord] Q1 *(Lord)*; L. Q2; Loue Q4; Lord
F   170 SD] F; *not in* Q   171 like] Q1; as Q2   172 to] Q1; toward Q2   172 SD.1] *Malone (after Capell); not in* Q,
F   172 SD.2] *This edn; not in* Q1; *Enter* Iuliet *againe.* Q2   173 Romeo, Romeo!] Q1 *(subst.);* Hist *Romeo* hist Q2   175
cry] Q1 *(crie);* speake Q2   177 voice as] Q1; tongue more Q2   177–8 as mine / With] Q1 *(subst.);* then / With Q2;
then myne / With Q4   178 Romeo's name] Q1 *(Romeos); Romeo* Q2   181 in] Q1; by Q2   183] Q1 *(Madame);* My
Neece Q2; My Deere Q4; My sweete F2; My niëss *Wilson–Duthie*   184 At what] Q1; What Q2   184 send] Q1; send
to thee Q2   185 At] Q1; By Q2

170 Following this line, Q2 has a seven-line passage absent from Q1 in which the Nurse calls twice
from within before Juliet exits.

177–9 Another passage which editors usually
emend by reference to Q1. Q2 lacks 'mine' at the
end of 177, and the following line ends after 'my
Romeo'. It has been plausibly conjectured that a
damaged manuscript accounts for the Q2 omissions in these lines. As Jowett points out, owing to
Q2's agreed omission, Q1 in fact provides the only
authoritative text here.

180 The line suggests that Q1's 'Romeo!' in the
preceding line, absent from Q2, is again correct.

181 In Q1, Romeo's speech lacks the last line
present in Q2: 'Like softest musicke to attending
eares'.

183 Q1's 'Madam' is more formal than 'My
niëss' (Dover Wilson's convincing emendation
of Q2's 'My Neece'), which addresses Juliet
as a young hawk who has not yet left its
nest. Note that at 189 Q1's Romeo addresses
Juliet as 'you' where Q2's 'thou' is again less
formal.

186–8 Only in Q1 does Juliet call back Romeo
('Romeo!') before confessing that she does
not know why she has done so. Editors usually

[*Juliet and Romeo about to exit separately. Juliet returns.*]
Romeo!
[*Romeo returns*]
I have forgot why I did call thee back.

ROMEO Let me stay here till you remember it.

JULIET I shall forget, to have thee still stay here,   190
Rememb'ring how I love thy company.

ROMEO And I'll stay still to have thee still forget,
Forgetting any other home but this.

JULIET 'Tis almost morning, I would have thee gone,
But yet no further than a wanton's bird,   195
Who lets it hop a little from her hand,
Like a poor prisoner in his twisted gyves,
And with a silk thread pulls it back again,
Too loving-jealous of his liberty.

ROMEO Would I were thy bird.

JULIET   Sweet, so would I,   200
Yet I should kill thee with much cherishing thee.
Good night, good night. Parting is such sweet sorrow,
That I shall say good night till it be morrow.   [*Exit*]

ROMEO Sleep dwell upon thine eyes, peace on thy breast.
I would that I were sleep and peace, so sweet to rest.   205
Now will I to my ghostly father's cell,
His help to crave and my good hap to tell.   [*Exit*]

---

186 SD] *This edn; not in* Q, F   187 Romeo!] Q1 *(Romeo); not in* Q2   187 SD] *This edn; not in* Q, F   187–8] *Lineation this edn; as one line* Q1   189 stay] Q1; stand Q2   189 you] Q1; thou Q2   190 forget,] Q3; forget Q1, Q2   190 stay here] Q1 *(staie);* stand there Q2   192 stay still] Q1; still stay Q2   195 But] Q1; And Q2   195 further] Q1; farther Q2   196 Who] Q1; That Q2   196 her] Q1; his Q2   198 silk] Q1 *(silke);* silken Q2   198 pulls] Q1 *(puls);* plucks Q2   199 Too] Q1; So Q2   201 cherishing thee] Q1 *(subst.);* cherishing Q2   203 SD] *Pope; not in* Q, F   204 SH] Q1 *(Rom:); Iu.* Q2, F; *Ro.* Q4   204 on] Q1; in Q2   205 I would that] Q1; Would Q2   205 so] Q2; of Q1   206 Now] Q1; Hence Q2   206 father's cell] Q1 *(subst.);* Friers close cell Q2   207 good] Q1; deare Q2   207 SD] Q2; *not in* Q1

seem to assume that Juliet's words refer to the earlier occasion when she called him back (173–9), but Juliet then clearly did so to ask at what time she is to send for him the next day. A straightforward explanation is that the lovers, after Juliet's ''tis twenty years till then', start retiring separately, before Juliet calls Romeo back a second time.

205 Following this line, Q2's Romeo speaks two couplets, absent from Q1, which Friar Laurence repeats with minor alterations at the beginning of the following scene.

[6]   *Enter* FRIAR [LAURENCE *with a basket*]

FRIAR LAURENCE The grey-eyed morn smiles on the frowning night,
           Check'ring the eastern clouds with streaks of light,
           And fleckèd darkness like a drunkard reels
           From forth day's path and Titan's fiery wheels.
           Now ere the sun advance his burning eye,   5
           The world to cheer and night's dark dew to dry,
           We must upfill this osier cage of ours
           With baleful weeds and precious-juicèd flowers.
           O, mickle is the powerful grace that lies
           In herbs, plants, stones, and their true qualities.   10
           For naught so vile that vile on earth doth live,
           But to the earth some special good doth give;
           Nor naught so good but, strained from that fair use,
           Revolts to vice and stumbles on abuse.

0 SD] *This edn (following* Q2, *Enter Frier alone with a basket.); Enter Frier Francis.* Q1   1 SH] Q1 *(Frier:)*   2 Check'ring] Q1 *(Checkring); Checking* Q2 *(1st version); Checkring* Q2 *(2nd version);*   3 fleckèd darkness] Q1 *(subst.);* darknesse fleckted Q2 *(1st version);* fleckeld darknesse Q2 *(2nd version)*   4 path] Q1 *;* pathway Q2 *(1st version);* path Q2 *(2nd version)*   4 and Titan's fiery] Q1 *(subst.);* made by *Tytans* Q2 *(1st version);* and *Titans* burning Q2 *(2nd version)*   6 world] Q1 *;* day Q2   6 dark] Q1 *(darke);* dancke Q2   7 We] Q1 *;* I Q2   10 herbs, plants] Q1 *(hearbes);* Plants, hearbes Q2   11 vile on] Q1 *;* on the Q2   13 naught] Q1 *(nought);* ought Q2   14 to ... stumbles] Q1 *;* from true birth, stumbling Q2

Scene 6
Act 2, Scene 3 in the NCS edition.
Apart from two short omitted passages totalling eight lines, this scene corresponds closely to the equivalent portion of Q2.
0 SD Q1 here calls the Friar 'Francis', though he is referred to as 'Laurence', as in Q2, later on in the text. The basket is specified in Q2's SD, though not in Q1's. It is implied, however, by 'this osier cage of ours' (a basket made of willow twigs) in line 7.
1 SH SHs for Friar Laurence throughout the play are either '*Frier:*', '*Fri:*', or (most commonly) '*Fr:*', except in the penultimate scene – as he needs to be distinguished from Friar John – where SHs refer to him as '*Laur:*'.
1–4 Q2 contains two versions of this passage which are similar to each other, at the beginning of this and, attributed to Romeo, at the end of the preceding scene. The collation distinguishes between Q2's first and second versions.
6 night's dark dew The night's dew can be

said to be both 'dark' (Q1) because of the night and 'dank' ('dancke', Q2) because of the dew, so either reading seems possible.
7 Q2's 'I must vpfill this osier cage of ours' suggests that the Friar refers not to his own, personal, but to his order's, the Franciscans', basket. Q1's 'We', however, clearly refers exclusively to the Friar himself, suggesting that he is using the royal we, a form that seems appropriate enough considering his sententious style and his later reference to 'Our Romeo' (6.37).
8 Following this line, Q1 lacks three couplets present in Q2. They introduce in highly metaphorical language the idea of the earth as nature's mother and flowers as children born from the earth's womb.
14 Revolts to vice While the revolt in Q2 is 'from true birth', it is, more unusually, 'to vice', in Q1. The *OED* records instances of 'to revolt to', in the sense of going over to a rival power, between 1560 and 1692.

Virtue itself turns vice being misapplied,   15
And vice sometimes by action dignified.

[*Enter* ROMEO]

Within the infant rind of this small flower
Poison hath residence, and medicine power:
For this, being smelt to, with that part cheers each heart,
Being tasted slays all senses with the heart.   20
Two such opposèd foes encamp them still
In man as well as herbs: grace and rude will;
And where the worser is predominant,
Full soon the canker death eats up that plant.

ROMEO Good morrow to my ghostly confessor.   25
FRIAR LAURENCE *Benedicite.*

What early tongue so soon saluteth me?
Young son, it argues a distempered head
So soon to bid good morrow to thy bed.
Care keeps his watch in every old man's eye,   30
And where care lodgeth, sleep can never lie;
But where unbruisèd youth with unstuffed brains
Doth couch his limbs, there golden sleep remains.
Therefore thy earliness doth me assure
Thou art uproused by some distemperature.   35
Or if not so, then here I hit it right:
Our Romeo hath not been abed tonight.

---

16 sometimes] Q1; sometime Q2   16 SD] Q2; *not in* Q1   17 small] Q1; weake Q2   19 smelt to] Q1 *(too)*; smelt Q2;
smelt, too *Eichhoff*   19 heart] Q1 *(hart)*; part Q2   20 slays] Q1 *(slaies)*; staies Q2; slayes Q3   21 foes] Q1; Kings
Q2   25 to...confessor] Q1 *(subst.)*; father Q2   26–7] *Arranged as in* Q2; *as one line* Q1   26 *Benedicite*] Q1; Benedicitie
Q2   27 soon] Q1 *(soone)*; sweete Q2   29 thy] Q2; my Q1   31 can] Q1; will Q2   31 lodgeth] Q1; lodges Q2; lodgeth
F2   32 brains] Q1 *(braines)*; braine Q2   33 remains] Q1 *(remaines)*; doth raigne Q2   35 by] Q1; with Q2   36 right]
Q2; righ Q1   37 abed] Q1 *(a bed)*; in bed Q2

16 SD The moment of Romeo's entrance is not
specified in Q1 and could conceivably come earlier or, more likely, later. Pope and other editors
as well as many directors have delayed Romeo's
entrance until line 24. It has been rightly pointed
out, however, that Romeo's presence lends the
Friar's words an ironic dimension, and I follow
Q2 in inserting the stage direction at this point.

19 Q1's 'smelt to' (as opposed to Q2's 'smelt') is
the usual early-modern construction for the sense
of smell exercised in relation to a specific object.
It was not until the nineteenth century that 'at'
became the usual preposition (*OED*).

19–20 The couplet has an antithetical structure:
the flower's smell cheers the heart, but the flower's
taste slays the heart. Q2 prints 'part' instead of
'heart' in the first of the two lines.

20 slays Editors have often preferred 'slays' to
Q2's 'stays'.

25 ghostly confessor These words are not
part of the equivalent Q2 passage, but they appear
in the later text in Juliet's salutation of Friar Laurence in the wedding scene (2.6.21) and thus constitute another anticipation (see 4.191–2, 8.5–6,
8.10–11).

ROMEO The last was true, the sweeter rest was mine.
FRIAR LAURENCE God pardon sin! Wert thou with Rosaline?
ROMEO With Rosaline? My ghostly father, no.   40
   I have forgot that name and that name's woe.
FRIAR LAURENCE That's my good son. But where hast thou been
   then?
ROMEO I tell thee ere thou ask it me again:
   I have been feasting with mine enemy,
   Where on the sudden one hath wounded me   45
   That's by me wounded. Both our remedies
   Within thy help and holy physic lies.
   I bear no hatred blessèd man; for lo,
   My intercession likewise steads my foe.
FRIAR LAURENCE Be plain, my son, and homely in thy drift,   50
   Riddling confession finds but riddling shrift.
ROMEO Then plainly know my heart's dear love is set
   On the fair daughter of rich Capulet.
   As mine on hers, so hers likewise on mine,
   And all combined, save what thou must combine   55
   By holy marriage. Where and when and how
   We met, we wooed, and made exchange of vows
   I'll tell thee as I pass. But this I pray,
   That thou consent to marry us today.
FRIAR LAURENCE Holy Saint Francis, what a change is here!   60
   Is Rosaline, whom thou didst love so dear,
   So soon forsook? Lo, young men's love then lies
   Not truly in their hearts but in their eyes.
   Jesu Maria, what a deal of brine
   Hath washed thy sallow cheeks for Rosaline.   65
   How much salt water cast away in waste
   To season love, that of love doth not taste.
   The sun not yet thy sighs from heaven clears,
   Thy old groans ring yet in my ancient ears,

38 The] Q1; That Q2   38 was true] Q1; is true Q2   39 Wert] Q1 *(wert);* wast Q2   45 the] Q1; a Q2   50 my] Q1; good Q2   54 likewise] Q1; is set Q2   56 Where and when] Q1 *(subst.);* when and where Q2   57 vows] Q1 *(vowes);* vow Q2   58 I pass] Q1 *(passe);* we passe Q2   60 Saint] Q1 *(S.)*   61 whom] Q1 *(whome);* that Q2   62 forsook? Lo] Q1 *(forsooke, lo);* forsaken? Q2   66 cast] Q1; throwne Q2   67 of love] Q1 *(loue);* of it Q2   69 ring yet] Q1; yet ringing Q2; yet ring Q4   69 my] Q1; mine Q2; my Q3

 67 love, that of love Q2 reads 'it' where Q1 has the second 'love'. Jowett believes that 'Q1 might   preserve an authorial improvement.'

And lo, upon thy cheek the stain doth sit   70
Of an old tear that is not washed off yet.
If ever thou wert thus and these woes thine,
Thou and these woes were all for Rosaline.
And art thou changed? Pronounce this sentence then:
Women may fall when there's no strength in men.   75
ROMEO Thou chid'st me oft for loving Rosaline.
FRIAR LAURENCE For doting, not for loving, pupil mine.
ROMEO And bad'st me bury love.
FRIAR LAURENCE   Not in a grave,
To lay one in, another out to have.
ROMEO I pray thee, chide not. She whom I love now   80
Doth grace for grace and love for love allow.
The other did not so.
FRIAR LAURENCE   O, she knew well
Thy love did read by rote and could not spell.
But come, young waverer, come, go with me,
In one respect I'll thy assistant be.   85
For this alliance may so happy prove,
To turn your households' rancour to pure love.

                                                        Exeunt

[7]   *Enter* MERCUTIO, BENVOLIO

MERCUTIO Why, what's become of Romeo? Came he not home
          tonight?
BENVOLIO Not to his father's; I spake with his man.
MERCUTIO Ah, that same pale hard-hearted wench, that Rosaline,
          Torments him so that he will sure run mad.

---

70 And lo] Q1 *(loe)*; Lo here Q2   72 ever] Q1 *(euer)*; ere Q2   72 wert thus] Q1; wast thy selfe Q2   80 pray] Q1 *(pree)*   80 not. She whom] Q1 *(not, she whom)*; me not, her Q2   83 and] Q1; that Q2   1 Why . . . Romeo?] Q1 *(subst.)*; Where the deule should this *Romeo* be? Q2   2 spake] Q1; spoke Q2   3 Ah] Q1; Why Q2

87 Following the end of the scene in Q1, Q2 adds another two lines of dialogue: '*Ro*[*meo*]. O let vs hence, I stand on sudden hast. / *Fri*[*ar*]. Wisely and slow, they stumble that run fast.'

Scene 7
Act 2, Scene 4 in the NCS edition.
For much of the scene, Q1 corresponds quite closely to the corresponding passage in Q2, though with an important number of local substitutions and short omissions or additions. Towards the end of the scene, Q1 first shows a different arrangement of a short passage in Q2 before omitting some twenty lines present in the longer text.

[BENVOLIO] Tybalt, the kinsman of old Capulet,   5
        Hath sent a letter to his father's house.
[MERCUTIO] Some challenge, on my life.
BENVOLIO Romeo will answer it.
MERCUTIO Ay, any man that can write may answer a letter.
BENVOLIO Nay, he will answer the letter's master, if he be
        challenged.   10
MERCUTIO Who, Romeo? Why, he is already dead, stabbed with
        a white wench's black eye, shot through the ear with a love
        song, the very pin of his heart cleft with the blind bow-boy's
        butt-shaft. And is he a man to encounter Tybalt?
BENVOLIO Why, what is Tybalt?   15
MERCUTIO More than the prince of cats, I can tell you. O, he is
        the courageous captain of compliments. Catso, he fights as you
        sing prick-song, keeps time, distance, and proportion, rests me
        his minim rest, one, two, and the third in your bosom; the very
        butcher of a silken button, a duellist, a duellist, a gentleman   20
        of the very first house of the first and second cause. Ah, the
        immortal *passado*, the *punto reverso*, the *hay*!
BENVOLIO The what?
MERCUTIO The pox of such limping, antic, affecting fantasticoes,
        these new tuners of accents. By Jesu, a very good blade, a very tall   25
        man, a very good whore. Why, grandsire, is not this a miserable

5 SH] Q2; *Mer:* Q1   5 of] Q1; to Q2   5 Capulet] Q2; *Capolet* Q1   7 SH] Q2 *(Mer.); not in* Q1   7 Some] Q1; A
Q2   9 Ay, any] Q1 *(I, anie)*; Any Q2   10 if . . . challenged] Q1 *(subst.);* how he dares, being dared Q2   11 Who . . .
Why] Q1 *(subst.);* Alas poore *Romeo* Q2   12 shot] Q1; runne Q2   16 the prince] Q1; Prince Q2   16 cats . . . you] Q1
(cattes); Cats Q2   16 he is] Q1; hees Q2   17 Catso, he] Q1; he Q2   18–19 rests . . . rest] Q1 *(subst.);* he rests, his
minum rests Q2; he rests his minum rests Q3   20 silken] Q1; silke Q2   24 limping, antic] Q1 *(subst.);* antique lisping
Q2   24 fantasticoes] Q1; phantacies Q2; phantasies Q5   26–7 Why . . . case] Q1 *(subst.);* Why is not this a lamtable
thing graundsir Q2

5–7 Q1 mistakenly attributes all three lines to
Mercutio, not only the last one, as Q2 does. As
Q1's SH, '*Mer:*', follows after two lines which are
attributed to the same character, Q1 cannot be correct.

17 Catso from Italian, 'cazzo', penis, also used
to designate 'rogue' in the seventeenth century
(*OED*). Absent from Q2, the word, which puns on
both 'cats' and 'prick-song', seems entirely appropriate in the given context.

18 rests me The so-called ethical dative pronoun (used to imply that a person other than the
subject or object has an indirect interest in the fact
stated) is found often in Shakespeare, but is not in
Q2.

24 limping Whereas Q2's 'lisping' designates
a speech affectation, Q1's 'limping' refers to
impaired movement, perhaps in the more general
sense of 'halting' (*OED ppl. a.* b).

24 fantasticoes 'An absurd and irrational person' (*OED*). Many editors since Capell have
adopted the word in Q1, while others, following
John Crow ('Editing and Emending', *Essays &
Studies*, 10 (1955), 1–20) have amended 'phantacies' to 'phantasimes' on the grounds that a
dropped tilde on the 'i' would suffice to explain
the misreading (NCS, Gibbons). For Q1's 'fantasticoes', see Nashe's 'new-fangled *Galiardos* and
Senior *Fantasticoes*' (*Saffron-Walden, Works*, III,
31).

case, that we should be still afflicted with these strange flies, these fashion-mongers, these pardon-me's, that stand so much on the new form that they cannot sit at ease on the old bench? O their bones, their bones!   30

[*Enter* ROMEO]

BENVOLIO Here comes Romeo.

MERCUTIO Without his roe, like a dried herring. O flesh, flesh, how art thou fishified. Sirrah, now is he for the numbers that Petrarch flowed in. Laura to his lady was but a kitchen drudge – yet she had a better love to berhyme her – Dido a dowdy,   35 Cleopatra a gypsy, Hero and Helen hildings and harlotries, Thisbe a grey eye or so, but not to the purpose. Signor Romeo, *bonjour*. There is a French curtsy to your French slop. Ye gave us the counterfeit fairly yesternight.

ROMEO What counterfeit, I pray you?   40

MERCUTIO The slip, the slip, can you not conceive?

ROMEO I cry you mercy. My business was great, and in such a case as mine a man may strain courtesy.

MERCUTIO O, that's as much to say as such a case as yours will constrain a man to bow in the hams.   45

ROMEO A most courteous exposition.

MERCUTIO Why, I am the very pink of courtesy.

ROMEO Pink for flower.

MERCUTIO Right.

ROMEO Then is my pump well flowered.   50

---

27 still] Q1 *(stil); thus* Q2   28 pardon-me's] Q1 *(pardonmees);* pardons mees Q2   28 that stand] Q1; who stand Q2   30 SD] Q2; *not in* Q1   31 Romeo] Q1 *(Romeo); Romeo, here comes Romeo* Q2   33 Sirrah, now] Q1 *(Sirra now);* now Q2   34 flowed in] Q2; flowdin Q1   34 was but] Q1; was Q2   34 drudge] Q1 *(drudg);* wench Q2   35 yet] Q1; marrie Q2   36 Hero and Helen] Q1 *(subst.); Hellen and Hero* Q2   36 harlotries] Q1 *(harletries);* harlots Q2   38 bonjour] Q1 *(bon iour); Bonieur* Q2   38 curtsy] Q1 *(curtesie);* salutation Q2; courtesy *Hubbard*   38 slop] Q2; flop Q1   38 Ye] Q1 *(yee);* you Q2   39 yesternight] Q1; last night Q2   40 I pray] Q1; did I giue Q2   41 slip, the] Q1 *(slip the);* slip sir, the Q2   42 I . . . mercy] Q1; Pardon good *Mercutio* Q2   44 O, that's] Q1 *(Oh thats);* Thats Q2   44 much to] Q1; much as to Q2   44–5 will constrain] Q1 *(subst.);* constrains Q2   47 Why] Q1; Nay Q2   48 flower.] Q2; flower? Q1   50 Then] Q1; Why then Q2

---

36 harlotries The term is here synonymous with 'harlots' (*OED n.* 4), the word used in Q2. See also 'A peevish self-willed harlotry' (*1H4* 3.1.194).

38 curtsy Q1's 'curtesie' has been variously modernised to 'courtesy' (Hubbard) and 'curtsy' (Levenson). The ensuing passage (lines 39–43) plays on the ambiguity, an ambiguity modernisation has to resolve. In the context of 'French slop', i.e. loose, short breeches, the physical movement of a curtsy here seems appropriate. On the diffi-

culty of modernising 'curtesie', see note at 4.54.

40 Q1 omits Romeo's salutation as present in Q2, 'Goodmorrow to you both'.

44 that's as much to say as Modern usage requires 'as much to say as', as in Q2, but Q1's wording also occurs in *TN* (1.5.52).

45 Following this line, Q2 has a short exchange absent from Q1 which explicates the wordplay: 'Ro[*meo*]. Meaning to cursie. / Mer[*cutio*]. Thou hast most kindly hit it.' See Introduction, p. 10.

MERCUTIO Well said. Follow me now that jest till thou hast worn
out thy pump, that when the single sole of it is worn, the jest
may remain, after the wearing, solely singular.

ROMEO O single-soled jest, solely singular for the singleness.

MERCUTIO Come between us, good Benvolio, for my wits fail.   55

ROMEO Swits and spurs, swits and spurs, or I'll cry 'a match'.

MERCUTIO Nay, if thy wits run the wild-goose chase, I have done,
for I am sure thou hast more of the goose in one of thy wits than
I have in all my five. Was I with you there for the goose?

ROMEO Thou wert never with me for anything when thou wert not   60
with me for the goose.

MERCUTIO I'll bite thee by the ear for that jest.

ROMEO Nay, good goose, bite not.

MERCUTIO Why, thy wit is a bitter sweeting, a most sharp sauce.

ROMEO And was it not well served into a sweet goose?   65

MERCUTIO O, here is a wit of cheverel that stretcheth from an inch
narrow to an ell broad.

ROMEO I stretched it out for the word 'broad', which, added to the
goose, proves thee fair and wide a broad goose.

MERCUTIO Why, is not this better now than groaning for love? Why,   70
now art thou sociable, now art thou thyself, now art thou what
thou art, as well by art as nature. This drivelling love is like a
great natural that runs up and down to hide his bauble in a hole.

BENVOLIO Stop there.

MERCUTIO Why, thou wouldst have me stop my tale against the   75
hair.

BENVOLIO Thou wouldst have made thy tale too long.

---

51 Well said] Q1; Sure wit Q2   51 now that jest] Q1 *(subst.);* this ieast, now Q2   53, 54 solely singular] *Theobald (subst.);*
solie singuler Q1; soly singular Q2; sole-singular F   55 wits fail] Q1 *(faile);* wits faints Q2; wits faint Q5; wit faints
F2   57 thy] Q1; our Q2   57 have] Q1 *(haue);* am Q2   58 I . . . thou] Q1; thou Q2   58 goose] Q1; wildgoose Q2   59
all my] Q1 *(al);* my whole Q2   60 wert . . . wert] Q1 *(subst.);* wast . . . wast Q2   60 with me] Q1; there Q2   62 I'll]
Q1 *(Ile);* I will Q2   64 Why, thy] Q1 *(Why thy);* Thy Q2   64 a most] Q1; it is a most Q2   65 was] Q1; is Q2   65
well] Q1; then well Q2; well Q3   65 into] F1; in to Q   66 stretcheth] Q1; stretches Q2   68 stretched] Q1 *(stretcht);*
stretch Q2   68 the word] Q1; that word Q2   69 fair] Q1 *(faire);* farre Q2   70–1 Why, now] Q1 *(why now);* now
Q2   71 thyself] Q1 *(thy selfe);* *Romeo* Q2   72 as . . . as] Q1 *(subst.);* by art as well as by Q2   72 This] Q1; for
this Q2   73 runs up] Q1 *(vp);* runs lolling vp Q2   73 bauble] F4; bable Q1, Q2   74 Stop there] Q1; Stop there, stop
there Q2   75 Why . . . stop] Q1 *(subst.);* Thou desirest me to stop in Q2   77 wouldst] Q1; wouldst else Q2   77 too
long] Q1; large Q2

---

55 wits fail Q1's 'fail' and Q2's 'faints' (Q5:
'faint') are roughly synonymous as 'faint' still had
the more general meaning of growing weak and
feeble (*OED v.* 2).

MERCUTIO Tut, man, thou art deceived. I meant to make it short, for I was come to the whole depth of my tale and meant indeed to occupy the argument no longer.   80

ROMEO Here's goodly gear.

Enter NURSE *and her man* [PETER]

MERCUTIO A sail, a sail, a sail!

BENVOLIO Two, two, a shirt and a smock.

NURSE Peter, prithee, give me my fan.

MERCUTIO Prithee do, good Peter, to hide her face, for her fan is   85
the fairer of the two.

NURSE God ye good morrow, gentlemen.

MERCUTIO God ye good e'en, fair gentlewoman.

NURSE Is it 'God ye good e'en', I pray you?

MERCUTIO 'Tis no less, I assure you, for the bawdy hand of the dial   90
is even now upon the prick of noon.

NURSE Fie, what a man is this?

ROMEO A gentleman, Nurse, that God hath made for himself to
mar.

NURSE By my troth, well said. 'For himself to mar', quoth he? I pray   95
you, can any of you tell where one may find young Romeo?

ROMEO I can; but young Romeo will be elder when you have found
him than he was when you sought him. I am the youngest of
that name, for fault of a worse.

NURSE Well said.   100

---

78 Tut, man] Q1 *(Tut man)*; O Q2   78 meant to make] Q1; would haue made Q2   81 PETER] *Gibbons; not in* Q, F   82 A sail, a sail, a sail] Q1 *(subst.)*; A sayle, a sayle Q2   83 SH] Q1 *(Ben:)*; *Mer.* Q2   84 prithee, ... fan] Q1 *(subst.); Peter.* Anon. / *Nur.* My fan *Peter* Q2   85 Prithee, do, good] Q1 *(subst.)*; Good Q2   85 fan is] Q1 *(fanne)*; fans Q2   86 of the two] Q1; face Q2   88 God ye good e'en] Q1 *(God ye good den)*   89 'God ... you] Q1 *(godyegooden)*; good den Q2   90 assure you] Q1; tell yee Q2   91 even now] Q1 *(euen)*; now Q2   92 Fie] Q1; Out vpon you Q2   92 is this] Q1; are you Q2   93 A ... Nurse] Q1 *(subst.)*; One gentlewoman Q2   93 for himself] Q1 *(himselfe)*; himself Q2   95 well] Q1; it is well Q2   95 quoth he] Q1; quoth a Q2   95–6 I pray you] Q1; Gētlemē Q2   96 tell] Q1; tel me Q2   96 one] Q1; I Q2   96 young] Q1 *(yong)*; the yong Q2   97 can] Q1; can tell you Q2   97 elder] Q1; older Q2   100 Well said] Q1; You say well Q2

82–3 Q2 assigns the first line to Romeo and the second to Mercutio. Capell, Malone, and most nineteenth-century editors followed Q1's speech headings, while more recent editors have mostly reverted to Q2's assignments (NCS, Gibbons, Oxford), partly because 83 seems more appropriate for Mercutio than for Benvolio. Jowett follows Q2 in attributing 83 to Mercutio but attributes 82 to Benvolio, arguing that 'the reporter of Q1 could easily have switched speech assignations, but pre-

sumably only if, as is attractive from a dramatic point of view, a new speaker spoke "A sayle, a sayle".'

84 Q2 inserts Peter's reply, 'Anon'.

93–4 Various editors from Collier to Jowett add Q1's 'for', absent from Q2. As Jowett points out, the line in Q2 is so crammed that a compositor may well have left out the word on purpose. Q1 and Q2 have 'For himself to mar' in the following speech, which further supports the reading in Q1.

MERCUTIO Yea, is the worst well? Mass, well noted, wisely, wisely.

NURSE [*To Romeo*] If you be he, sir, I desire some conference with
ye.

BENVOLIO O, belike she means to invite him to supper.

MERCUTIO So ho, a bawd, a bawd, a bawd!   105

ROMEO Why, what hast found, man?

MERCUTIO No hare, sir, unless it be a hare in a Lenten pie, that is
somewhat stale and hoar ere it be eaten.

He walks by them and sings
And an old hare hoar,
And an old hare hoar,   110
Is very good meat in Lent.
But a hare that's hoar
Is too much for a score,
If it hoar ere it be spent.
You'll come to your father's to supper?   115

ROMEO I will.

MERCUTIO Farewell, ancient lady, farewell, sweet lady.

Exeunt Benvolio, Mercutio

NURSE Marry, farewell. Pray, what saucy merchant was this that was
so full of his rope-ripe?

---

101 Mass, well noted] Q1 *(subst.)*; very wel took, ifaith Q2   102 conference] Q1; confidence Q2   102 SD] *Jowett*;
not in Q, F   103 ye] Q1; you Q2   104 O, . . . invite] Q1 *(subst.)*; She will endite Q2   104 supper] Q1; some supper
Q2   105 So . . . bawd!] Q1 *(subst.)*; A baud, a baud, a baud. So ho. Q2   106 Why, what] Q1 *(Why what)*; What
Q2   106 found, man] Q1 *(found man)*; found Q2   107 unless it be] Q1 *(vnlesse)*; vnlesse Q2   107 hare] Q1; hare
sir Q2   108 somewhat] Q1; something Q2   108 eaten] Q1; spent Q2   108 SD] Q1; *not in* Q2   109–14 *Arranged as
in Capell*; And . . . hore / . . . Lent: / . . . score, / . . . spent. Q1; An . . . lent. / . . . spent. Q2   109 And an] Q1;
An Q2   114 If it hoar] Q1 *(if it hore)*; when it hores Q2   115 You'll] Q1 *(Youl)*; Romeo, will you Q2   115 father's
to supper?] Q1 *(fathers)*; fathers? weele to dinner thither. Q2   116 will] Q1; will follow you Q2   117 sweet lady] Q1
(subst.); Lady, Lady, Lady Q2   117 SD] Q1 *(subst.)*; Exeunt. Q2; Exit. Mercutio, Benuolio. F   118 Marry . . . Pray,] Q1
(subst.); I pray you sir, Q2   119 rope-ripe] Q1 *(roperipe)*; roperie Q2; roguery F4

102–3 In place of Q1's 'conference', Q2 has
the malapropism 'confidence' (cf. Dogberry in
Ado, 'I would have some confidence with you',
3.5.2–3). Did the players, for some reason, get rid
of the malapropisms in the playhouse? Or were
they omitted when copy of Q1 was composed? Or
did the compositors 'correct' the words when setting the type in the printing house? It is possible to
speculate but impossible to determine what occasioned Q1's elimination of the malapropism in this
and the following lines.

104 invite Q1 has again the grammatically correct word where Q2 has a malapropism, Benvolio
countering the Nurse's 'confidence' with 'endite'
for 'invite'.

119 rope-ripe Q2 has 'roperie', though the two

words, as Richard Levin ('Grumio's "rope-tricks"
and the Nurse's "ropery"', *SQ* 22 (1971), 82–86)
has pointed out, may have been interchangeable,
meaning 'lewd jesting' in the given context.
See also Robert Wilson's *The Three Ladies of
London* (1584): 'Thou art very pleasant & ful
of thy roperipe (I would say Retorick)' (B1r).
Q2's 'roperie' also functions as a malapropism for
'roguery' (to which the word was emended in F4).
In addition, 'rope' was a slang word for 'penis'
(unrecorded in Partridge's *Shakespeare's Bawdy*,
but see Anne Lancashire, 'Lyly and Shakespeare
on the ropes', *JEGP* 58 (1969), 237–44), a meaning whose presence is here corroborated by the
pun on 'stand to'.

ROMEO A gentleman, Nurse, that loves to hear himself talk and will   120
speak more in an hour than he will stand to in a month.

NURSE If he stand to anything against me, I'll take him down, if he
were lustier than he is. If I cannot take him down, I'll find them
that shall. I am none of his flirt-gills, I am none of his skains
mates.   125

She turns to Peter, her man

And thou like a knave must stand by and see every jack use me
at his pleasure.

PETER I see nobody use you at his pleasure. If I had, I would soon
have drawn. You know my tool is as soon out as another's, if I
see time and place.   130

NURSE Now, afore God, he hath so vexed me that every member
about me quivers. Scurvy jack! But, as I said, my lady bade
me seek ye out, and what she bade me tell ye, that I'll keep
to myself. But if you should lead her into a fool's paradise, as
they say, it were a very gross kind of behaviour, as they say,   135
for the gentlewoman is young. Now, if you should deal doubly
with her, it were very weak dealing, and not to be offered to any
gentlewoman.

ROMEO Nurse, commend me to thy lady; tell her, I protest –

NURSE Good heart, i'faith, I'll tell her so. O, she will be a joyful   140
woman.

ROMEO Why, what wilt thou tell her?

NURSE That you do protest, which, as I take it, is a gentlemanlike
proffer.

121 hour] Q1 *(houre); minute* Q2   122 If . . . to] Q1 *(subst.);* And a speake Q2   122 if he] Q1; and a Q2   123 is.
If] Q1 *(is: if);* is, and twentie such Iacks: and if Q2   123 cannot . . . down] Q1 *(downe);* cannot Q2   123 them] Q1;
those Q2   125 SD] Q1 *(subst.); not in* Q2   126 thou . . . must] Q1 *(subst.);* thou must Q2   126 by . . . jack] Q1 *(subst.);*
by too and suffer euery knaue to Q2   126 see . . . use] Q1 *(subst.);* saw no man Q2   128–30 I would . . . place.] Q1
(subst.); my weapon shuld quickly haue bin out: I warrant you, I dare draw assoone as an other man, if I see occasion
in a goodquarel, & the law on my side. Q2   131 he . . . me] Q1 *(subst.);* I am so vext Q2   131 member] Q1; part
Q2   132 jack] Q1 *(Iacke);* knaue Q2   132 But, . . . said] Q1 *(subst.);* pray you sir a word: and as I told you Q2   132
lady] Q1 *(Ladie);* young Lady Q2   132 bade] Q1 *(bad);* bid Q2   133 seek ye] Q1 *(seeke);* enquire you Q2   133 and]
Q1; *not in* Q2   133 bade] Q1 *(bad);* bid Q2   133 tell ye] Q1 *(yee);* say Q2   134 But] Q1 *(but);* but first let me tell ye
Q2   134 you] Q1; ye Q2   134 into] Q1; in Q2   136 Now] Q1; and therefore Q2   136 doubly] Q1; double Q2   137 it]
Q1; truly it Q2   137 very . . . not] Q1 *(subst.);* an ill thing Q2   138 gentlewoman] Q1 *(Gentlewoman);* Gentlewoman,
and very weake dealing Q2   139 lady . . . protest –] Q1 *(subst.);* Lady and Mistresse, I protest vnto thee. Q2   140
i'faith I'll] Q1 *(subst.);* and yfaith I wil Q2   140 so] Q1; as much Q2   140 O] Q1 *(oh);* Lord, Lord Q2   142 Why]
Q1; not in Q2   142 her] Q1; her Nurse Q2   143 That] Q1; I will tell her sir, that Q2   144 proffer] Q1; offer Q2

128–30 Peter's speech differs significantly in
wording and length from that in Q2.

142 **tell her?** Q2 here adds another expression
of Romeo's impatience: 'thou dooest not marke
me?'

144 **proffer** Q2 has the synonymous 'offer'.
Shakespeare uses 'proffer' as a verb elsewhere (e.g.

Cym. 3.5.49) and 'proffered' as an adjective (e.g.
R3 3.7.192), but the only instances of the noun
'proffer' in the Shakespearean canon occur in what
are probably un-Shakespearean portions of *1H6*
(5.1.41, 5.6.137), *Per.* (7.65 (= 2.3.65)), and *PP*
(4.10).

ROMEO Bid her get leave tomorrow morning   145
     To come to shrift to Friar Laurence' cell,
     And stay thou, Nurse, behind the abbey wall.
     My man shall come to thee and bring along
     The cords, made like a tackled stair,
     Which to the high topgallant of my joy   150
     Must be my conduct in the secret night.
     [*Offering money*] Hold, take that for thy pains.
NURSE No, not a penny, truly.
ROMEO I say you shall not choose.
NURSE [*Taking the money*] Well, tomorrow morning, she shall not
     fail.   155
ROMEO Farewell. Be trusty, and I'll quit thy pain.   *Exit*
NURSE Peter, take my fan and go before.

                                     Ex[eunt] omnes

[8]   *Enter* JULIET

JULIET The clock struck nine when I did send my Nurse,
     In half an hour she promised to return.

---

145 get . . . morning] Q1 *(subst.)*; deuise some means Q2   145–6] Q1 *(subst.)*; Bid her deuise some means to come to shrift this afternoon, / And there she shall at Frier *Lawrence* Cell / Be shrieued and married: Q2   146 shrift to] Q1; shrift this afternoon, / And there she shall at Q2   147 thou] Q1; good Q2; thou good F1   148–9 My . . . cords] Q1 *(subst.)*; Within this houre my man shall be with thee, / And bring thee cordes Q2   151 conduct] Q1; conuoy Q2   152 SD] *Jowett, not in* Q, F   152 Hold, take] Q1; here is Q2   153 not . . . truly] Q1 *(subst.)*; truly sir not a penny Q2   154 I] Q1; Go too, I Q2   154 not choose] Q1 *(chuse)*; not in Q2   155 SD] *Jowett, not in* Q, F   155 Well . . . morning] Q1 *(subst.)*; This afternoone sir, well Q2   155 not fail] Q1 *(faile)*; be there Q2   156 quit] Q2; quite Q1   156 pain] Q1 *(paine)*; paines Q2   157] Q1 *(subst.)*; Nur. . . . Peter. / Pet. Anon. / Nur. Before and apace. Q2   157 SD] Q1 *(Ex. omnes.)*   1 struck] *Rowe*; stroke Q1; strooke Q2   1 my] Q1; the Q2

---

145 tomorrow morning In Q2, the appointed time is 'this afternoon'. For inconsistencies in Q1 concerning the time of Romeo and Juliet's marriage, see Introduction, pp. 34–5.

145–6 Intriguingly, Q1's Romeo, contrary to Q2's, does not explicitly say that Juliet, at Friar Laurence's cell, is to be not only shriven but also married. In Q2, Romeo insists on shriving twice: Juliet is 'to come to shrift' and to 'Be shrieued and married'. Perhaps the second mention of shriving was omitted to avoid the repetition, thereby accidentally omitting the reference to marriage. The context, in particular the Nurse's acquiescence to the scheme and her words to Juliet in the following scene ('There stays a bridegroom to make you a bride', line 35), clearly indicates that marriage is the purpose of Romeo's plan.

147–55 These lines appear in a different order in Q1 and Q2. In Q2, lines closely corresponding to 152–5 appear before the equivalent of Q1's 147–51.

148–9 The one major difference from the equivalent speech in Q2 seems again a matter of the different time at which the marriage is planned in the two texts. In Q2, where the marriage is to take place the same day, Romeo's man is to bring her the cords 'Within this houre' (see Introduction, pp. 34–5).

155 tomorrow morning Q2, by contrast, again reads 'This afternoon' (see Introduction, pp. 34–5).

156 Following these words, Q1 omits a passage of some twenty lines present in Q2 in which the talkative Nurse prolongs her conversation with Romeo. The omission in no way affects the plot and seems likely to reflect a theatrical cut.

Scene 8

Act 2, Scene 5 in the NCS edition. This is the first scene with significantly less correspondence between Q1 and Q2. Throughout the

Perhaps she cannot find him. That's not so;
O, she is lazy. Love's heralds should be thoughts
And run more swift than hasty powder fired   5
Doth hurry from the fearful cannon's mouth.

Enter NURSE

O now she comes. Tell me, gentle Nurse,
What says my love?
NURSE O I am weary, let me rest a while.
Lord, how my bones ache. O where's my man?   10
Give me some aqua-vitae.
JULIET I would thou hadst my bones and I thy news.
NURSE Fie, what a jaunt have I had! And my back a' t'other side!
Lord, Lord, what a case am I in.

---

3 find] Q1 *(finde);* meete Q2   4 lazy] Q1 *(lazie);* lame Q2   7 now] Q1; God Q2   7 gentle] Q1; hony Q2   8 says my love] Q1 *(subst.);* newes Q2   9–11] *Arranged as in Hubbard; as prose* Q1   9 weary] Q1 *(wearie);* a wearie Q2   9 let me rest] Q1 *(mee);* giue me leaue Q2   13 jaunt] Q1 *(iaunt);* iaunce Q2; iaunt Q4, F1   13 have I had] Q1 *(haue);* haue I Q2; haue I had Q3; had I *Daniel (conj.)*

scene, there are lines and passages where the relationship is very close (1–4, 9, 12, 29, 33, 35–6) or at least close (20–7), but much of the scene is essentially made of different linguistic material (some of it transposed from elsewhere in the play), even though the basic dramatic structure is the same. Another significant difference is length: the scene in Q1 has a mere 44 lines as opposed to 77 in Q2; Juliet's part in particular is reduced by more than one half.

5–6 These lines do not resemble the equivalent passage in Q2 ('Which ten times faster glides then the Suns beames, / Driuing backe shadowes ouer lowring hills'), but they anticipate a later passage in a speech by Romeo: 'And that the trunk may be discharged of breath / As violently as hasty powder fired / Doth hurry from the fatal cannon's womb' (5.1.63–5). The Q1 equivalent to the Q2 passage 5.1.63–5 corresponds in fact less closely to the lines in the present scene: 'As suddenly as powder being fired / From forth a cannon's mouth' (18.45–6). The anticipation has been taken as evidence for memorial reconstruction. Q2's comparison of 'loues heraulds' to sunbeams may at first seem more appropriate than Q1's to cannon fire, but the latter may not be inadequate in a play in which violent delights have violent ends.

6 Following this line, Q1 omits ten lines present in Juliet's Q2 soliloquy in which she further expresses her impatience.

8 Among the omitted material following this line is what may be a specifically literary passage insofar as it insists on the Nurse's facial expression, something a reader needs to be told but a spectator would be able to see: 'Now good sweete Nurse, O Lord, why lookest sad? / Though newes be sad, yet tell them merily. / If good, thou shamest the musicke of sweete newes, / By playing it to me, with so sower a face.' Q1 omits or modifies a number of similar passages (e.g. 10.55, 11.45, 14.120 SD, 16.14, 20.75) by eliminating references to what a reader needs to be told but a spectator would be able to see. It therefore seems possible that the omission was deliberate and part of the script's preparation for performance. On the other hand, passages which tell spectators what they can see may not be devoid of a specifically theatrical logic: they can enhance the emotional significance of what is seen or serve as implicit SDs for spectators who are too far away to see details, as with the 'mole, cinque-spotted' (2.2.38) on Innogen's breast in *Cymbeline*.

10–11 O . . . aqua-vitae. In Q2, the Nurse's first words in this scene are addressed to Peter, who may remain offstage or exit immediately following his entrance: 'Peter stay at the gate.' The Q1 passage constitutes another anticipation or transposition (cf. 8.5–6 above). In the following scene Q2's Nurse says: 'Ah wheres my man? giue me some Aqua-vitae' (3.2.88).

13 Both exclamations are present in Q2, but the first occurs earlier, the second later in the scene.

13 jaunt As lower case 't' is easily misread for lower case 'c' in secretary hand, Q2's 'jaunce' may be a misreading, though Barry Gaines has made a strong case for 'jaunce' reflecting dialect pronunciation ('Another example of dialect from the Nurse in *Romeo and Juliet*', *SQ* 32 (1981), 96–7).

JULIET But tell me, sweet Nurse, what says Romeo?   15
NURSE Romeo? Nay, alas, you cannot choose a man. He's nobody,
    he is not the flower of courtesy, he is not a proper man; and for
    a hand, and a foot, and a body – well, go thy way, wench, thou
    hast it, i'faith. Lord, Lord, how my head beats.
JULIET What of all this? Tell me, what says he to our marriage?   20
NURSE Marry, he says, like an honest gentleman,
    And a kind, and, I warrant, a virtuous –
    Where's your mother?
JULIET Lord, Lord, how oddly thou repliest:
    'He says, like a kind gentleman,   25
    And an honest, and a virtuous:
    "Where's your mother?"'
NURSE Marry, come up, cannot you stay a while?
    Is this the poultice for mine aching bones?
    Next errand you'll have done, even do't yourself.   30
JULIET Nay, stay, sweet Nurse, I do entreat thee now,
    What says my love, my lord, my Romeo?
NURSE Go, hie you straight to Friar Laurence' cell,
    And frame a scuse that you must go to shrift.
    There stays a bridegroom to make you a bride.   35
    Now comes the wanton blood up in your cheeks.
    I must provide a ladder made of cords
    With which your lord must climb a bird's nest soon.
    I must take pains to further your delight,

---

16 cannot] Q1; know not how to Q2   18 a body] Q2; a baudie Q1; body Q4; a bawdy F2; a Baw-dy *Rowe;* a bo-dy *Pope*   21–30] *Arranged as in Levenson; as prose* Q1   22 kind] Q1 *(*kinde*)*; Courteous, and a kinde, and a handsome Q2   25 He] Q1; Your loue Q2   25–6 a . . . virtuous] Q1 *(subst.)*; an honest gentleman Q2   30 errand] Q1 *(*arrant*)*; messages Q2   33 Go] Q1 *(*Goe*)*; Then Q2   33 straight] Q1; hence Q2   35 bridegroom] Q1 *(subst.)*; husband Q2   35 bride] Q1 *(*Bride*)*; wife Q2   39 further] Q1; toyle Q2

15 Juliet's simple and straightforward question strikingly contrasts with the elaborate seven-line passage in which Juliet lengthily (and somewhat paradoxically, given her emphasis on haste) laments the Nurse's delay in revealing her news.

18 body The bawdy pun is emphasised by the spelling in Q1, 'baudie'.

20 Following the Q2 equivalent of this line, the longer text contains a seven-line passage in which the Nurse further evades Juliet's question.

34 This line is absent from Q2, where the Nurse's speech is preceded by the question 'Haue

you got leaue to go to shrift to day?', answered affirmatively by Juliet. The emphasis is thus somewhat different, Q2's Juliet being allowed to go to Friar Laurence's, whereas Q1's more actively makes up her own excuse.

34 scuse 'Aphetic form of excuse' (*OED*), implying the loss of a short unaccented vowel at the beginning of a word, as in 'squire' for 'esquire'.

35 bridegroom Q2's 'husband' makes the line strictly speaking contradictory, a contradiction that is avoided by Q1's substitution of 'bridegroom'.

But you must bear the burden soon at night.   40
Doth this news please you now?
JULIET [*Aside*] How doth her latter words revive my heart.
[*To the Nurse*] Thanks, gentle Nurse, dispatch thy
     business,
And I'll not fail to meet my Romeo.

                                                        Exeunt

[9]   *Enter* ROMEO, FRIAR [LAURENCE]

ROMEO Now, Father Laurence, in thy holy grant
     Consists the good of me and Juliet.
FRIAR LAURENCE Without more words I will do all I may
     To make you happy, if in me it lie.
ROMEO This morning here she pointed we should meet   5
     And consummate those never-parting bands,
     Witness of our hearts' love, by joining hands,
     And come she will.
FRIAR LAURENCE   I guess she will indeed.
     Youth's love is quick, swifter than swiftest speed.

---

42 SD] *This edn; not in* QI   43 SD] *This edn; not in* QI   0 SD] QI *(Enter Romeo, Frier.)*

41 Starting with this line and for the last four lines of this and all of the following scene, Q1 is completely different from Q2.

42 Juliet's rather moving exclamation – offering a glimpse of Juliet's emotions, spoken as an aside, in what has been a mostly comic scene – is absent from Q2 where Juliet's final speech reads: 'Hie to high fortune, honest Nurse farewell.'

43 gentle Nurse In this scene, Juliet addresses the Nurse as 'gentle' (7), 'sweet' (15, 31), and again here, 'gentle'. Q2's Juliet shows more variety, moving from 'hony Nurse' to 'good sweete Nurse' to 'good, good Nurse' to 'Sweete, sweete, sweete Nurse', only to end up on 'honest Nurse' once she has been given the news she wanted (2.4.18, 20, 28, 54, 78).

Scene 9
Act 2, Scene 6 in the NCS edition.
Although this scene dramatises the same event as the corresponding one in Q2, the text is almost completely different, as is its tone (see Urkowitz). With twenty-eight lines as opposed to thirty-seven in Q2, Q1 is again somewhat shorter. See Introduction, pp. 29–30.

5 This morning This time indication is consistent with Romeo's instruction to the Nurse (7.145–6) but contradicted by the Nurse's advice to Juliet to 'hie you straight to Friar Laurence' cell' (8.33). See Introduction, pp. 34–5.

5 pointed an archaic form of 'appointed' (*OED* Point *v.* 2) which could mean not only to fix or determine but also to agree upon. As it was not Juliet but Romeo who appointed the time and place of their betrothal (8.33), it is this last meaning which is here implied.

5–8 Peter Brook substituted these lines for some of Q2's in his Stratford production of 1947 (Loehlin).

6–7 From here on, much of the scene in Q1 (though not in Q2) consists of rhyming couplets (see also note at 9.17).

8–9 Q1 omits the Friar's moralising warning that 'These violent delights haue violent endes' and his admonition to 'loue moderately' (2.6.9, 14).

9 Youth's love is quick As elsewhere, Friar Laurence sounds sententious and proverbial, though no corresponding proverb seems to have been identified.

Enter JULIET, *somewhat fast, and embraceth Romeo*

    See where she comes.   10
    So light of foot ne'er hurts the trodden flower.
    Of love and joy, see, see the sovereign power.
JULIET Romeo.
ROMEO My Juliet, welcome. As do waking eyes,
    Closed in night's mists, attend the frolic day,   15
    So Romeo hath expected Juliet,
    And thou art come.
JULIET   I am, if I be day,
    Come to my sun. Shine forth, and make me fair.
ROMEO All beauteous fairness dwelleth in thine eyes.

JULIET Romeo, from thine all brightness doth arise.   20
FRIAR LAURENCE Come, wantons, come, the stealing hours do pass.
    Defer embracements till some fitter time.
    Part for a while; you shall not be alone
    Till holy Church have joined ye both in one.
ROMEO Lead, holy Father, all delay seems long.   25
JULIET Make haste, make haste, this ling'ring doth us wrong.

9 SD] Q1 *(subst.); Enter* Iuliet. Q2   10] Q1*;* Here comes the Lady Q2   11] Q1 *(subst.);* Oh so light a foote / Will nere
weare out the euerlasting flint Q2   21 Come . . . come] Q1 *(subst.);* Come, come, with me Q2   23–4 you . . . one] Q1
(subst.); you shall not stay alone, / Till holy Church incorporate two in one Q2

9 SD This descriptive stage direction, probably
reflecting early performance practice, is confined
to Q1. Q2 more soberly reads: '*Enter Iuliet*'.

11–12 Describing Juliet's gait and 'sovereign
power', the Friar, somewhat surprisingly, seems
to liken her to a goddess. Venus, in her encounter
with Aeneas, reveals herself as a true goddess by
her gait (*Aeneid*, 1.405). The common compliment
'to walk like a goddess' is alluded to in Shakespeare's Sonnet 130: 'I grant I never saw a goddess go: / My mistress when she walks treads on
the ground.' The equivalent passage in Q2 reads:
'Here comes the Lady, Oh so light of foote /
Will nere weare out the euerlasting flint' (2.6.16–
17), meaning that 'Juliet moves so lightly that she
barely touches the ground and hence will never
wear out the flint cobble-stones over which she has
"walked"' (NCS). The phrase 'euerlasting flint'
looks subtly forward to the stone tomb and monument in which the lovers will end up. Q1 and Q2
are here entirely different, yet both are so carefully
composed that the passage strengthens the case for
a deliberate and careful rewriting. See Introduction, pp. 29–30.

13 Romeo Q2's more polite and less sponta-

neous Juliet addresses her first words to the Friar.

14 waking eyes The collocation does not occur
elsewhere in Shakespeare, but it is present in
Samuel Daniel's Sonnet 45 in *Delia* of 1592 ('Care-
charmer Sleep, son of the sable Night') which also
dwells on the contrast between 'day' and 'night'
and 'light' and 'clouds' (9, 1, 3, 13).

15 frolic joyous, merry, mirthful. Not till later
centuries was the sense derived from the verb
(*OED*).

17 day This takes up Romeo's 'day' two lines
earlier, and both rhyme with the final words in the
Friar's concluding couplet in what may be seen as
a playful poetic enactment of the spousal rites.

19–20 The short and simple one-line speeches,
forming a rhyming couplet (cf. 25–6 below), contrast with the elaborate rhetoric of Romeo and
Juliet's corresponding two speeches in Q2 which
total eleven lines (2.6.24–34).

21 stealing hours Cf. 'the stealing hours of
time' (*R3* 3.7.158).

23–4 you . . . one The only passage in this scene
which is verbally quite close to Q2.

25–8 In Q2, the scene ends after the Friar's preceding speech.

FRIAR LAURENCE O, soft and fair makes sweetest work, they say.
　　Haste is a common hind'rer in cross' way.

Exeunt omnes

[10]　*Enter* BENVOLIO, MERCUTIO, [*and his* PAGE]

BENVOLIO I prithee, good Mercutio, let's retire.
　　The day is hot, the Capels are abroad.
MERCUTIO Thou art like one of those that, when he comes into the
　　confines of a tavern, claps me his rapier on the board and says:
　　'God send me no need of thee.' And, by the operation of the　　5
　　next cup of wine, he draws it on the drawer, when indeed there
　　is no need.
BENVOLIO Am I like such a one?
MERCUTIO Go to, thou art as hot a jack, being moved, and as soon
　　moved to be moody, and as soon moody to be moved.　　10
BENVOLIO And what to?
MERCUTIO Nay, and there were two such, we should have none
　　shortly. Didst not thou fall out with a man for cracking of nuts,
　　having no other reason but because thou hadst hazel eyes? What
　　eye but such an eye would have picked out such a quarrel?　　15
　　With another for coughing, because he waked thy dog that lay
　　asleep in the sun? With a tailor for wearing his new doublet

0 SD] *This edn; Enter Benuolio, Mercutio.* Q1; *Enter* Mercutio, Benuolio, *and men.* Q2　　2 Capels are] Q1 *(Capels)*
are, *Capels* Q2; *Capulets* Q4, F　　3 those] Q1; these fellowes Q2　　3 comes into] Q1; enters Q2　　4 rapier] Q1; sword
Q2　　6 next] Q1; second Q2　　6 cup of wine] Q1; cup Q2　　6 it] Q1; him Q2　　8 one] Q1; fellow Q2　　9 being moved]
Q1 *(mooude)*; in thy moode Q2　　11 to] Q1 *(too)*; Pope; too Q, F　　13 fall out] Q1; quarrell Q2　　14 hadst] Q1; hast
Q2　　15 have picked] Q1 *(subst.)*; spie Q2　　16 waked] Q1 *(wakd)*; hath wakened Q2　　16 lay] Q1; hath laine Q2

27 'Soft and fair' is proverbial (Dent, s601). See
also *Ado*: FRIAR . . . to the chapel let us presently. /
BENEDICK Soft and fair, Friar, which is Beatrice?
(5.4.71–2).

28 The way of the cross ('cross' way') is the way
to salvation; haste, according to Friar Laurence,
provides an obstacle to it. See also the proverbs
'the more haste the less speed' and 'marry in haste
and repent at leisure' (Dent H196, H198).

Scene 10
Act 3, Scene 1 in the NCS edition.
Much of this scene (1–52, 76–114, 132–43) corre-
sponds quite closely to passages in Q2 (3.1.1–74,

100–45, 169–84), though other parts do significantly less so (53–75, 115–31, 144–5). A number
of cuts reduce the total length from 188 to 145
lines.

10 Q2 here adds the second term of the
comparison: 'as any in Italie'. Q1 does not, which
means that the present comparison reiterates that
made in Mercutio's previous speech: Benvolio,
Mercutio says, is as hot a jack as 'one of those' (line
3) quarrelsome gallants he has just described.

12–19 Mercutio's speech lacks two passages –
after 'shortly' (13) and 'quarrel' (15) – present
in Q2 which add up to more than a third of the
speech's length in the longer text.

before Easter, and with another for tying his new shoes with old
ribbons? And yet thou wilt forbid me of quarrelling.

BENVOLIO By my head, here comes a Capulet.   20

Enter TYBALT

MERCUTIO By my heel, I care not.

TYBALT Gentlemen, a word with one of you.

MERCUTIO But one word with one of us? You had best couple it
with somewhat, and make it a word and a blow.

TYBALT I am apt enough to that if I have occasion.   25

MERCUTIO Could you not take occasion?

TYBALT Mercutio, thou consorts with Romeo.

MERCUTIO Consort? Zounds, consort? [*To Benvolio*] The slave will
make fiddlers of us. [*To Tybalt*] If you do, sirrah, look for nothing
but discord, [*Touching his rapier*] for here's my fiddlestick.   30

Enter ROMEO

TYBALT Well, peace be with you, here comes my man.

MERCUTIO But I'll be hanged if he wear your livery. Marry, go
before into the field, and he may be your follower; so in that
sense your worship may call him 'man'.

---

19 forbid me of] Q1; tuter me from Q2   20 a Capulet] Q1 *(Capolet)*; the *Capulets* Q2   20 SD] Q1 *(subst.); Enter* Tybalt, Petruchio, *and others. (one line earlier)* Q2   22 Gentlemen] Q1; Gentlemen, Good den Q2   23 You . . . couple] Q1; couple Q2   24 somewhat] Q1; something Q2   25 I am] Q1; You shall find me Q2   25 that] Q1; that sir Q2   25 occasion] Q1; some occasion without giuing Q2   27 consorts] Q1; consortest Q2   27 Romeo.] Q2 *(Romeo.)*; Romeo? Q1   28 SD] *This edn; not in* Q, F   28–9 The . . . us.] Q1 *(subst.);* doest thou make vs Minstrels? Q2   29 SD] *This edn; not in* Q, F   30 SD] *Jowett; not in* Q, F   31 you] Q1; you sir Q2   32 hanged] Q1; hangd sir Q2

19 **forbid me of** The preposition 'of' has become archaic (*OED* Forbid *v.* e.).

19 Following Mercutio's speech, Q1 omits a three-line passage present in Q2 consisting of short speeches by Benvolio and Mercutio.

20 SD In Q2, Tybalt enters with 'Petruchio, *and others*'.

22 In Q2, Tybalt begins this speech by addressing his companions, 'Follow me close, for I will speake to them', a line Q1, which has Tybalt enter alone, understandably omits.

22–31 Q2's Tybalt begins by saluting the Montagues ('Gentlemen, Good den') and twice addresses Mercutio as 'sir', three marks of (ironic?) politeness which Q1 omits in a passage which is otherwise close to Q2. See Introduction, pp. 31–2.

24 **somewhat** Q1 has the now archaic 'somewhat' (*OED n.* 1.a.) instead of Q2's synonymous 'something'.

27 **consorts** 'In verbs ending with "-*t*", "-*test*" final in the second person sing[ular] often becomes "-*ts*"' (Abbott 340).

28 **Zounds, consort?** In Q2, this exclamation occurs at the end of Mercutio's speech, the first of a number of transpositions in this scene.

30 **fiddlestick** Q2's Mercutio adds: 'heeres that shall make you daunce'.

30 Following this line, Q2 adds a six-line passage in which Benvolio urges the belligerents to refrain from conflict or at least to withdraw to some private place.

TYBALT   Romeo, the hate I bear to thee can afford   35
            No better words than these: thou art a villain.
ROMEO   Tybalt, the love I bear to thee doth excuse
            The appertaining rage to such a word.
            Villain am I none; therefore, I well perceive
            Thou know'st me not.   40
TYBALT   Base boy,
            This cannot serve thy turn, and therefore draw.
ROMEO   I do protest I never injured thee,
            But love thee better than thou canst devise
            Till thou shalt know the reason of my love.   45
MERCUTIO   O dishonourable, vile submission.
            'Alla stoccata' carries it away. [*Draws*]
            [*To Tybalt*] You rat-catcher, come back, come back.
TYBALT   What wouldst with me?
MERCUTIO   Nothing, king of cats, but borrow one of your nine lives.   50
            Therefore come draw your rapier out of your scabbard, lest mine
            be about your ears ere you be aware.
                       [*Mercutio and Tybalt fight*]
ROMEO   Stay, Tybalt! Hold, Mercutio! Benvolio, beat down their
            weapons.

35–40] *Arranged as in Levenson (following* Q2*); as prose* Q1   35 hate] Q1; loue Q2   36 words] Q1; terme Q2   37 love
. . . thee] Q1 *(subst.);* reason that I haue to loue thee Q2   38 word] Q1; greeting Q2   39 therefore] Q1; Therefore
farewell Q2   39 well perceive] Q1 *(perceiue);* see Q2   41–2] *Arranged as in Hubbard; as prose* Q1   41 Base boy]
Q1 *(*Bace*);* Boy Q2   42 This . . . turn] Q1 *(subst.);* shall not excuse the iniuries / That thou hast done me Q2   42
therefore draw] Q1 *(*drawe*);* therefore turne and draw Q2   43–8] *Arranged as in Levenson (following* Q2*); as prose*
Q1   46 dishonourable] Q1 *(subst.);* calme, dishonourable Q2   47 'Alla stoccata'] *Knight;* Allastockado Q1; *Alla stu-*
catho Q2   47 SD] *Capell; not in* Q, F   48 SD] *This edn; not in* Q, F   48 come . . . back] Q1 *(subst.);* will you walke
Q2   49 wouldst] Q2; wouldest Q1; woulds Q3   50 borrow] Q1; *not in* Q2   51 rapier] Q1; sword Q2   51 scabbard]
Q1 *(*scabard*);* pilcher Q2   52 you be aware] Q1; it be out Q2   52 SD] *Rowe; not in* Q, F

35–48 This passage is set as prose in Q1 while
the corresponding passage in Q2 is in verse.

35 hate The straightforward 'hate' instead of
Q2's ironic 'loue', along with Q1's omission of
Tybalt's (mock-)polite greetings (see note above
at 22–31), raises the question of whether Q1 consistently presents a different Tybalt from its Q2
counterpart. See Introduction, pp. 31–2.

39–42 Q2's Romeo here bids 'farewell', and Q2's
Tybalt, three lines later, not only asks him to 'draw'
but to 'turne and draw', suggesting a stage action
– Romeo beginning to exit – that is not implied by
the shorter text.

45 Following this line, Q2's Romeo adds two
more lines: 'And so good Capulet, which name I
tender / As dearely as mine owne, be satisfied.'

50–2 In a short passage absent from Q1, Q2's
Mercutio wants not only 'one of [Tybalt's] nine

liues' but also to 'drie beate the rest of the eight'.

51 scabbard This is synonymous with Q2's
lesser-known term 'pilcher', the word's only
occurrence in all of Shakespeare. Scabbard, by
contrast, is also used in other plays (e.g. *Ado*
5.1.126, *TN* 3.4.267, and *Cym.* 3.4.80).

53–4 Instead of this single speech, Q2 has four
speeches, three very short ones by Tybalt, Romeo,
and Mercutio, and a five-line speech by Romeo
in which he reminds Mercutio and Tybalt that 'the
Prince expressly hath / Forbid this bandying in
Verona [sic] streetes'. As in the opening scene (see
1.48 SD and note), Q1's stage action substitutes
for Q2's words, possibly because the exact words
may not have greatly mattered or may have been
impossible to understand in the heat of the action.
See Introduction, pp. 17–18.

Tybalt under Romeo's arm thrusts Mercutio, in and flies

MERCUTIO Is he gone? Hath he nothing? A pox on your houses!   55
ROMEO What, art thou hurt, man? The wound is not deep.
MERCUTIO No, not so deep as a well, nor so wide as a barn-door,
but it will serve, I warrant. What meant you to come between
us? I was hurt under your arm.
ROMEO I did all for the best.   60
MERCUTIO A pox of your houses! I am fairly dressed. [*To Page*]
Sirrah, go fetch me a surgeon.
PAGE I go, my lord.   [*Exit*]

MERCUTIO I am peppered for this world, I am sped, i'faith; he
hath made worms' meat of me. And ye ask for me tomorrow,   65
you shall find me a grave man. A pox of your houses! I shall
be fairly mounted upon four men's shoulders, for your house
of the Montagues and the Capulets. And then some peasantly
rogue, some sexton, some base slave shall write my epitaph,
that Tybalt came and broke the Prince's laws, and Mercutio   70
was slain for the first and second cause.

[*Enter* PAGE]

[*To Page*] Where's the surgeon?
PAGE He's come, sir.

---

55 pox] Q1 (*poxe*); plague Q2   56 wound . . . deep] Q1 (*deepe*); hurt cannot be much Q2   57 barn-door] Q1 (*subst.*);
Church doore Q2   61 SD] *This edn; not in* Q, F   63 SH] *Levenson; Boy:* Q1   63 SD] *Capell; not in* Q, F   66 grave man]
Q1 (*graue-man*)   71 SD] *Levenson; not in* Q1   72 SD] *This edn; not in* Q1   73 SH] *Levenson; Boy:* Q1

55–75 This passage consists partly of rear-
ranged verbal material present in Q2 and partly
of material unique to Q1 (esp. after line 66). Since
Q1 and Q2 correspond quite closely to each other
before and after this passage and since both texts
make good sense, Shakespearean revision may
well be responsible for the existence of the two
versions. Jowett shows that 'Most idioms in the
Q1 passage can be paralleled in Shakespeare' and
argues that the evidence points 'towards Shakespeare's authorship, though not conclusively'.
He adds that 'An editor accepting Shakespeare's
authorship of the Q1 passage might take Q1 as
control-text here'. See Introduction, pp. 23–4.
55 The two small additional passages in Q2, 'I
am hurt' and 'I am sped', tell readers what they
would not otherwise know but can be suggested

through action rather than words onstage.
55 **pox** Q1 substitutes this blunter word for Q2's
'plague', and Q1's Mercutio utters the curse four
times as opposed to three in Q2. See also notes at
19.7 and 20.177.
61 **dressed** prepared (for death); see *OED*
Dressed *ppl. a.*
70 **Tybalt . . . laws** In fact, it was Mercutio who
challenged Tybalt and thus broke the Prince's laws
too, arguably even before Tybalt did.
71 **first and second cause** two grounds for
a duel. The phrase also occurs above (7.21) and
in the corresponding Q2 passage. The transposition has been taken as another sign of memorial
reconstruction.
71 SD Only in Q1 does Mercutio's man re-enter.

MERCUTIO Now he'll keep a-mumbling in my guts – on the other
    side – come, Benvolio, lend me thy hand. A pox of your houses!   75
               Exeunt [Mercutio, his Page, and Benvolio]
ROMEO This gentleman, the Prince's near ally,
    My very friend hath ta'en this mortal wound
    In my behalf, my reputation stained
    With Tybalt's slander; Tybalt that an hour
    Hath been my kinsman. Ah Juliet,   80
    Thy beauty makes me thus effeminate,
    And in my temper softens valour's steel.

               Enter BENVOLIO

BENVOLIO Ah Romeo, Romeo, brave Mercutio is dead.
    That gallant spirit hath aspired the clouds,
    Which too untimely scorned the lowly earth.   85
ROMEO This day's black fate on more days doth depend;
    This but begins what other days must end.

               Enter TYBALT

BENVOLIO Here comes the furious Tybalt back again.
ROMEO Alive in triumph and Mercutio slain?
    Away to heaven, respective lenity,   90
    And fire-eyed fury be my conduct now.
    Now, Tybalt, take the 'villain' back again
    Which late thou gav'st me. For Mercutio's soul
    Is but a little way above the clouds

74–5 guts – . . . – come] *Levenson;* guts on the other side, come Q1; guts on the other side. Come *Hubbard*   75 SD] *This edn;* Exeunt Q1; Exit. Q2; Exeunt Mercutio and Benvolio Hubbard; Exit Mercutio with Benvolio Levenson   77 ta'en] Q1 *(tane);* got Q2   80 kinsman] Q1, *Capell;* Cozen Q2   80 Juliet] Q1 *(Iuliet);* sweete *Iuliet* Q2   81 makes me thus] Q1; hath made me Q2   82 softens] Q1; softned Q2   85 scorned the lowly] Q1 *(scornd);* here did scorne Q2   87 what other days] Q1 *(dayes);* the wo others Q2   87 SD] Q1 *(subst.); not in* Q2–Q4; Enter Tybalt. F   89 Alive] Q1 *(A liue);* He gan Q2; He gon Q3; He gone Q5; He live *NCS (conj.)*   91 fire-eyed] Q1 *(fier eyed);* fier end Q2; fier and Q3   94 the clouds] Q1 *(cloudes);* our heads Q2

74 **a-mumbling in my guts** For similar constructions – 'a-killing' (*Oth.* 4.1.174); 'a-going'
(*H8* 1.3.50); 'a-hanging' (*Lear* 5.3.249) – see
Abbott 24. Note that Q2's Capulet uses the word
'mumbling' at 3.5.173, a line with no equivalent
in Q1.

74–5 **on the other side** The exact meaning
of these words does not seem clear, all the more
so as Q1's punctuation provides little help: 'heele
keepe a mumbling in my guts on the other side,

come'. Perhaps the best explanation is that Mercutio interrupts his train of thought, has it change
direction ('on the other side') and decides to seek
the help of Benvolio and the surgeon. For a similar usage of 'on the other side', see *R3*, additional
passage H, line 7. Eichhoff argued that the words
are addressed to the surgeon.

89 **Alive** Q1's 'A liue' can be modernised as
either 'Alive' or 'He live', which also 'makes excellent sense' (NCS).

> And stays for thine to bear him company. 95
> Or thou, or I, or both shall follow him.

[They] fight. Tybalt [is wounded. He] falls [and dies]

BENVOLIO Romeo, away, thou seest that Tybalt's slain.
The citizens approach; away, be gone!
Thou wilt be taken.
ROMEO   Ah, I am fortune's slave.   *[Exit]*

*Enter [*WATCHMAN *and other] citizens*

WATCHMAN Where's he that slew Mercutio, Tybalt, that villain? 100
BENVOLIO There is that Tybalt.
[WATCHMAN]   Up, sirrah, go with us.

Enter PRINCE *[and]* CAPULET'S WIFE

PRINCE Where be the vile beginners of this fray?
BENVOLIO Ah, noble Prince, I can discover all
The most unlucky manage of this brawl.
Here lies the man, slain by young Romeo, 105
That slew thy kinsman, brave Mercutio.
CAPULET'S WIFE Tybalt, Tybalt, O, my brother's child,
Unhappy sight! Ah, the blood is spilled
Of my dear kinsman. Prince, as thou art true,
For blood of ours shed blood of Montague. 110

---

95 And stays] Q1 *(staies)*; Staying Q2   95 bear] Q1 *(beare)*; keepe Q2   96 Or] Q1; Either Q2   96 shall follow] Q1; must go Q2   96 SD] *Jowett*; Fight, Tibalt falles. Q1; They fight. Tibalt falles. Q2   98 approach] Q1; are vp Q2   99 SD.1] Q2 *(Exit Romeo.)*; Exeunt Q1   99 WATCHMAN *and other*] *This edn; not in* Q1   100 SH] Q1 *(Watch.)*   100 Where's] Q1 *(Wher's)*; Which way ran Q2   100 slew] Q1 *(slue)*; kild Q2   100 villain] Q1 *(villaine)*; murtherer Q2   101 is] Q1; lies Q2   101 SH WATCHMAN] *Mommsen (Watch.); no SH, but 'Watch:* Vp' *catchword on preceding page* Q1; Citi. Q2   101 sirrah] Q1 *(sirra)*; sir Q2   101 us] Q1 *(vs)*; me Q2   101 SD] Q1 *(Enter Prince, Capolets wife.)*; Enter Prince, olde* Mountague, Capulet, *their wiues and all.* Q2   102 be] Q1; are Q2   104 most unlucky] Q1 *(vnlucky)*; vnluckie Q2   104 brawl] Q1 *(brawle)*; fatall brall Q2   105 Here] Q1 *(Heere)*; There Q2   107 Tybalt, Tybalt] Q1 *(subst.)*; Tybalt, my Cozin Q2   108 Unhappy sight] Q1 *(subst.)*; O Prince, O Cozen, husband Q2

96 Following this line, Q2 adds three lines in which Tybalt threatens Romeo – 'Thou wretched boy that didst cosort him here, / Shalt with him hence.'

99 Following this line, Q2's Romeo appears to delay his exit, prompting Benvolio's question, 'Why dost thou stay?'

99 SD [WATCHMAN *and other*] Q1 and Q2's stage direction reads '*Enter Citizens*', but the SH in Q1, '*Watch.*' (in Q2: '*Citti.*'/'*Citi.*'), specifies that the speaker is a watchman. At least three watchmen appear in the last scene.

101 Following this line, Q2 adds another line to the Watchman's speech: 'I charge thee in the Princes name obey.'

101 SD As elsewhere in the play, Q1 greatly reduces Q2's casting requirements, omitting the entrance of Montague and Capulet as well as of other unspecified characters ('*and all*'). See also note at 135–6 below.

108 The line in Q1 is a syllable short. Malone conjectured that it should read, 'Unhappy sight! ah *me*, the blood is spill'd.'

PRINCE Speak, Benvolio, who began this fray?
BENVOLIO Tybalt, here slain, whom Romeo's hand did slay.
　　　Romeo, who spake him fair, bid him bethink
　　　How nice the quarrel was.
　　　But Tybalt still persisting in his wrong,   115
　　　The stout Mercutio drew to calm the storm,
　　　Which Romeo seeing called 'Stay, gentlemen!'
　　　And on me cried, who drew to part their strife.
　　　And with his agile arm young Romeo
　　　As fast as tongue cried 'Peace!' sought peace to make.   120
　　　While they were interchanging thrusts and blows,
　　　Under young Romeo's labouring arm to part,
　　　The furious Tybalt cast an envious thrust
　　　That rid the life of stout Mercutio.
　　　With that he fled but presently returned,   125
　　　And with his rapier bravèd Romeo,
　　　That had but newly entertained revenge.
　　　And ere I could draw forth my rapier
　　　To part their fury, down did Tybalt fall,
　　　And this way Romeo fled.   130
CAPULET'S WIFE He is a Montague and speaks partial.
　　　Some twenty of them fought in this black strife,
　　　And all those twenty could but kill one life.
　　　I do entreat, sweet Prince, thou'lt justice give:

---

111 Speak, Benvolio] Q1 *(subst.); Benuolio* Q2   111 fray] Q1; bloudie fray Q2   113 who spake] Q1; that spoke Q2   119 agile] Q1 *(agill); aged* Q2; agill Q4; able F2   124 rid] Q1; hit Q2   134 do ... give] Q1 *(subst.);* beg for Iustice which thou Prince must giue Q2

114 In Q2, the line continues with 'and vrgd withall', turning Q1's trimeter into a regular iambic pentameter.

115–30 Contrary to the first three, the last sixteen lines of Benvolio's speech are very different from Q2. A few isolated phrases parallel Q2 – 'an enuious thrust' (123), 'the life / Of stout *Mercutio*' (124), 'had but newly entertaind reuenge' (127), 'ere I / Could draw' (128) – but the passage as a whole seems clearly of independent origin (possibly owing to revision) rather than an imperfect rendering of the version in Q2.

116 Benvolio's description of Mercutio's motive seems inaccurate (see 46–52 above). Q2's Benvolio, by contrast, states that, following Tybalt's aggression, Mercutio 'all as hot, turnes deadly poynt to poynt'.

121 This corresponds to a line in Benvolio's report to the Prince in 1.1: 'While we were enterchaunging thrusts and blowes' (1.1.104). The Q2 verse is part of an eight-line passage that is absent from Q1. Since the present Q1 speech seems of good quality and independent origin from Q2, it seems possible that Shakespeare himself transposed the line to its new location.

122 An elliptic line (of which Q1 contains a certain number – see, for instance, 20.12–13 and 20.166 and notes): Under young Romeo's labouring arm *which was striving* to part *Mercutio and Tybalt*.

Romeo slew Tybalt, Romeo may not live.   135
PRINCE And for that offence
Immediately we do exile him hence.
I have an interest in your hate's proceeding,
My blood for your rude brawls doth lye a-bleeding.
But I'll amerce you with so large a fine   140
That you shall all repent the loss of mine.
I will be deaf to pleading and excuses,
Nor tears nor prayers shall purchase for abuses.
Pity shall dwell and govern with us still;
Mercy to all but murderers, pardoning none that kill.   145
                    Exeunt omnes [*with Tybalt's body*]

[11]   *Enter* JULIET

JULIET Gallop apace, you fiery-footed steeds,
To Phoebus' mansion. Such a wagoner
As Phaëton would quickly bring you thither
And send in cloudy night immediately.

---

138 hate's] Q1 *(hates); hearts Q2   140 large] Q1; strong Q2   142 I] Q1; It Q2; I Q4   143 for] Q1; out Q2   145 *with Tybalt's body*] *This edn (following Jowett); not in* Q, F   0 SD] Q1 *(Enter* Iuliet.); *Enter* Iuliet alone. Q2   1 SH] Q1 (Iul:); *not in* Q2   2 To] Q1; Towards Q2   2 mansion] Q1; lodging Q2   3 quickly ... thither] Q1 (thether); whip you to the west Q2   4 send] Q1; bring Q2   4 SD] Q1 (subst.); *Enter Nurse with cords.* Q2*

135–6 Q2, where Capulet's Wife and the Prince share a pentameter that forms a rhyming couplet with the following line, provides a smoother transition between the two speeches. The passage may well provide evidence for Q1's derivative nature. Between these two lines, Q2 also inserts Montague's only speech in this scene (3.1.175–7). Q1 omits not only the speech but disposes of Montague and Capulet's presence altogether (see note at 101 SD above).

144–5 The end of the scene rewrites and condenses that in Q2, substituting one couplet where Q2 has two. In the penultimate couplet in Q2, the Prince points out that if Romeo is found in Verona, he will be sentenced to death, a statement Q1 omits. In the final couplet Q2's Prince concludes with the point made in Machiavelli's *Prince* that too much mercy only leads to further bloodshed: 'mercie but murders, pardoning those that kill'. To quote Evans's paraphrase, 'Mercy only leads to further murders by pardoning murderers' (NCS). Q1's Prince establishes a sharp contrast between murderers (who will not be pardoned) and all others (who will be treated mercifully), which arguably stands in contradiction to the stiff fine he has just promised to inflict on the Capulets and the Montagues. It seems again impossible to determine whether the lines in Q1 result from a failure of memory or from a conscious effort at rewriting.

Scene 11
Act 3, Scene 2 in the NCS edition.
The length of this scene in Q1 is less than half that of Q2. Juliet's part, in particular, is heavily abridged, from almost 120 to only forty lines. A number of Q2 passages leave no trace in Q1, most notably a twenty-seven line passage in Juliet's opening soliloquy. Later in the scene, the Q1 abridgement is at times less clear-cut with occasional transpositions and condensations of material in Q2.

4 Following this line, Juliet's soliloquy in Q2 has a passage of twenty-seven lines which are absent from Q1.

Enter NURSE *wringing her hands, with the ladder of cords in her lap*

        But how now, Nurse? O Lord, why look'st thou sad?   5
        What hast thou there, the cords?
NURSE Ay, ay, the cords. Alack, we are undone,
        We are undone, lady, we are undone.
JULIET What devil art thou that torments me thus?
NURSE Alack the day, he's dead, he's dead, he's dead.   10
JULIET This torture should be roared in dismal hell.
        Can heavens be so envious?
NURSE Romeo can if heavens cannot.
        I saw the wound, I saw it with mine eyes –
        God save the sample – on his manly breast.   15
        A bloody corpse, a piteous, bloody corpse,
        All pale as ashes. I swoonèd at the sight.
JULIET Ah Romeo, Romeo, what disaster hap
        Hath severed thee from thy true Juliet?
        Ah, why should heaven so much conspire with woe,   20
        Or fate envy our happy marriage,
        So soon to sunder us by timeless death?
NURSE O Tybalt, Tybalt, the best friend I had,
        O honest Tybalt, courteous gentleman.
JULIET What storm is this that blows so contrary?   25
        Is Tybalt dead and Romeo murderèd?
        My dear-loved cousin and my dearest lord?
        Then let the trumpet sound a general doom.
        These two being dead, then living is there none.

---

6 the cords?] Q1 *(cordes); The cords that Romeo bid thee fetch?* Q2   12 heavens] Q1 *(heauens);* heauen Q2   13 if heavens] Q1 *(heauens);* Though heauen Q2   15 sample] Q1; marke Q2   16 bloody . . . bloody] Q1 *(subst.);* piteous coarse, a bloudie piteous Q2   16 corpse] Q1 *(coarse)*   17 All pale] Q1; Pale, pale Q2   17 swoonèd] Q1 *(swounded);* sounded Q2   24 honest . . . courteous] Q1; curteous *Tybalt*, honest Q2   26 Tybalt . . . murderèd?] Q1 *(subst.); Romeo* slaughtred? and is *Tybalt* dead? and is *Tybalt* dead? Q2   27 dear-loved] Q1 *(subst.);* dearest Q2   27 dearest] Q1; dearer Q2   28 let the] Q1; the Q2

---

4 SD This SD has been ridiculed by several scholars (Hart, 423; Hoppe, 88), but, as Farley-Hills (29) points out, 'lap' here seems to refer to 'the skirt or apron pocket' (*OED* Lap *n.* 4). This also explains why Juliet, in Q1 and Q2, asks, 'What hast thou there.'

9 torments See note at 10.27.

11 In Q2, the equivalent line is followed by a seven-line passage, absent from Q1, with Juliet's elaborate puns on 'ay', 'I', the vowel 'i' and 'eye'.

15 God . . . sample An explanatory phrase, a variant of Q2's 'God saue the marke.' It does not appear elsewhere in Shakespeare, but see Damon's

short closing speech in George Gascoigne, *Supposes* (London, 1566).

16 corpse Q1's spelling is 'coarse'; see Wells, *Modernizing*, pp. 9–10.

16 It is noticeable that in this as well as a number of other lines in this scene (24, 26, 39, 54–5), Q1 and Q2 use the same words but arrange them in a different order. Such transpositions may be the result of imperfect memorisation.

18–22 This is the only passage in this scene consisting of lines that seem altogether independent of Q2.

NURSE   Tybalt is dead and Romeo banishèd;   30
          Romeo, that murdered him, is banishèd.

JULIET   Ah heavens, did Romeo's hand shed Tybalt's blood?

NURSE   It did, it did, alack the day, it did.

JULIET   O serpent's hate hid with a flow'ring face,
          O painted sepulchre, including filth!   35
          Was never book containing so foul matter
          So fairly bound? Ah, what meant Romeo?

NURSE   There is no truth, no faith, no honesty in men.
          All false, all faithless, perjured, all forsworn.
          Shame come to Romeo!   40

JULIET   A blister on that tongue! He was not born to shame.
          Upon his face shame is ashamed to sit.
          But wherefore, villain, didst thou kill my cousin?
          That villain cousin would have killed my husband.
          All this is comfort. But there yet remains   45
          Worse than his death, which fain I would forget.
          But ah, it presseth to my memory:
          Romeo is banished. Ah, that word 'banishèd'
          Is worse than death. 'Romeo is banishèd'
          Is father, mother, Tybalt, Juliet,   50
          All killed, all slain, all dead, all banishèd.
          Where are my father and my mother, Nurse?

NURSE   Weeping and wailing over Tybalt's corpse.
          Will you go to them?

---

30 dead] Q1; gone Q2   31 murdered him] Q1 (murdred); kild him he Q2   32 Ah heavens] Q1 (heauens); O God Q2   33 alack] Q1 (alacke); alas Q2   34 serpent's hate] Q1 (serpents); serpent heart Q2   36 never] Q1 (neuer); euer Q2   36 so foul] Q1 (foule); such vile Q2   38 There is] Q1; Theres Q2   39 All . . . forsworn] Q1 (subst.); All periurde, all forsworne, all naught, all dissemblers Q2   41 A . . . tongue] Q1 (tung); Blisted be thy Q2   42 face] Q1; brow Q2   46 which . . . forget] Q1 (subst.); I would forget it faine Q2   52 are] Q1; is Q2

33 This line is correctly given to the Nurse in Q1 but misattributed to Juliet in Q2, an error that is corrected in Q5 and F4.

35 This line, which has no exact equivalent in Q2, replaces a nine-line passage made up of a series of oxymora. The omitted Q2 passage includes a phrase – 'Rauenous douefeatherd rauen' – which modern editors believe to be a 'false start'.

43–5 Lines 43–4 is all that survives of a fourteen-line passage in Q2 in which Juliet further develops her conflict of loyalty between Romeo and Tybalt. Note that the removed lines explain better than Q1 alone what exactly *is* comfort, namely that Romeo is still alive, which provides further evidence of Q1's derivative nature. See Introduction, pp. 9–10.

45 All . . . comfort Q2's verse continues with the rhetorical question, 'wherefore weepe I then?', containing an implied stage action of which a spectator, unlike a reader, would be aware.

48–51 Q1 has a four-line lamentation where Q2 has a passage of sixteen lines. The lament for 'Tybalt's death' (repeated three times in the longer text) is conspicuously absent from Q1.

JULIET   Ay, ay, when theirs are spent,
　　　Mine shall be shed for Romeo's banishment.   55
NURSE Lady, your Romeo will be here tonight.
　　　I'll to him, he is hid at Laurence' cell.
JULIET Do so, and bear this ring to my true knight,
　　　And bid him come to take his last farewell.

Exeunt

[12] *Enter* FRIAR [LAURENCE]

FRIAR LAURENCE Romeo, come forth, come forth, thou fearful man.
　　　Affliction is enamoured on thy parts,
　　　And thou art wedded to calamity.

Enter ROMEO

ROMEO Father, what news, what is the Prince's doom?
　　　What sorrow craves acquaintance at our hands   5
　　　Which yet we know not?
FRIAR LAURENCE   Too familiar
　　　Is my young son with such sour company.
　　　I bring thee tidings of the Prince's doom.
ROMEO What less than doomsday is the Prince's doom?
FRIAR LAURENCE A gentler judgement vanished from his lips: 10
　　　Not body's death, but body's banishment.

---

55 be] *Eichhoff;* he Q1   56 Lady] Q1 *(Ladie);* Harke ye Q2   56 tonight] Q1 *(to night);* at night Q2   58 Do ... bear]
Q1 *(subst.);* O find him, giue Q2   59 SD] Q1; *Exit.* Q2   0 SD] Q1 *(Enter* Frier.*); Enter Frier and* Romeo. Q2   2 on]
Q1; of Q2   5–6 our ... we] Q1; my hand, / That I yet Q2   7 young] Q1 *(yong);* deare Q2

54–5 In Q1, contrary to Q2, 'theirs' and 'mine'
are not preceded by 'tears', meaning that the pronouns' referent is implied and not spelt out.

55 Following this line, Q2 prints another eight
lines, all absent from Q1, in which Juliet addresses
the 'poore ropes', likening her plight to theirs.

Scene 12
Act 3, Scene 3 in the NCS edition.
In general, this scene corresponds quite closely
to its equivalent in the second quarto. However, it omits some thirty-five lines present in the
longer text, mostly from Friar Laurence's lengthy
admonitory speech to Romeo, which is reduced
from fifty-one to twenty-five lines.

2 enamoured on 'on' meaning 'of' is com-

monly found in Elizabethan texts (e.g. *Ado*
2.1.154).

5–6 our hands . . . we In this awkwardly
pompous passage, Romeo says 'our' and 'we'
where Q2 has 'my' and 'I'. For the use of 'our'
in the 'royal style', see Abbott 222.

7 young It is striking that Q1, in this scene, has
a variety of different words where Q2 has the word
'dear': 'young son' (here; Q2: 'deare sonne'), 'mere
mercy' (line 27; Q2: 'deare mercie'), 'fair Juliet's
skin' (line 35; Q2: 'deare Iuliets hand'), 'For whose
sweet sake' (line 113; Q2: 'For whose deare sake').
Q2 further has 'deare loue' in a line of Friar Laurence's long speech that is absent from Q1. All in
all, the word occurs thus five times in Q2 but not
a single time in Q1.

ROMEO Ha, banishèd? Be merciful, say 'death'.
   For exile hath more terror in his looks
   Than death itself; do not say 'banishment'.
FRIAR LAURENCE Hence from Verona art thou banishèd.   15
   Be patient, for the world is broad and wide.
ROMEO There is no world without Verona walls
   But purgatory, torture, hell itself.
   Hence banishèd is banished from the world,
   And world-exiled is death. Calling death 'banishment', 20
   Thou cut'st my head off with a golden axe,
   And smilest upon the stroke that murders me.
FRIAR LAURENCE O monstrous sin, O rude unthankfulness!
   Thy fault our law calls death, but the mild Prince,
   Taking thy part, hath rushed aside the law   25
   And turned that black word 'death' to 'banishment'.
   This is mere mercy, and thou seest it not.
ROMEO 'Tis torture and not mercy. Heaven is here
   Where Juliet lives. And every cat and dog
   And little mouse, every unworthy thing   30
   Live here in heaven and may look on her,
   But Romeo may not. More validity,
   More honourable state, more courtship lives
   In carrion-flies than Romeo. They may seize
   On the white wonder of fair Juliet's skin   35
   And steal immortal kisses from her lips;
   But Romeo may not, he is banishèd.
   Flies may do this, but I from this must fly.

---

12 banishèd] Q1 *(Banished)*; banishment Q2   14 Than death itself] Q1 *(it selfe)*; Much more then death Q2   15 Hence] Q1; Here Q2   20 world-exiled] Q1 *(world exilde)*; worlds exile Q2   20 'banishment'] Q1 *(banishment)*; banished Q2   23 monstrous] Q1; deadly Q2   24 mild] Q1 *(milde)*; kind Q2   27 mere] Q1 *(meere)*; deare Q2   35 fair . . . skin] Q1 *(subst.)*; deare *Iuliets* hand Q2   36 kisses] Q1; blessing Q2

20 world-exiled exiled from the world. Instead of Q2's 'world's exile' (an objective genitive), Q1 has a compound adjective, a compound of which there is no other occurrence in Shakespeare's work.

20 death Q2 inserts here a few words absent from Q1 ('Then banished, / Is death, mistermd'), the first, short passage in this scene that is absent from Q1.

27 mere pure.

36 kisses In the two earliest versions, Romeo variously laments that he may not steal kisses (Q1)

or blessing (Q2) from Juliet's lips. Q2's Romeo thus construes kissing in religious terms, as he already did when the lovers first met (1.5.92–109).

36 Following this line, Q2 has a four-line passage which is absent from Q1. In the first two lines, Romeo stresses Juliet's 'vestall modestie'. The last two lines, 'This may flyes do, when I from this must flie, / And sayest thou yet, that exile is not death?', is often considered a false start and omitted from modern editions, including NCS (see Evans's long note, p. 202). Pope follows Q1 in omitting all four lines.

O father, hadst thou no strong poison mixed,
No sharp-ground knife, no present mean of death,   40
Though ne'er so mean, but 'banishment'
To torture me withal? Ah, 'banishèd'.
O Friar, the damnèd use that word in hell;
Howling attends it. How hadst thou the heart,
Being a divine, a ghostly confessor,   45
A sin-absolver, and my friend professed,
To mangle me with that word 'banishment'?
FRIAR LAURENCE Thou fond madman, hear me but speak a word.
ROMEO O, thou wilt talk again of banishment.
FRIAR LAURENCE I'll give thee armour to bear off this word,   50
Adversity's sweet milk, philosophy,
To comfort thee though thou be banishèd.
ROMEO Yet 'banishèd'? Hang up philosophy.
Unless philosophy can make a Juliet,
Displant a town, reverse a prince's doom,   55
It helps not, it prevails not, talk no more.
FRIAR LAURENCE O, now I see that madmen have no ears.
ROMEO How should they, when that wise men have no eyes?
FRIAR LAURENCE Let me dispute with thee of thy estate.
ROMEO Thou canst not speak of what thou dost not feel.   60
Wert thou as young as I, Juliet thy love,
An hour but married, Tybalt murderèd,
Doting like me, and like me banishèd,
Then mightst thou speak, then mightst thou tear thy hair
And fall upon the ground as I do now,   65
Taking the measure of an unmade grave.
                    Nurse knocks [within]
FRIAR LAURENCE Romeo, arise, stand up, thou wilt be taken.
I hear one knock, arise, and get thee gone.

---

39 strong poison] Q1 *(poyson)*; poyson Q2   40 present] Q1; sudden Q2   44 hadst] Q1; hast Q2   47 'banishment']
Q1 *(Banishment)*; banished Q2   48 Thou] Q1; Then Q2; Thou Q4   48 but . . . word] Q1 *(subst.)*; a little speake
Q2; heare me speake F   49 talk] Q1 *(talke)*; speake Q2   50 bear off this] Q1 *(beare)*; keepe off that Q2; bear
off that *Pope*   52 be] Q1; art Q2   57 now] Q1; then Q2   57 madmen] Q1; mad man Q2   60 what] Q1; that
Q2   62 murderèd] Q2 *(murdered)*; murdred Q1   64] Q1; *as two lines (* . . . speake / . . . hayre*)* Q2   64 mightst] Q1;
mightest Q2   66 *within*] *Rowe; not in* Q, F

50 bear ward.
67–74 The present passage, while dramatising
the same *action* as in Q2, stands alone in this scene
in departing markedly from the *words* used in Q2.
This may be typical for an action-packed moment
containing much movement and a quick succes-
sion of short speeches in which the exact words
used may be of smaller significance than in a long
speech.

NURSE [*Within*] Ho, Friar!

FRIAR LAURENCE God's will, what wilfulness is this?   70

                She knocks again

NURSE [*Within*] Ho, Friar, open the door!

FRIAR LAURENCE By and by, I come. Who is there?

NURSE [*Within*] One from Lady Juliet.

FRIAR LAURENCE [*Opening the door*] Then come near.

              [*Enter* NURSE]

NURSE O holy Friar, tell me, O holy Friar,   75

    Where is my lady's lord, where's Romeo?

FRIAR LAURENCE There on the ground, with his own tears made

    drunk.

NURSE O, he is even in my mistress' case,

    Just in her case. O woeful sympathy,

    Piteous predicament! Even so lies she,   80

    Weeping and blubb'ring, blubb'ring and weeping.

    Stand up, stand up. Stand and you be a man.

    For Juliet's sake, for her sake, rise and stand.

    Why should you fall into so deep an O?

                  He rises

ROMEO Nurse.   85

NURSE Ah sir, ah sir. Well, death's the end of all.

ROMEO Spakest thou of Juliet? How is it with her?

    Doth she not think me an old murderer

    Now I have stained the childhood of her joy

    With blood removed but little from her own?   90

    Where is she, and how doth she, and what says

    My concealed lady to our cancelled love?

---

69 SD] *Rowe; not in* Q, F   70 wilfulness] Q1 *(wilfulnes);* simplenes Q2   71 SD] *Rowe; not in* Q, F   73 SD] *Rowe; not in* Q, F   74 SD.1] *Capell; not in* Q, F   74 SD.2] *Rowe; not in* Q1   76 Where is] Q1; Wheres Q2   77] Q1; *as two lines (. . . ground, / . . . drunke.)* Q2   81] Q1 *(subst.);* Blubbring and weeping, weeping and blubbring, Q2   84 SD] Q1; *not in* Q2   86 Well, death's] Q1 *(subst.);* deaths Q2   88 she not] Q1; *not* she Q2; she *not* Q5   89 her] Q1; *our* Q2

76 Here as in other lines, Q1 is metrically regular and decasyllabic, whereas Q2, printing 'Wheres' instead of 'Where is', is not. A number of modern editors adopt the reading in Q1.

86 The line is a regular iambic pentameter in Q1, but it is one syllable short in Q2, where Q1's interjection 'Well' is missing.

NURSE   O, she saith nothing, but weeps and pules,
             And now falls on her bed, now on the ground,
             And 'Tybalt' cries, and then on Romeo calls.   95
ROMEO   As if that name, shot from the deadly level of a gun,
             Did murder her, as that name's cursèd hand
             Murdered her kinsman. Ah, tell me, holy Friar,
             In what vile part of this anatomy
             Doth my name lie? Tell me, that I may sack   100
             The hateful mansion?
             He offers to stab himself, and Nurse snatches the dagger away
NURSE   Ah!
FRIAR LAURENCE   Hold, stay thy hand! Art thou a man? Thy form
             Cries out thou art, but thy wild acts denote
             The unreasonable furies of a beast;   105
             Unseemly woman in a seeming man,
             Or ill-beseeming beast in seeming both.
             Thou hast amazed me. By my holy order,

93 but] Q1; sir, but Q2   93 and pules] Q1; and weeps Q2   95 cries . . . calls] Q1 *(subst.)*; calls, and then on *Romeo* cries Q2   98 Ah . . . Friar] Q1 *(subst.)*; Oh tell me Frier, tell me Q2   100 lie] Q1 *(lye)*; lodge Q2   101 SD] Q1; *not in* Q2   102 Ah!] Q1 *(Ah?)*   103 Hold . . . hand] Q1; Hold thy desperate hand Q2   104 denote] Q1; deuote Q2; denote Q4; doe note F2; do note F3   105 furies] Q1 *(furyes)*; furie Q2   107 Or] Q1; And Q2

93 In this line, contrary to line 86 above, Q1 is a syllable short whereas Q2, which adds 'sir' after 'nothing', is a regular iambic pentameter.

95 Following this line, Q2 adds a half line that further insists on Juliet's turmoil: 'And then downe falls againe.'

101 SD Q1's SD, absent from the early editions of the longer text, may provide important information about how this passage was originally acted. Only the first quarto suggests that it is the Nurse who intervenes, and directors, basing their productions on editions of Q2, have often had the Friar grab Romeo's dagger (e.g. the film directed by Franco Zeffirelli of 1968, the BBC version of 1978, or the RSC production of 1995, directed by Adrian Noble). The Nurse's following interjection, also exclusive to Q1, seems to accompany the stage action as described by the SD. In Q2 (which lacks the SD and the Nurse's interjection), the Friar's words, 'Hold thy desperate hand', might look like an implicit SD and be taken to imply that he intervenes. In Q1, by contrast, his many *words* contrasts with the Nurse's *deed* as described by the SD and corroborated by her interjection. Modern editors variously adopt Q1's stage direction

(e.g. NCS) or do not (e.g. Gibbons). See also Erne and Kidnie, Introduction, pp. 2–3, Alan Dessen, *Rescripting Shakespeare: The Text, the Director, and Modern Productions* (Cambridge, 2002), pp. 143–4, and Loehlin, note at 3.3.108 SD.

102 The Nurse's interjection, clearly related to her intervention as spelled out by the preceding stage direction, is absent from the early editions of the longer text.

103–7 The Friar's lines seem ironic in the light of the preceding SD, in which it is the woman and not the man who bravely intervenes.

103–27 At twenty-five lines, Q1's speech is less than half the length of its equivalent in Q2. Garrick's eighteenth-century adaptation omits twenty-seven lines from Q2's speech and is close to Q1 in what it omits and preserves. Modern productions also regularly abridge the speech, most notably, as Loehlin (3.3.108–58n) points out, with a long cut that corresponds almost precisely to the seventeen-line passage of Q2 between what corresponds to Q1's lines 111 and 112. Pope calls this passage 'a great deal of nonsense' and follows Q1 in not including it.

I thought thy disposition better tempered.
Hast thou slain Tybalt? Wilt thou slay thyself   110
And slay thy lady, too, that lives in thee?
Rouse up thy spirits. Thy lady Juliet lives,
For whose sweet sake thou wert but lately dead;
There art thou happy. Tybalt would kill thee,
But thou slewest Tybalt; there art thou happy, too.   115
A pack of blessings lights upon thy back.
Happiness courts thee in his best array,
But like a misbehaved and sullen wench
Thou frown'st upon thy fate that smiles on thee.
Take heed, take heed, for such die miserable.   120
Go, get thee to thy love as was decreed.
Ascend her chamber-window, hence, and comfort her,
But look thou stay not till the watch be set,
For then thou canst not pass to Mantua.
Nurse, provide all things in a readiness.   125
Comfort thy mistress, haste the house to bed,
Which heavy sorrow makes them apt unto.

NURSE   Good Lord, what a thing learning is! I could
      Have stayed here all this night to hear good counsel.
      Well, sir, I'll tell my lady that you will come.   130
ROMEO   Do so, and bid my sweet prepare to chide.
      Farewell, good Nurse.

---

111 that lives in thee] Q1 *(liues); that* in thy life lies Q2   112] Q1 *(subst.);* What rowse thee man, thy *Iuliet* is aliue,
Q2   113 sweet] Q1; deare Q2   113 wert] Q1; wast Q2   115 happy, too] Q1 *(happy too);* happie Q1   116 lights]
Q1; light Q2; lights Q4   117 his] Q1; her Q2   118 misbehaved] Q1 *(misbehaude);* mishaued Q2; misbehau'd Q4
    119] Q1 *(subst.);* Thou puts vp thy fortune and thy loue: Q2; Thou powts vpon thy fortune and thy loue: Q4   122
chamber-window] Q1 *(Chamber Window);* chamber Q2   125–6] Q1 *(subst.);* Go before Nurse, commend me to thy
Lady, / And bid her hasten all the house to bed, Q2   128 what . . . learning] Q1; what learning Q2   128–30] *Arranged
as in Hubbard;* . . . learning is. / . . . night / . . . Sir, / . . . come. Q1   129 this] Q1; the Q2   130 Well, sir] Q1 *(Well
Sir);* My Lord Q2   131 chide] Q2; childe Q1

115 Following this line, Q2's Friar adds another
reason why Romeo may be happy: 'The law that
threatned death becomes thy friend, / And turnes
it to exile, there are thou happie.'
    124 Following this line Q2 has a five-line pas-
sage that is absent from Q1, in which the Friar
mentions the prospect of future reconciliation and
pardon after which Romeo can be called back
to Verona. Because of the absence of a similarly

optimistic outlook at the end of Q1's speech, the
present version seems altogether bleaker.
    128–9 In Q2, the order of these two lines is
inversed: 'O Lord, I could haue staid here all the
night, / To heare good counsel, oh what learning
is:'.
    132 This line and the following SD are unique
to Q1.

Nurse offers to go in and turns again

NURSE Here is a ring, sir, that she bade me give you.

ROMEO How well my comfort is revived by this.

Exit Nurse

FRIAR LAURENCE Sojourn in Mantua. I'll find out your man,   135
    And he shall signify from time to time
    Every good hap that doth befall thee here.
    Farewell.

ROMEO But that a joy past joy cries out on me,
    It were a grief so brief to part with thee.   140

[Exeunt]

[13] *Enter old* CAPULET *and his* WIFE, *with County* PARIS

CAPULET Things have fallen out, sir, so unluckily
    That we have had no time to move my daughter.
    Look ye, sir, she loved her kinsman dearly,
    And so did I. Well, we were born to die.
    Wife, where's your daughter? Is she in her chamber?   5
    I think she means not to come down tonight.

PARIS These times of woe afford no time to woo.
    Madam, farewell. Commend me to your daughter.

Paris offers to go in, and Capulet calls him again

CAPULET Sir Paris, I'll make a desperate tender of my child.
    I think she will be ruled in all respects by me.   10
    But soft, what day is this?

133] Q1 *(subst.)*; Here sir, a Ring she bid me giue you sir: Q2   137 that ... here] Q1 *(heere)*; to you, that chaunces here Q2   139 cries] Q1 *(cryes)*; calls Q2   140 SD] Q2; *not in* Q1   2 my] Q1; our Q2   3 ye, sir] Q1 *(yee Sir)*; you Q2   3 kinsman] Q1; kinsman *Tybalt* Q2   7 time] Q1; times Q2   8 farewell] Q1 *(farwell)*; goodnight Q2   9 child] Q1; childes loue Q2

Scene 13

Act 3, Scene 4 in the NCS edition.
This scene is somewhat shorter than its Q2 equivalent (twenty-seven lines as opposed to thirty-five), as a few brief passages present in the longer text (including Lady Capulet's only two lines) leave no trace in Q1. The remaining lines usually have their equivalent in the second quarto, although they are rarely altogether identical.

5 Capulet's questions have no equivalent in Q2.
6 Following the equivalent of this line, Q2 prints two verses ('I promise you, but for your companie, / I would haue bene a bed an houre ago.') which appear in Q1 in identical form in a Capulet speech in an earlier scene (see 4.191–2 and note).

8 SD Q1's SD has no equivalent in Q2. Instead, Q2 inserts a two-line speech by Lady Capulet ('I will, and know her mind early to morrow, / To night shees mewed vp to her heauines') which is absent from Q1.

10 Following this line, Q2 adds three and a half lines to Capulet's speech which leave no trace in Q1: 'nay more, I doubt it not. / Wife go you to her ere you go to bed, / Acquaint her here, of my sonne Paris loue, / And bid her, marke you me? On wendsday next.' As Capulet, in these lines, already plans the wedding for Wednesday, the statement in his next speech, 'then Wednesday is too soon' (in Q1 and Q2), refers back in Q2 to words not present in Q1, which supports the view that Q2 was

PARIS Monday, my lord.

CAPULET O, then Wednesday is too soon.

    On Thursday let it be, you shall be married.

    We'll make no great ado, a friend or two or so.   15

    For look ye, sir, Tybalt being slain so lately,

    It will be thought we held him carelessly,

    If we should revel much. Therefore we will have

    Some half a dozen friends and make no more ado.

    But what say you to Thursday?   20

PARIS My lord, I wish that Thursday were tomorrow.

CAPULET Wife, go you to your daughter ere you go to bed.

    Acquaint her with the County Paris' love.

    Farewell, my lord, till Thursday next.

    Wife, get you to your daughter. Light to my chamber!   25

    Afore me, it is so very very late

    That we may call it early by and by.

                                             Exeunt

[14] *Enter* ROMEO *and* JULIET *at the window*

JULIET Wilt thou be gone? It is not yet near day.

    It was the nightingale and not the lark

14] Q1 *(subst.);* A thursday let it be, a thursday tell her / She shall be married to this noble Earle: / Will you be ready? do you like this haste? Q2   **15** make] Q1; keepe Q2   **16** look ye] Q1; harke you Q2   **16** lately] Q1; late Q2   **17** will] Q1; may Q2   **18** should revel] Q1 *(reuell);* reuell Q2   **19** make . . . ado] Q1 *(adoe);* there an end Q2   **21** wish] Q1 *(wishe);* would Q2   **26** very very] Q1; very Q2   **0** SD *at the window*] Q1; *aloft* Q2

abridged, not Q1 expanded. The omitted lines in fact correspond quite closely to lines 22 to 23. Q2 thus contains a repetition which Q1 avoids. See Introduction, pp. 9–10.

23 This line in Q1 corresponds closely to a Q2 line in an earlier speech by Capulet in this scene that is absent from Q1 ('Acquaint her here, of my sonne Paris loue'; see note at 10 above) but has no direct equivalent in Capulet's final speech in Q2.

25–6 Light . . . me Capulet's words may or may not be addressed to a servant onstage who might have entered with the other characters at the beginning of the scene or enter at this point. 'Afore me', while it is quite possibly a simple interjection, could also be a direction to a servant to carry the light ahead of him.

27 Following the end of this scene, at the bottom of G2v, Q1 indicates a break by a row of printer's ornament, followed by another row at the top of the following page, above the beginning of the next scene.

Scene 14

Act 3, Scene 5 in the NCS edition.

This scene reduces the 242 lines in Q2 to 196 lines by means of short cuts (all fewer than ten lines) as well as through a number of condensations and substitutions. The scene can in fact be divided into two unequal parts in terms of their relationship to Q2: the initial dialogue between Romeo and Juliet (1–55) omits (and, in fact, partly transposes) a five-line passage in the longer text (3.5.37–41), but otherwise corresponds closely to Q2 with more than two thirds of the lines having identical or almost identical lines in Q2. The rest of the scene (56–196) corresponds far less closely to Q2 and contains a good number of substitutions within and between lines, with less than one third of its lines having equivalents or near-equivalents in the longer text. The resulting text is often metrically irregular, although the corresponding Q2 lines are not (e.g. lines 7, 43, 57, 67, 79–80, 130). Capulet and the Nurse's speeches are particularly irregular: more than a third of their lines are either short or long.

That pierced the fearful hollow of thine ear.
Nightly she sings on yon pomegranate tree.
Believe me, love, it was the nightingale.   5
ROMEO It was the lark, the herald of the morn,
And not the nightingale. See, love, what envious streaks
Do lace the severing clouds in yonder east.
Night's candles are burnt out, and jocund day
Stands tiptoes on the misty mountain tops.   10
I must be gone and live, or stay and die.
JULIET Yon light is not daylight, I know it, I.
It is some meteor that the sun exhaled
To be this night to thee a torch-bearer
And light thee on thy way to Mantua.   15
Then stay awhile, thou shalt not go so soon.
ROMEO Let me stay here, let me be ta'en and die.
If thou wilt have it so, I am content.
I'll say yon grey is not the morning's eye,
It is the pale reflex of Cynthia's brow.   20
I'll say it is the nightingale that beats
The vaulty heaven so high above our heads,
And not the lark, the messenger of morn.
Come, death, and welcome. Juliet wills it so.
What says my love? Let's talk, 'tis not yet day.   25
JULIET It is, it is. Be gone, fly hence, away!
It is the lark that sings so out of tune,
Straining harsh discords and unpleasing sharps.
Some say the lark makes sweet division.

4 yon] Q1; yond Q2   7 And not the] Q1; No Q2   7 See] Q1; looke Q2   7 streaks] Q1 *(strakes)*   10 tiptoes] Q1;
tipto Q2   12 yon] Q1; Yond Q2   13 exhaled] *Hosley;* exhales Q1, Q3; exhale Q2   14 this . . . thee] Q1; to thee this
night Q2   16 Then . . . awhile] Q1; Therefore stay yet Q2   16 shalt . . . soon] *Pope;* shalt not goe soone Q1; needst
not to be gone Q2   17 stay here] Q1; be tane Q2   17 ta'en and die] Q1 *(subst.);* put to death Q2   18] Q1 *(subst.);* I
am content, so thou wilt haue it so. Q2   20 It is] Q1; Tis but Q2   21] Q1 *(subst.);* Nor that is not the Larke whose
noates do beate Q2   23] Q1 *(subst.);* I haue more care to stay then will to go: Q2   25 What . . . love?] Q1 *(subst.);* How
ist my soule Q2   25 'tis not yet] Q1 *(tis);* it is not Q2   26 Be . . . hence] Q1 *(subst.);* hie hence be gone Q2

13 Richard Hosley ('The corrupting influence
of the bad quarto on the received text of *Romeo and
Juliet*', *SQ* 4 (1953), 11–33, 20) argues convincingly that 'exhaled' must be the correct reading:
the present light is precisely not daylight emanat-
ing from the sun but a meteor which was thought
to result from vapours drawn up ('exhaled') from
the earth to the sun and then ignited. Q1 reads
'exhales', Q2 'exhale'.
    16 Pope preferred Q1's reading to Q2's ('There-
fore stay yet, thou needst not to be gone'), but

emended the irregular 'shalt not goe soone' to the
more natural 'shalt not go so soon', an emendation that was taken over by Hubbard. The word
'so' may have been accidentally omitted because
the following word, 'soon', begins with the same
letters.
    27–31 These lines are so close to Q2 – with only
two variants, incidental or substantive – that the
Q2 compositor seems likely to have made use of Q1
(Jowett).

This doth not so, for this divideth us.   30
Some say the lark and loathèd toad changed eyes.
I would that now they had changed voices too,
Since arm from arm her voice doth us affray,
Hunting thee hence with hunt's-up to the day.
So now, be gone, more light and light it grows.   35

ROMEO   More light and light, more dark and dark our woes.
Farewell, my love, one kiss, and I'll descend.

He goeth down [using the rope ladder].

JULIET   Art thou gone so, my lord, my love, my friend?
I must hear from thee every day in the hour,
For in an hour there are many minutes.   40
Minutes are days, so will I number them.
O, by this count I shall be much in years
Ere I see thee again.

ROMEO   Farewell.
I will omit no opportunity   45
That may convey my greetings, love, to thee.

JULIET   O, think'st thou we shall ever meet again?

ROMEO   No doubt, no doubt, and all this woe shall serve
For sweet discourses in the time to come.

JULIET   O God, I have an ill-divining soul!   50
Methinks I see thee, now thou art below
Like one dead in the bottom of a tomb.
Either mine eyesight fails, or thou look'st pale.

---

30 this] Q1; she Q2   **31** changed] *Rowe* (chang'd); change Q, F   **32** I . . . now] Q1; O now I would Q2   **33** her] Q1; that Q2   **35** So] Q1; O Q2   my love] Q1 (Loue); farewell Q2   **37** SD *using the rope ladder*] *This edn, following Jowett; not in* Q1   **38** my lord . . . friend] Q1 (*subst.*); loue, Lord, ay husband, friend Q2   **40** an . . . minutes] Q1 (*subst.*); a minute there are many dayes Q2   **43** see thee again] Q1 (againe); againe behold my *Romeo* Q2   **44-5**] *Arranged as in* Q2; *as one line* Q1   **48** No . . . doubt] Q1; I doubt it not Q2   **48** this woe] Q1; these woes Q2   **49** the time] Q1; our times Q2   **51** below] Q1; so lowe Q2   **52** Like] Q1; As Q2   **53** mine] Q1; my Q2

36 Following this line, Q2 has a short passage in which the Nurse enters and announces the arrival of Juliet's mother. The effect of this is that Q1, contrary to Q2, begins with a self-contained movement with Romeo and Juliet alone. See Introduction, p. 31.

37 SD The rope ladder probably has to be disposed of at this stage, perhaps, as Hosley suggests, by Juliet's 'dropping it to Romeo, who carries it off stage' ('Upper stage', 376).

40-1 The equivalent passage in Q2, 'For in a minute there are many dayes', also expresses the slow passage of time by means of a paradox, although its logic differs slightly from Q1: minutes feel as long as days, according to Q1, whereas, even more extravagantly, one minute feels like many days, according to Q2. Either version resembles but is not identical with passages in Brooke's narrative poem: 'Eche minute seemed an howre, and every howre a day' (line 747); 'eche howre seemes twenty yere' (line 823).

43 In Q1's short line, as elsewhere, the language is more immediate and direct than in Q2 ('Ere I againe behold my Romeo').

ROMEO And trust me, love, in my eye so do you.
      Dry sorrow drinks our blood. Adieu, adieu.   *Exit*   55

Enter NURSE *hastily [below]*

NURSE Madam, beware, take heed, the day is broke.
      Your mother's coming to your chamber, make all sure.
      [Juliet] goeth down from the window.

Enter CAPULET'S WIFE *[below]*

CAPULET'S WIFE Where are you, daughter?
NURSE What lady, lamb, what Juliet?
JULIET *[Within]* How now, who calls?   60
NURSE It is your mother.

*[*JULIET *enters below]*

CAPULET'S WIFE Why, how now, Juliet?
JULIET Madam, I am not well.

---

55 SD.2 *below*] *This edn; not in* Q, F   57 SD.1 *Juliet*] *This edn; She* Q1   57 SD.2] *This edn; Enter Juliets Mother, Nurse*
Q1   57 SD.2 *below*] NCS; *not in* Q, F   60 SD] *This edn; not in* Q1   61 SD] *This edn; not in* Q1

---

55 After Romeo's departure, Q2 has a five-line speech by Juliet in which she complains to 'fickle Fortune', followed by Lady Capulet's arrival signalled by the simple SD, '*Enter Mother*'.

57 SD.1, 2 Between the two SDs, '*She goeth down from the window*' and '*Enter Iuliets Mother, Nurse*', Q1 inserts a row of printer's ornaments which elsewhere occur between scenes. The action is continuous, however, and the Nurse may remain onstage. Q1 provides in fact two entrances for the Nurse. The original SD at this point reads '*Enter Iuliets Mother, Nurse*', even though the Nurse already entered two lines earlier. The fact that Q2's Nurse makes her first appearance earlier in the scene (see note at 36 above) may suggest that the Nurse's double entrance results from local revision. The present SD ambiguously states that '*She*' goes down from the window. Even though the preceding speech is by the Nurse, the ensuing dramatic sequence makes clear that Juliet descends to the main stage. What happens is that Juliet's bedroom moves from the upper to the lower platform. As Levenson points out, 'Elizabethan staging would have allowed Juliet to descend from upper to main level by an inner staircase . . . the audience imagining a change of scene from bedroom window to chamber itself' (Oxford, 3.5.67.1n; see also NCS and Hosley, 'Upper stage', 374, for discussions of the staging of this passage; and see Introduction, pp. 28–9).

58–61 These lines parallel the beginning of the third scene (3.1–6; Q2 is substantively identical). Q2 provides no dialogue during the moment of Juliet's descent offstage, and the resulting awkwardness in performance may have led to the present addition in Q1. See Introduction, pp. 28–9.

60 SD This and the SD in the following line follow the compelling analysis of the staging of this moment by Hosley ('Upper stage', 374). See also Irace, p. 87.

62 Hubbard starts a new scene with this verse.

62 SH In earlier Q1 scenes, the SH for Capulet's Wife is '*Wife*' (or '*W*'), but it is '*Moth*' (or '*Mo*'), short for 'Mother', throughout this scene, emphasising her role in interacting with her daughter. The speech headings for Juliet's father, by contrast, are '*Capo*' (which, incidentally, is Italian for 'head' or 'chief', from Latin 'caput') and '*Cap*' throughout the scene. In the equivalent scene in Q2, '*Ca*' alternates with '*Fa*' (for 'Father') and '*Mo*' (or '*M*') with '*La*' (for 'Lady') – plus one occurrence of '*Wi*' (for Capulet's Wife). These alternations in Q2 may well reflect Shakespeare's manuscript in which he seems to have chosen SHs to reflect the way he thought of characters at the particular moments when he composed their speeches.

CAPULET'S WIFE What, evermore weeping for your cousin's death?
　　　　I think thou'lt wash him from his grave with tears.   65
JULIET I cannot choose, having so great a loss.
CAPULET'S WIFE I cannot blame thee,
　　　　But it grieves thee more that villain lives.
JULIET What villain, madam?
CAPULET'S WIFE That villain Romeo.   70
JULIET Villain and he are many miles asunder.
CAPULET'S WIFE Content thee, girl. If I could find a man,
　　　　I soon would send to Mantua, where he is,
　　　　That should bestow on him so sure a draught
　　　　As he should soon bear Tybalt company.   75
JULIET Find you the means, and I'll find such a man.
　　　　For whilst he lives my heart shall ne'er be light
　　　　Till I behold him – dead – is my poor heart
　　　　Thus for a kinsman vexed.
CAPULET'S WIFE Well, let that pass. I come to bring thee joyful
　　　　news.   80
JULIET And joy comes well in such a needful time.
CAPULET'S WIFE Well, then, thou hast a careful father, girl,
　　　　And one who, pitying thy needful state,
　　　　Hath found thee out a happy day of joy.
JULIET What day is that, I pray you?

---

64 What] Q1; *not in* Q2   65 I think thou'lt] Q1 *(subst.);* What wilt thou Q2   68 it . . . more] Q1 *(subst.);* thou weepst
not so much Q2   69 villain] Q1 *(Villaine);* same villaine Q2   71 are] Q1; be Q2   74 should] Q1; shall Q2   74 bestow
on him] Q1; giue him Q2   74 draught] Q1; dram Q2   75 should] Q1; shall Q2   75 bear] Q1 *(beare);* keepe Q2   78
him – dead –] *Pope;* him, dead Q1; him. Dead Q2   79 Thus] Q1; so Q2   80 news] Q1 *(newes);* tidings Q2   81
needful] Q1; needie Q2   82 then] Q1; well Q2   82 girl] Q1 *(Girle);* child Q2   83 pitying . . . state] Q1 *(subst.);* to
put thee from thy heauines Q2   84 found thee] Q1; sorted   84 happy] Q1 *(happie);* sudden Q2

65 Following this line, Q2 prints a six-line passage absent from Q1 that develops Capulet's Wife's
exhortations to Juliet.

71 As Levenson points out, this line need not
necessarily be spoken as an aside as 'Villain' and
'he' can be understood not only as opposites but
also as synonyms: that villainous Romeo is far
away. After this line, Q2 prints a five-line passage absent from Q1 in which, as in lines 76–79,
Juliet's intentionally ambiguous words deceive her
mother.

72–5 In Q1, Capulet's Wife formulates a hypo-
thetical intention to have Romeo killed ('If I
could find a man'), whereas in Q2 she unam-
biguously asserts that 'We will haue vengeance

for it, feare thou not' and 'Ile send to one in
Mantua.'

76 This line appears thirteen lines later in Q2
and is assigned to Juliet's mother (who addresses
her daughter with 'thou' as opposed to Juliet's
'you'). Q1 thus adds here another deliberately
ambiguous statement, Juliet making her mother
understand that she would like to take an active
part in the revenge for Tybalt's death, but also
covertly asserting that she herself would like to go
to Mantua where Romeo is, if only her mother will
provide the means to get her there.

79 Following this line, Q2's speech continues
for seven more lines in which Juliet is deliberately
ambiguous about Romeo.

CAPULET'S WIFE   Marry, my child,   85
     The gallant, young, and youthful gentleman,
     The County Paris, at Saint Peter's Church,
     Early next Thursday morning must provide
     To make you there a glad and joyful bride.
JULIET   Now by Saint Peter's Church and Peter too,   90
     He shall not there make me a joyful bride.
     Are these the news you had to tell me of?
     Marry, here are news indeed! Madam,
     I will not marry yet. And when I do,
     It shall be rather Romeo, whom I hate,   95
     Than County Paris, that I cannot love.

Enter old CAPULET

CAPULET'S WIFE   Here comes your father, you may tell him so.
CAPULET   [*To Juliet*] Why, how now, evermore show'ring? In one
     little body
     Thou resemblest a sea, a bark, a storm.
     For this thy body, which I term a bark,   100
     Still floating in thy ever-falling tears
     And tossed with sighs arising from thy heart,
     Will without succour shipwreck presently.
     But hear you, wife, what, have you sounded her?
     What says she to it?   105
CAPULET'S WIFE   I have, but she will none; she thanks ye.
     Would God that she were married to her grave.

---

86 youthful] Q1 *(youthfull)*; Noble Q2   88 morning] Q1; morne Q2   89 you] Q1; thee Q2   89 glad and joyful] Q1 *(ioyfull)*; ioyfull Q2   91 there make me] Q1; make me there Q2   93–5] *Arranged as in Hubbard;* Marrie . . . yet / . . . hate, Q1   93 here] Q1; these Q2   94 do,] Q1 *(doo)*; do, I sweare Q2   95–6 rather . . . Paris] Q1 *(subst.)*; Romeo . . . / Rather then Paris Q2   96 SD] Q1; *Enter* Capulet *and Nurse.* Q2   97 you . . . so] Q1; tell him so your selfe Q2   98 SD] *This edn; not in* Q1   98–9] *Arranged as in Hubbard;* Why . . . showring? / . . . storme: Q1   99 resemblest] Q1; countefaits Q2   104–5] *Arranged as in Hubbard; as one line* Q1   106 thanks ye] Q1 *(thankes)*; giue you thankes Q2   107 Would . . . she] Q1; I would the foole Q2

89 you In Q1, Juliet's mother uses 'you' at the moment she announces to her daughter the planned wedding, whereas Q2 preserves 'thee' which she has used earlier in the scene (in Q1 and Q2). For 'thou' and 'you' in Shakespeare, see Crystal, 450–1.

98–105 Q1 condenses into eight lines a speech that consists of twelve in Q2. Part of the condensation results from the fact that Q2 spells out the various correspondences of its extended metaphor ('thy eyes, which I may call the sea'; 'the windes thy sighes'), whereas Q1 does not.

106 Q1's spelling is 'thankes ye' which, if pronounced as three syllables (analogously to 'thanketh ye'), makes the line regular. With modernised spelling, the line is irregular and short.

CAPULET   What, will she not? Doth she not thank us?
      Doth she not wax proud?
JULIET   Not proud ye have, but thankful that ye have.   110
      Proud can I never be of that I hate,
      But thankful even for hate that is meant love.
CAPULET   'Proud' and 'I thank you' and 'I thank you not'
      And yet 'not proud'? What's here, chop-logic?
      Proud me no prouds, nor thank me no thanks,   115
      But fettle your fine joints on Thursday next
      To go with Paris to Saint Peter's Church,
      Or I will drag you on a hurdle thither.
      Out, you green-sickness baggage! Out, you tallow-face.
JULIET   Good father, hear me speak.   120

She kneels down

CAPULET   I tell thee what: either resolve on Thursday next
      To go with Paris to Saint Peter's Church,
      Or henceforth never look me in the face.
      Speak not, reply not, for my fingers itch.
      Why, wife, we thought that we were scarcely blessed   125
      That God had sent us but this only child,

108–9] *Arranged as in Hubbard; as prose* Q1   **108** not] Q1; none Q2   **108** thank us] Q1 *(thanke vs); giue vs thanks* Q2   **109** wax] Q1 *(wexe); not in* Q2   **110** ye . . . ye] Q1 *(subst.);* you . . . you Q2   **111** that] Q1; what Q2   **114** chop-logic] Q1 *(chop logicke);* chopt lodgick Q2   **115** thanks] Q1 *(thankes);* thankings Q2   **116** on] Q1; gainst Q2   **118** you] Q1; thee Q2   **119** Out, you tallow-face] Q1 *(subst.);* You tallow face Q2; Out you Tallow-face F4   **120** SD] Q1 *(subst.); not in* Q2   **123** henceforth never] Q1 *(neuer);* neuer after Q2   **125** thought . . . blessed] Q1 *(blest);* scarce thought vs blest Q2   **126** sent] Q1; lent Q2

108–9 Like Capulet's previous speech, the present one is significantly shorter than its five-line equivalent in Q2.

109 wax become.

113–19 While consisting of material of which almost all is present in Q2, Capulet's speech contains various minor transpositions and abridges Q2's eight-and-a-half lines to seven.

118 you Like Juliet's mother, her father addresses her with 'you' at a point where Q2 has 'thee' (see note at 89 above).

120 In Q2, Juliet's speech is preceded by a speech by Capulet's Wife: 'Fie, fie, what are you mad?' In Q1 Juliet's mother does not intervene until line 137.

120 SD Q2 has no SD at this point, but Juliet's speech implies the equivalent stage action: 'Good Father, I beseech you on my knees, / Heare me with patience, but to speake a word.' The more theatrical Q1 thus omits verbal material which a spectator sees and therefore does not need to be told. In other words, if we assume that the passage in Q2 ensures that the actor kneels down – the words thus constituting a playwright's implicit SD for the actor – then it may be significant that this implicit SD has been eliminated from the more theatrical Q1. Another assumption is that the implicit SD is there for readers in general, readers who only know that Juliet kneels down because she says so. Regarding such implicit SDs, see Ann Pasternak Slater, *Shakespeare the Director* (Brighton, 1982) and David Bevington, *Action Is Eloquence: Shakespeare's Language of Gesture* (Cambridge, MA, 1984).

121–2 Q2's Capulet is even fiercer than his equivalent in Q1: 'Hang thee young baggage, disobedient wretch, / I tell thee what, get thee to Church a Thursday.'

But now I see this one is one too much,
And that we have a cross in having her.
NURSE Marry, God in heaven bless her, my lord,
You are to blame to rate her so.   130
CAPULET And why, my Lady Wisdom? Hold your tongue,
Good Prudence, smatter with your gossips, go.
NURSE Why, my lord, I speak no treason.
CAPULET O God 'i' good e'en!
Utter your gravity over a gossip's bowl,   135
For here we need it not.
CAPULET'S WIFE My lord, ye are too hot.
CAPULET God's blessèd mother, wife, it mads me.
Day, night, early, late, at home, abroad,
Alone, in company, waking, or sleeping,   140
Still my care hath been to see her matched.
And having now found out a gentleman
Of princely parentage, youthful, and nobly trained,
Stuffed, as they say, with honourable parts,
Proportioned as one's heart could wish a man,   145
And then to have a wretched whining fool,
A puling mammet in her fortune's tender,

---

128 cross] Q1 *(crosse)*; curse Q2   134 e'en] Q1 *(den)*   137 ye] Q1; You Q2   138 mads me] Q1; makes me mad
Q2   139 early . . . abroad] Q1; houre, tide, time, worke, play Q2   141 see] Q1; haue Q2   142 found out] Q1; prouided
Q2   143 princely] Q1 *(Princely)*; noble Q2   143 trained] Q1 *(trained)*; liand Q2; allied Q3; ligned *Gibbons;* lined
Jowett   145 heart could] Q1 *(coulde)*; thought would Q2   146–7 whining . . . mammet] Q1 *(subst.)*; puling foole, /
A whining mammet Q2

130 **to blame** The spelling in Q1 is 'too blame'
which could mean either 'to blame' or 'too blame-
worthy'. See David Bevington, 'Modern spelling:
the hard choices', in Erne and Kidnie, pp. 145–6.

136 After the equivalent line, Q2 inserts a short
speech by the Nurse, 'May not one speake?', followed by the first line of Capulet's ensuing speech:
'Peace you mumbling foole'.

138–59 Capulet's speech is often metrically
irregular with a number of short or long lines (lines
138, 143, 149, 153, 157).

138 **mads** maddens, makes insane (*OED v.* 2).

139–40 Q1 and Q2 present Capulet's anger
through a series of opposites: 'Day, night' and
'Alone, in company' (Q1 and Q2); 'early, late',
'at home, abroad', and 'waking, or sleeping' (Q1
only), and 'worke, play' (Q2 only). Q2 interrupts

the series of opposites with the words 'houre, tide,
time', leading some recent editors to conclude that
these words constitute an 'unclearly deleted "first
shot"' (NCS).

142 **found out** Q2 and Brooke (line 1962), in a
closely parallel passage, agree on the word 'provided' where Q1 has 'found out'. See Introduction,
pp. 10–11.

143 **princely** As in the previous line, Q1 is different from both Q2 ('noble') and Brooke, where
Juliet's father comments on the 'noblenes . . . of
the race, / From whence his [County Paris'] father
came' (lines 1967–8). See Introduction, pp. 10–11.

143 **trained** Q2's 'liand' is problematic. Later
editions – starting with Q3 – have tried to clarify
the passage, occasionally by adopting the reading
in Q1 (e.g., Capell, Hudson, Furness).

To say 'I cannot love, I am too young,
I pray you pardon me.'
[*To Juliet*] But if you cannot wed, I'll pardon you!   150
Graze where you will, you shall not house with me.
Look to it, think on't. I do not use to jest.
I tell ye what: Thursday is near.
Lay hand on heart, advise, bethink yourself.
If you be mine, I'll give you to my friend.   155
If not, hang, drown, starve, beg, die in the streets!
For, by my soul, I'll never more acknowledge thee,
Nor what I have shall ever do thee good.
Think on't, look to't. I do not use to jest.   *Exit*

JULIET Is there no pity hanging in the clouds   160
That looks into the bottom of my woes?
[*To her mother*] I do beseech you, madam, cast me not away.
Defer this marriage for a day or two,
Or, if you cannot, make my marriage bed
In that dim monument where Tybalt lies.   165

CAPULET'S WIFE Nay, be assured, I will not speak a word.
Do what thou wilt, for I have done with thee.   *Exit*

JULIET Ah Nurse, what comfort? What counsel canst thou give me?
NURSE Now trust me, madam, I know not what to say.
Your Romeo, he is banished, and all the world to nothing.   170
He never dares return to challenge you.

---

148 say] Q1; answere Q2   148–9] *Arranged as in Hubbard; as one line* Q1   150 SD] *This edn; not in* Q, F   150 if] Q1; and Q2   150 cannot] Q1; will not Q2   155 If] Q1; And Q2   156–7] *Arranged as in Hubbard;* If . . . beg, / . . . Soule / . . . thee, Q1   156 If not] Q1; And you be not Q2   156 drown . . . beg] Q1 *(subst.);* beg, starue Q2   157 never more] Q1 *(neuer);* nere Q2   158 I have] Q1 *(haue);* is mine Q2   158 ever] Q1 *(euer);* neuer Q2   159] Q1 *(subst.);* Trust too't, bethinke you, ile not be forsworne. Q2   160 hanging] Q1; sitting Q2   161 looks] Q1 *(lookes);* sees Q2   161 woes] Q1; greefe Q2   162 SD] *This edn; not in* Q, F   162 I . . . madam] Q1 *(subst.);* O sweet my Mother Q2   163 Defer] Q1; Delay Q2   163 a day or two] Q1; a month, a weeke Q2   164 cannot] Q1; do not Q2   164 marriage] Q1 *(mariage);* Bridall Q2   166 Nay, be assured] Q1 *(subst.);* Talke not to me Q2   167 what] Q1; as Q2   170 Your Romeo] Q1 *(Romeo);* Romeo Q2   171 He . . . return] Q1 *(subst.);* That he dares nere come back Q2

159 I do . . . jest Q1, contrary to Q2, repeats words Capulet has already spoken a few lines earlier in the same speech (152 above).

162 I . . . madam Juliet's address to her mother is more formal in Q1 than in Q2, which is in keeping with the more formal pronouns used by her parents (see notes at 89 and 118 above).

164 marriage bed Q2 has 'Bridall bed'. Shakespeare uses both: 'marriage bed', for instance, in *John* (3.1.171, 5.2.93) and 'bridal bed' in *Rom.* (5.3.12; see below, 20.7).

168 In Q2, the speech has an additional eight lines in which Juliet analyses in rhetorically intricate language her impossible situation.

169–78 The Nurse's speech is metrically irregular and contains several short and long lines (170, 173–5), some of which have been relineated.

171 Q1's Nurse, contrary to Q2's, does not go on to mention the alternative possibility that 'if he do [i.e. if Romeo does return], it needs must be by stealth'.

Now I think good you marry with this County.
O, he is a gallant gentleman.
Romeo is but a dish-clout in respect of him.
I promise you,   175
I think you happy in this second match.
As for your husband, he is dead, or 'twere
As good he were, for you have no use of him.

JULIET Speak'st thou this from thy heart?

NURSE Ay, and from my soul, or else beshrew them both.   180

JULIET Amen.

NURSE What say you, madam?

JULIET Well, thou hast comforted me wondrous much.
I pray thee, go thy ways unto my mother.
Tell her I am gone, having displeased my father,   185
To Friar Laurence' cell, to confess me
And to be absolved.

NURSE I will, and this is wisely done.   [*Exit*]

She looks after Nurse

JULIET Ancient damnation! O most cursèd fiend!
Is it more sin to wish me thus forsworn,   190
Or to dispraise him with the self-same tongue
That thou hast praised him with above compare
So many thousand times? Go, counsellor,
Thou and my bosom henceforth shall be twain.
I'll to the Friar to know his remedy.   195
If all fail else, I have the power to die.   *Exit*

---

172 good] Q1; best Q2   172 marry] Q1; married Q2   172 this] Q1; the Q2   173–5] *Arranged as in Levenson;* Oh . . . dishclout / . . . you Q1   173 gallant] Q1; louely Q2   174 in respect of] Q1 (In); to Q2   176 you happy] Q1; you are happie Q2   177–8] *Arranged as in Hubbard;* As . . . dead: / . . . him. Q1   179 this] Q1; *not in* Q2   180 Ay . . . soul] Q1 *(subst.);* And from my soule too Q2   180 or else] Q1 *(els);* else Q2   183 wondrous] Q1; maruellous Q2   184 mother] Q1; Lady Q2   186 Friar Laurence'] Q1 *(subst.); Laurence* Q2   186 confess me] Q1 *(confesse);* make confession Q2   188 SD.1] Q4 *(subst.); not in* Q1, Q2   188 SD.2] Q1 *(subst.); not in* Q2   189 cursèd] Q1 *(cursed);* wicked Q2   191 him] Q1; my Lord   191 the self-same] Q1 *(selfe same);* that same Q2   196 fail else] Q1 *(faile els);* else faile Q2   196 I have the] Q1 *(haue);* my selfe haue Q2

174 **in respect of** in comparison with (*OED* Respect *n.* 3.a.).

175 Q2's Nurse at this point likens Paris to an eagle in a short, two-line passage with no equivalent in Q1.

176 **I think you** I consider you (*OED* Think *v.²* 10.a).

176–8 The conclusion to the Nurse's speech condenses into three lines what occupies four lines in Q2, where she adds that the second match 'excels

your first, or if it did not, / Your first is dead'.

188 SD.2 It is very rare for stage directions in Shakespeare's plays to record characters looking at something or someone (as opposed to out of a window, as in *Shr.* 5.1.13). Lady Anne, in Folio *R3*, 'looks scornfully' at Richard (1.2.158). The only other instance recorded in Dessen and Thomson is also in Q1 *Rom.*, Friar Laurence who, in the last scene, '*stoops and looks on the blood and weapons*' (20.94 SD).

[15]   *Enter* FRIAR [LAURENCE] *and* PARIS

FRIAR LAURENCE   On Thursday, say ye? The time is very short.
PARIS   My father Capulet will have it so,
      And I am nothing slack to slow his haste.
FRIAR LAURENCE   You say you do not know the lady's mind?
      Uneven is the course, I like it not.   5
PARIS   Immoderately she weeps for Tybalt's death,
      And therefore have I little talked of love,
      For Venus smiles not in a house of tears.
      Now sir, her father thinks it dangerous
      That she doth give her sorrow so much sway,   10
      And in his wisdom hastes our marriage
      To stop the inundation of her tears,
      Which, too much minded by herself alone,
      May be put from her by society.
      Now do ye know the reason of this haste.   15
FRIAR LAURENCE   [*Aside*] I would I knew not why it should be slowed.

                    Enter [JULIET]

              Here comes the lady to my cell.
PARIS   Welcome, my love, my lady, and my wife.
JULIET   That may be, sir, when I may be a wife.
PARIS   That 'may be' must be, love, on Thursday next.   20
JULIET   What must be shall be.
FRIAR LAURENCE   That's a certain text.

---

0 SD] Q1 *(Enter Fryer and Paris.)*; Enter Frier and Countie Paris. Q2   1 say ye] Q1; sir Q2   3 slack to slow] Q1 *(slacke)*; slow to slacke Q2   7 talked] Q1 *(talkt)*; talke Q2   9 thinks] Q1 *(thinkes)*; counts Q2   10 doth] Q1; do Q2   15 ye] Q1; you Q2   16 SD.1] *Theobald; not in* Q, F   16 SD.2] Q2 *(Iuliet)*; *Enter Paris.* Q1   17 Here] Q1 *(Heere)*; Looke sir, here Q2   17 to] Q1; toward Q2   18 Welcome, my love] Q1 *(subst.)*; Happily met Q2

Scene 15
Act 4, Scene 1 in the NCS edition.
This scene can be divided into two parts, a first part up to and a second part after Paris's exit. The first part (lines 1–42) corresponds very closely to the text in Q2 (4.1.1–43). The rest of the scene reduces 83 lines in Q2 (4.1.44–126) to 50 (lines 43–92): a nine-line passage in Juliet's first long speech (4.1.50–67) leaves no trace in Q1, and the last twenty-eight lines in Q2 (4.1.99–126) are reduced to seven in the shorter text. The scene in Q1 thus consists of two parts of almost identical length, whereas the second part is by far the longer in Q2. The main difference is that Q1 telescopes and

speeds up Juliet's encounter with Friar Laurence. Q1 indicates a break by a row of printer's ornaments above the beginning of the scene.
     3 slack to slow This inverses the order of Q2's 'slow to slacke'.
     7 talked Modern editors usually prefer Q1's 'talked' to Q2's 'talk'.
     10 doth Unlike Q2's 'do', Q1's 'doth' does not have a subjunctive effect.
     16 SD.2 Q1's SD, '*Enter Paris*', is an obvious slip. Q2's correct SD occurs one line later.
     17 The first of several short lines in this scene (see also lines 33 and 72).

PARIS What, come ye to confession to this friar?

JULIET To tell you that were to confess to you.

PARIS Do not deny to him that you love me.

JULIET I will confess to you that I love him.   25

PARIS So, I am sure, you will that you love me.

JULIET And if I do, it will be of more price
    Being spoke behind your back than to your face.

PARIS Poor soul, thy face is much abused with tears.

JULIET The tears have got small victory by that,   30
    For it was bad enough before their spite.

PARIS Thou wrong'st it more than tears by that report.

JULIET That is no wrong, sir, that is a truth,
    And what I spake I spake it to my face.

PARIS Thy face is mine, and thou hast slandered it.   35

JULIET It may be so, for it is not mine own. –
    Are you at leisure, holy father, now,
    Or shall I come to you at evening mass?

FRIAR LAURENCE My leisure serves me, pensive daughter, now. –
    My lord, we must entreat the time alone.   40

PARIS God shield I should disturb devotion!
    Juliet, farewell, and keep this holy kiss. [*Kissing her*]
                                    Exit Paris

JULIET Go, shut the door, and when thou hast done so,
    Come weep with me that am past cure, past help.

FRIAR LAURENCE Ah Juliet, I already know thy grief.   45
    I hear thou must, and nothing may prorogue it,
    On Thursday next be married to the County.

JULIET Tell me not, Friar, that thou hear'st of it,
    Unless thou tell me how we may prevent it.
    Give me some sudden counsel; else, behold,   50
             [*She draws a knife*]

---

22 What, come ye to] Q1 *(What come);* Come you to make Q2   22 friar] Q1 *(Fryer);* Father Q2   23 tell you] Q1; aunswere Q2   23 were to] Q1; I should Q2   26 So . . . will] Q1; So will ye, I am sure Q2   27 And if I do] Q1 *(doe);* If I do so Q2   32 by] Q1; with Q2   33 wrong] Q1; slaunder Q2   33 that] Q1; which Q2   42] Q1 *(subst.);* Iuliet, on Thursday early will I rowse yee, / Till then adue, and keepe this holy kisse. Q2   42 SD.1] *Jowett; not in* Q, F   42 SD.2] Q1; *Exit* Q2   43 Go] Q1 *(Goe);* O Q2   44 that am] Q1; past hope, Q2   44 cure] Q1; care Q2   45 Ah] Q1; O Q2   46 nothing] Q1 *(nothiug)*   47 the] Q1; this Q2   48 it] Q1; this Q2   49 we] Q1; I Q2   50 sudden] Q1; present Q2   50 else] Q1 *(els);* or Q2   50 SD] *Jowett; not in* Q, F

44 **cure** Most modern editors follow Rowe in preferring Q1's 'cure' to Q2's 'care'.

45 Q2's Friar here adds a line not present in the shorter text: 'It straines me past the compasse of my wits.'

49 In a nine-line passage that follows this verse, Juliet threatens Friar Laurence with suicide if he does not help her.

> 'Twixt my extremes and me this bloody knife
> Shall play the umpire, arbitrating that
> Which the commission of thy years and art
> Could to no issue of true honour bring.
> Speak not, be brief, for I desire to die,   55
> If what thou speak'st speak not of remedy.
> FRIAR LAURENCE Stay, Juliet, I do spy a kind of hope,
> Which craves as desperate an execution
> As that is desperate we would prevent.
> If rather than to marry County Paris   60
> Thou hast the strength or will to slay thyself,
> 'Tis not unlike that thou wilt undertake
> A thing like death to chide away this shame,
> That cop'st with death itself to fly from blame.
> And if thou dost, I'll give thee remedy.   65
> JULIET O bid me leap, rather than marry Paris,
> From off the battlements of yonder tower,
> Or chain me to some steepy mountain's top,
> Where roaring bears and savage lions are,
> Or shut me nightly in a charnel-house   70
> With reeky shanks and yellow chapless skulls,
> Or lay me in tomb with one new dead –

55 Speak . . . desire] Q1 *(subst.);* Be not so long to speake, I long Q2   57 Stay, Juliet] Q1 *(Stay Juliet);* Hold daughter Q2   59 we] Q1; which we Q2   2; of Q2   61 or] Q1; of Q2   61 slay] Q1; stay Q2; slay Q4; lay F2   62 'Tis not unlike] Q1 *(subst.);* Then it is likely Q2   64 itself] Q1 *(it selfe);* himselfe Q2   64 fly] Q1 *(flye);* scape Q2   64 blame] Q1; it Q2   65 dost] Q1 *(doost);* darest Q2   67 off] Q1; of Q2; off Q5   67 yonder] Q1, *Pope;* any Q2   70 shut] Q1, *Pope;* hide Q2   71 yellow] Q1 *(yeolow)*   71 chapless] Q1 *(chaples);* chapels Q2; chaples Q4

55 Juliet's irrational staccato orders, asking Friar Laurence not to speak at the same time as she is asking him to speak, captures the emotional intensity of the moment but loses the pun on 'long' in Q2's equivalent line, 'Be not so long to speak, I long to die' (4.1.66).

64 **death itself** The reflexive personal pronoun is neuter in Q1 but masculine in Q2. Shakespeare uses both elsewhere: for instance, 'And look on death itself' (*Mac.* 2.3.77); 'For I will throw my glove to Death himself' (*Tro.* 4.5.62).

68–9 In the equivalent lines in Q2 Juliet phrases her despair rather differently: 'Or walke in thieuish wayes, or bid me lurke / Where Serpents are; chaine me with roaring Beares' (4.1.79–80). Q2's lines call up the dangers of city life (lanes haunted by thieves) and the bear-baiting which was practised near Elizabethan playhouses. By contrast, Q1 seems to allude to Prometheus' punishment, even though the dangerous animals are

not eagles but bears and lions. There is no other 'steepy mountain' in Shakespeare, but the expression occurs in Marlowe's poem, 'The Passionate Shepherd to His Love', which had been written a few years before *Rom.*: 'Come live with mee, and be my love / And we will all the pleasure prove, / That Valleys, groves, hills, and fieldes, / Woods or steepie mountaine yeeldes' (1–4).

70 Following this line, Q2's Juliet speaks another verse which adds to the horror of her imagined charnel-house: 'O'ercovered quite dead men's rattling bones' (4.1.82).

71 **chapless** Editors usually adopt the Q1 reading rather than Q2's 'chapels'.

72 This short line condenses two lines present in the longer text: 'Or bid me go into a new made graue, / And hide me with a dead man in his shroud' (4.1.83–4; 'shroud' is not present in Q2 and is supplied from Q4).

Things that, to hear them named, have made me
    tremble –
And I will do it without fear or doubt,
To keep myself a faithful, unstained wife   75
To my dear lord, my dearest Romeo.
FRIAR LAURENCE Hold, Juliet, hie thee home, get thee to bed.
Let not thy Nurse lie with thee in thy chamber.
And when thou art alone, take thou this vial,
And this distillèd liquor drink thou off;   80
When presently through all thy veins shall run
A dull and heavy slumber, which shall seize
Each vital spirit, for no pulse shall keep
His natural progress, but surcease to beat.
No sign of breath shall testify thou liv'st.   85
And in this borrowed likeness of shrunk death
Thou shalt remain full two-and-forty hours.
And when thou art laid in thy kindred's vault,
I'll send in haste to Mantua to thy lord,
And he shall come and take thee from thy grave.   90
JULIET Friar, I go.
Be sure thou send for my dear Romeo.

Exeunt

---

73 named] Q1 *(namde)*; told Q2   79] Q1 *(subst.)*; Take thou this Violl being then in bed, Q2   80 distillèd] Q1
(distilled); distilling Q2   82 dull and heavy slumber] Q1 *(heauie)*; cold and drowzie humour Q2   84 natural] Q1
(naturall); natiue Q2   84 surcease to beat] Q1 *(beate)*; surcease Q2   85 sign of breath] Q1 *(signe)*; warmth, no breast
Q2; warmth, no breath Q3   87 remain full] Q1 *(remaine)*; continue Q2   88 laid] Q1; borne to buriall Q2   88 vault]
Q1 *(Vault)*; graue Q2   89–90] Q1 *(subst.)*; In the meane time against thou shalt awake, / Shall *Romeo* by my Letters
know our drift, / And hither shall he come, an he and I / Will watch thy walking Q2 *(waking* Q3*)*   91–2] *Arranged as
in Hubbard; as one line* Q1   92 SD] Q1; *Exit.* Q2

74–5 Contrary to the usual pattern, this Q1
passage expands a single line in Q2: 'To liue an
vnstaind wife to my sweete loue' (4.1.88).

77 Q2 is more specific at this point: 'Hold then,
go home, be merrie, giue consent / To marrie
Paris: wendsday is to morrow; / To morrow night
looke that thou lie alone' (4.1.89–91). Q2's Friar
Laurence thus explicitly recommends to Juliet to
mislead her parents ('be merry, give consent'),
whereas Q1's does not. For the different time
scheme Q1 and Q2 here seem to adopt, see Introduction, pp. 34–5.

82 For Q2's 'humour', meaning 'fluid', Q1
metonymically substitutes the effect of this fluid,
'slumber'.

82–3 which . . . spirit This short passage has
no equivalent in Q2.

84 surcease to beat Q2 simply has 'surcease'.
'Surcease to' is rare in Shakespeare, but there

are two other instances: 'Lest I surcease to honour mine own truth' (*Cor.* 3.2.121), and 'O time,
cease thou thy course and last no longer, / If they
surcease to be that should survive' (*Lucr.* 1766).

85 Following the equivalent line, Q2's speech
continues for twenty-three more lines, whereas Q1
does so for a mere five. Lines that are exclusive to
Q2 include predictions of the potion's effect on
Juliet's body in Petrarchan terms ('The roses in
thy lips and cheeks shall fade'), of how she will be
found and thought dead as dramatised in Scene 17
(4.4), and of Romeo's escape with her to Mantua
after she has woken up.

91–2 Q2 has a less abrupt leave-taking with
another short speech each by Friar Laurence and
Juliet. Q2's Juliet does not explicitly ask Friar Laurence to send for Romeo, but the Friar himself
asserts that 'I'll send a friar with speed / To Mantua with my letters to thy lord' (4.2.123–4).

[16]   *Enter old* CAPULET, *his* WIFE, NURSE, *and*
SERVING-MAN

CAPULET Where are you, sirrah?
SERVING-MAN Here, forsooth.
CAPULET Go, provide me twenty cunning cooks.
SERVING-MAN I warrant you, sir, let me alone for that. I'll know
        them by licking their fingers.   5
CAPULET How canst thou know them so?
SERVING-MAN Ah, sir, 'tis an ill cook cannot lick his own fingers.
CAPULET Well, get you gone.

                                        Exit Serving-man

      But where's this headstrong?
CAPULET'S WIFE She's gone, my lord, to Friar Laurence' cell   10
    To be confessed.
CAPULET Ah, he may hap to do some good of her.
    A headstrong self-willed harlotry it is.

                Enter JULIET

CAPULET'S WIFE See, here she cometh from confession.
CAPULET [*To Juliet*] How now, my headstrong, where have you
    been gadding?   15
JULIET Where I have learnèd to repent the sin
    Of froward wilful opposition
    'Gainst you and your behests, and am enjoined
    By holy Laurence to fall prostrate here

---

0 SD] Q1 *(subst.); Enter Father* Capulet, Mother, Nurse, *and* Seruing men, *two or three.*   **3** provide] Q1 *(prouide);* hire
Q2   **4–5** know . . . fingers] Q1 *(knowe);* trie if they can lick their fingers Q2   **6** know] Q1; trie Q2   **8** SD] Q1 *(Exit
Seruingman.); not in* Q2   **12** of] Q1; on Q2   **13** self-willed] Q1 *(selfewild)*   **14** confession] Q1 *(Confession);* shrift
with merie looke Q2   **15** SD] *Jowett; not in* Q, F   **17** froward wilful] Q1 *(wilfull);* disobedient Q2   **18** 'Gainst] Q1
(Gainst); To Q2

Scene 16

Act 4, Scene 2 in the NCS edition.
While Q1 and Q2's versions of this scene follow
the same course of action, the language is usually
quite different, at times altogether different. In
the entire scene, only two lines, 15 and 19, show
no substantive variants. Q1 indicates a break by a
row of printer's ornaments above the beginning of
the scene.

    0 SD Q2's permissive SD calls for 'two or three'
servants, and Capulet's commands with which
Q2's scene opens – 'So many guests invite as here
are writ', 'Sirrah, go hire me twenty cunning
cooks' – presuppose the presence of more than
one servant. By contrast, Q1's SD, in keeping with

the ensuing dialogue, requires only a single servant.

    3 provide get ready, arrange (*OED* Provide *v.*
3).

    10–11 This and Capulet's Wife's following
speech are assigned to the Nurse in Q2.

    12 do . . . her do her some good (see *OED* Of
prep., 55, 60).

    14 Q2's equivalent line adds 'with merry look'
(4.2.14), an implied stage direction which in performance can be acted and therefore does not have
to be spoken.

    17 froward wilful The two words are synony-
mous.

And crave remission of so foul a fact.   20

She kneels down

CAPULET'S WIFE Why, that's well said.

CAPULET Now, before God, this holy reverend Friar
　　　All our whole city is much bound unto.
　　　Go, tell the County presently of this,
　　　For I will have this knot knit up tomorrow.   25

JULIET Nurse, will you go with me to my closet,
　　　To sort such things as shall be requisite
　　　Against tomorrow.

CAPULET'S WIFE I prithee do, good Nurse, go in with her.
　　　Help her to sort tires, rebatos, chains,   30
　　　And I will come unto you presently.

NURSE Come, sweetheart, shall we go?

JULIET   I prithee, let us.

Exeunt Nurse and Juliet

CAPULET'S WIFE Methinks on Thursday would be time enough.

CAPULET I say I will have this dispatched tomorrow.
　　　Go one, and certify the Count thereof.   35

CAPULET'S WIFE I pray, my lord, let it be Thursday.

CAPULET I say tomorrow, while she's in the mood.

CAPULET'S WIFE We shall be short in our provision.

CAPULET Let me alone for that. Go, get you in.
　　　Now, before God, my heart is passing light,   40
　　　To see her thus conformèd to our will.

Exeunt

---

20 crave remission] Q1 *(craue)*; beg your pardon Q2   20 SD] Q1 *(subst.)*; *not in* Q2   22 before] Q1; afore Q2   22 holy reverend] Q1 *(reuerent)*, *Capell*; reuerend holy Q2; holy reverend Q5   23 unto] Q1 *(vnto)*; to him Q2   26 to] Q1; into Q2   27 things] Q1; needfull ornaments Q2   27–8 shall . . . / Against] Q1; you thinke fit to furnish me Q2   32 SD] Q1 *(Iuliet)*; *Exeunt.* Q2   33 would be] Q1; there is Q2   40 passing] Q1; wondrous Q2

20 **crave remission of** ask forgiveness for.

21 This speech has no equivalent in Q2.

27 **requisite** necessary, indispensable (*OED* Requisite *a.* A.a).

28 **Against** with respect to, in regard to (*OED* Against *prep.* 3).

29–41 Up to line 28, speeches in Q1 have their equivalent in Q2 (with the exception of line 21), but they do not in the rest of the scene. In Q2, Lady Capulet does not ask the Nurse to go in with Juliet (Capulet does so in the following speech) but instead asks her husband not to advance the wedding to Wednesday, a suggestion he roundly rejects. Q2's scene closes with a nine-line speech by Capulet, while Q1 concludes with a dialogue between the spouses, still arguing over the wedding date.

30 **tires** attire, apparel (*OED* Tire *n.*¹).

30 **rebatos** 'A kind of stiff collar worn by both sexes from about 1590 to 1630' (*OED*).

35 **certify** assure, inform certainly (*OED* Certify *v.* 3.a.).

[17]   *Enter* NURSE, JULIET

NURSE Come, come, what need you anything else?
JULIET Nothing, good Nurse, but leave me to myself,
     For I do mean to lie alone tonight.
NURSE Well, there's a clean smock under your pillow, and so good
     night.   *Exit*

          Enter CAPULET'S WIFE

CAPULET'S WIFE What, are you busy? Do you need my help?   5
JULIET No, madam, I desire to lie alone,
     For I have many things to think upon.
CAPULET'S WIFE Well then, good night. Be stirring, Juliet,
     The County will be early here tomorrow.   *Exit*
JULIET Farewell. God knows when we shall meet again.   10
     Ah, I do take a fearful thing in hand.
     What if this potion should not work at all?
     Must I of force be married to the County?
     This shall forbid it. Knife, lie thou there.
          [*She lays down a knife*]
     What if the Friar should give me this drink   15
     To poison me, for fear I should disclose
     Our former marriage? Ah, I wrong him much.

---

5 Do you need] Q1 *(doo);* need you Q2   11] Q1 *(subst.);* Come Violl Q2   12 potion] Q1 *(Potion);* mixture Q2   12
should] Q1*; do* Q2   13] Q1 *(subst.);* Shall I be married then to morrow morning? Q2*;* Shall I of force be marry'd to the
Count? *Pope*   14] Q1 *(subst.);* No, no, this shall forbid it, lie thou there, Q2   14 SD] *Johnson (Laying down a dagger.);*
not in Q, F

Scene 17
Act 4, Scenes 3, 4, and 5 in the NCS edition. (For
the question of scene division, see Appendix A,
pp. 157–8.)
This scene spans from Juliet drinking the potion
to her being discovered as 'dead' (followed by a
coda with the musicians). While it dramatises the
same events as the equivalent scenes in Q2, the relationship is less close than elsewhere: several short
speeches in Q2 have no equivalent in Q1; Capulet's
Wife and the Nurse at one point remain onstage
in Q1, whereas they exit in Q2 and re-enter a little later; throughout the scene, only six lines are
present in both texts with no substantive variant
(10, 37, 47, 53, 68–9). As for length, Q2 adds up to
224, Q1 to 136 lines. Most notably, Juliet's potion
speech has seventeen lines in Q1, forty-four in Q2;
and Friar Laurence speaks seven lines in Q1 but

twenty-four in Q2. Q1 indicates a break by a row
of printer's ornaments above the beginning of the
scene.
     1–4 In Q2, the scene opens with a five-line
speech by Juliet, starting with a reply to the Nurse
('Ay, those attires are best'), but the Nurse herself
is not assigned any speeches until quite a bit later
in the scene.
     4 smock a woman's under-garment, a chemise
(*OED* Smock *n.* 1).
     7 Q2's Juliet asks to be alone not so much to
think as to pray ('I haue need of many orysons /
To moue the heauens', 4.2.3–4) in keeping with
Brooke's, who claims that 'this night, my purpose
is to pray' (l. 2326). See Introduction, p. 13.
     13 of force by constraint, of necessity, compul-
sorily (*OED n.*[1] 5b).

He is a holy and religious man;
I will not entertain so bad a thought.
What if I should be stifled in the tomb,   20
Awake an hour before the appointed time?
Ah, then I fear I shall be lunatic,
And, playing with my dead forefathers' bones,
Dash out my frantic brains. Methinks I see
My cousin Tybalt welt'ring in his blood,   25
Seeking for Romeo. Stay, Tybalt, stay!
Romeo, I come. This do I drink to thee.
She [drinks from the vial and] falls upon her bed within the curtains

Enter NURSE *with herbs,* CAPULET'S WIFE

CAPULET'S WIFE That's well said, Nurse, set all in readiness.
The County will be here immediately.

Enter CAPULET

CAPULET Make haste, make haste, for it is almost day.   30
The curfew bell hath rung, 'tis four o'clock.
Look to your baked meats, good Angelica.
NURSE Go, get you to bed, you cotquean. I'faith, you will be sick
anon.

18] Q1 *(subst.)*; he hath still bene tried a holy man Q2   19] Q1 *(subst.); not in* Q2   20 tomb] Q1 *(*Toomb*); Vault
Q2   21 an hour...time] Q1 *(*houre*); before the time that* Romeo / Come to redeeme me Q2   22 lunatic] Q1 *(*lunaticke*);
distraught Q2   23] Q1 *(subst.);* And madly play with my forefathers ioynts? Q2   25 cousin ... blood] Q1 *(subst.)*;
Cozins Ghost Q2   27 SD.1 *drinks from the vial and*] *Jowett; not in* Q1   27 SD.2 CAPULET'S WIFE] Q1 *(Mother); Lady
of the house* Q2   29 SD] Q1 *(Enter Oldeman);* Enter old Capulet Q2   30 it ...day] Q1; the second Cock hath crowed
Q2   31 rung] Q1; roong Q2; roung Q3; rung F1   31 four] Q1 *(*foure*);* three Q2   32 your] Q1; the Q2   34 anon] Q1
*(*anone*);* to morrow / For this nights watching Q2

21 Q2 here has a lengthy, fifteen-line passage
which leaves no trace in Q1, in which Juliet
expands on her macabre fantasy.

24 Q1's Juliet, unlike Q2's, does not imagine
to 'pluck the mangled Tybalt from his shrowde'
(4.3.52).

25 The image of Tybalt 'welt'ring in his blood'
is exclusive to Q1, though Q2's Juliet, in a passage absent from Q1, refers to 'bloudie Tybalt'
(4.3.42) earlier in this speech, and Q2's Romeo,
in the final scene, addresses Tybalt lying in the
Capulets' tomb in his 'bloudie sheet' (5.3.97).

27 SD.1 For the staging of this moment, see
Introduction, pp. 27–8. A few editors have been
concerned by the presence of the vial, including
Capell who added to the SD that Juliet '*throws away
the Vial*'. Following this SD, Q1 marks a break by
another row of printer's ornaments, though the
action is continuous.

27 SD.2 Q1 is alone in pointing out that the
Nurse enters '*with herbs*', though Q2, in lines not
present in Q1, has the Nurse and Lady Capulet
mention other food required for the preparation
of the wedding feast, 'spices', 'dates', and 'quinces'
(4.4.1–2). Q2 thus establishes verbally what Q1
suggests visually.

31 four NCS argues that Q2's 'three a'clock'
(4.4.5) 'is extremely early' and that Q1 is
right, though Gibbons, quoting Thomas Tusser's
Husbandry (1573), suggests that Q2 is correct as
cocks crow 'At midnight, at three, and an hour ere
day'.

32 Q2's Capulet adds, 'Spare not for cost'
(4.4.6), a line that may be indebted to Brooke
where Capulet promises Paris 'a costly feast' (line
2258). See Introduction, p. 13.

CAPULET I warrant thee, Nurse, I have ere now watched all night   35
and have taken no harm at all.

CAPULET'S WIFE Ay, you have been a mouse-hunt in your time.

Enter SERVING-MAN *with logs and coals*

CAPULET A jealous hood, a jealous hood! [*To serving-man*] How now,
sirrah, what have you there?

SERVING-MAN Forsooth, logs.   40

CAPULET Go, go, choose drier. Will will tell thee where thou shalt
fetch them.

SERVING-MAN Nay, I warrant, let me alone. I have a head, I trow,
to choose a log.   *Exit*

CAPULET Well, go thy way, thou shalt be loggerhead.   45
[*To his wife*] Come, come, make haste, call up your
daughter.
The County will be here with music straight.
                                          [*Exit Capulet's Wife*]
[*Play music within*]
God's me, he's come. Nurse, call up my daughter.

NURSE Go, get you gone.
                                          [*Exit Capulet*]

35–6 ere . . . all] Q1 *(subst.)*; watcht ere now, / All night for lesser cause, and nere bene sicke Q2   37 SD] Q1 *(subst.)*;
Enter three or foure with spits and logs, and Baskets. Q2   38 SD] *This edn; not in* Q, F   39 have you] Q1 *(*haue*)*; is
Q2   40] Q1 *(subst.)*; Things for the Cooke sir, but I know not what. Q2   41 choose drier] Q1 *(*dryer*)*; fetch drier logs
Q2   41 Will] Q1; *Peter* Q2   41 tell] Q1; shew Q2   41–2 thou . . . them] Q1; they are Q2   43 trow] Q1 *(*troe*)*   44
to . . . log] Q1 *(*Log*)*; that will find out logs Q2   46 SD] *This edn; not in* Q1   47 SD.1] *This edn; not in* Q1   47 SD.2]
Cam.; not in Q1; *Play Musicke.* Q2; *Music within Hubbard*   49 SD] *This edn (Hubbard, following 46); Exeunt Capulet
and his Wife Levenson*

---

37 This line exists in identical form in Q2, where Lady Capulet adds: 'But I will watch you from such watching now' (4.4.12). Q2 then provides a SD, '*Exit Lady and Nurse*', which has no equivalent in Q1 where the two women remain onstage.

37 SD As at the beginning of the previous scene, Q1 requires a single Serving-man where Q2's permissive SD asks for several.

41 Will Probably not an allusion to Shakespeare's name but to Will Kempe, the famous comedian of the Lord Chamberlain's Men, who played Peter, 'Peter' being the name here in Q2.

46 This line has no equivalent in Q2 where Lady Capulet has already left the stage.

47 SD.1 The text provides no indication as to when exactly Capulet's Wife exits, and she may also do so a line earlier or slightly later. Hubbard provides no exit for her. In Levenson, she leaves with her husband (line 49).

49 Q1's Nurse, contrary to Q2's, begins her speech with Capulet still onstage which reinforces the impression that the action is continuous. Most editions of *Romeo and Juliet* start a new scene here, however. See Appendix A, pp. 157–8.

What lamb, what ladybird! Fast, I warrant.   50
What Juliet! Well, let the County take you in your bed;
Ye sleep for a week now, but the next night
The County Paris hath set up his rest
That you shall rest but little. What lamb, I say.
Fast still? What lady, love, what bride, what Juliet!   55
Gods me, how sound she sleeps. Nay, then I see
I must wake you indeed.
                [*She draws back the curtains*]
                            What's here?
Laid on your bed, dressed in your clothes, and down?
Ah me, alack the day, some aqua-vitae, ho!

                Enter CAPULET'S WIFE

CAPULET'S WIFE How now, what's the matter?   60
NURSE Alack the day, she's dead, she's dead, she's dead.
CAPULET'S WIFE Accursed, unhappy, miserable time!

                Enter CAPULET

CAPULET Come, come, make haste. Where's my daughter?
CAPULET'S WIFE Ah, she's dead, she's dead.
CAPULET Stay, let me see – all pale and wan.   65
Accursèd time, unfortunate old man.

50–9] *Arranged as in Levenson; as prose* Q1   50 What . . . ladybird] Q1 *(subst.);* Why Lambe, why Lady Q2   52 Ye . . . now] Q1 *(subst.);* Sleepe for a weeke Q2   57 SD] *Capell (undraws the Curtains); not in* Q, F   59 SD CAPULET'S WIFE] Q1 *(Mother)*   62 SD CAPULET] Q1 *(Oldeman)*   66 SD] Q1 *(Enter Fryer and Paris.); Enter Frier and the Countie.* Q2

50–9 The Nurse's speech – set in prose in Q1 – compresses and rearranges much of the material in the equivalent Q2 lines. See Erne, pp. 212–13.

50 ladybird A term of endearment (cf. Q2's 'sweet heart', 4.5.3).

56 Gods me See note at 1.101.

61 The last speech by the Nurse in the mourning sequence. Three later Q2 speeches assigned to her (4.5.23, 29, 49–54) have no equivalent in Q1.

62 This anticipates line 75 (assigned to Paris), which begins with the same three adjectives, as well as a Q2 line later in the scene, assigned to Lady Capulet ('Accurst, vnhappie, wretched hatefull day!', 4.5.43).

64 In Q2, the Nurse precedes Lady Capulet in announcing the news: 'Shees dead: deceast, shees dead, alack the day' (4.5.23).

65 Capulet's assessment of Juliet is purely visual. In Q2, by contrast, 'shees cold, / Her bloud is setled, and her ioynts are stiffe' (4.5.25–6).

65–6 The brevity of Capulet's reaction to his supposedly dead daughter contrasts with Q2 where he lyricises the situation – 'Death lies on her like an vntimely frost / Vpon the sweetest flower of all the field' (4.5.28–9) – and contradictorily goes on to claim that 'Death . . . / Ties vp my tongue and will not let me speake' (4.5.31–2).

Enter FRIAR [LAURENCE] *and* PARIS

PARIS What, is the bride ready to go to church?

CAPULET Ready to go, but never to return.
   O son, the night before thy wedding day
   Hath death lain with thy bride. Flower as she is,   70
   Deflowered by him. See where she lies.
   Death is my son-in-law; to him I give all that I have.

PARIS Have I thought long to see this morning's face,
   And doth it now present such prodigies?
   Accursed, unhappy, miserable man,   75
   Forlorn, forsaken, destitute I am,
   Born to the world to be a slave in it,
   Distressed, remediless, and unfortunate.
   O heavens, O nature, wherefore did you make me
   To live so vile, so wretched as I shall?   80

CAPULET O here she lies that was our hope, our joy,
   And being dead, dead sorrow nips us all.

---

67 SH] Q1 *(Par:); Fri.* Q2   **67** What] Q1*; Come* Q2   **67** bride] Q1*; wife* Q2   **70–1**] Flower . . . lies.] Q1 *(subst.);* there she lies / Flower as she was, deflowred by him, Q2   **73** long] Q1*; loue* Q2*; long* Q3   **74** now . . . prodigies] Q1 *(*Prodegies*);* giue me such a sight as this Q2   **82** SD] Q1*; not in* Q2

67 The line is assigned to Friar Laurence in Q2. Melchiori thinks that the enquiry 'is more suited to the Friar than to Paris', but given Paris's impatience when we last saw him in Scene 15, Q1's ascription seems suitable enough.

72 to . . . have. A clumsy and extrametrical passage, in contrast to Q2's 'Death is my heir' (4.5.38).

74 prodigies abnormal or monstrous things (*OED* Prodigy 2).

82 SD Like other SDs in Q1, these words may have been composed as part of the redaction of the manuscript that served as copy for Q1 or they may have been added later. See Introduction, pp. 39–41. This SD raises a number of questions to which no simple answers are forthcoming: is the intended effect parodic or would it be 'dangerously unhistorical' (NCS) to assume so? Or is the desired effect chiefly musical, as Melchiori has argued? Does the simultaneous delivery apply only to the two lines which the SH assigns to 'all' or also to the following five-line speeches by Capulet, his wife, and Paris? And does the choric delivery of at least part of this passage suggest that the six lines each attributed to Capulet, his wife, Paris, and the Nurse in Q2 should also be spoken simultaneously, as Charles B. Lower ('*Romeo and Juliet*, IV.v: a stage direction and purposeful comedy', *S.St.* 8 (1975), 177–94) and Jowett have argued? (For a slightly different theory regarding the simultaneous delivery, see Melchiori.) Irace reports that 'In an effective variation of the Q1 stage direction, Terry Hands's 1989 Royal Shakespeare Company production presented the lamentations as half song, half chorus' (77). Jonson's *The Alchemist* (4.5) offers a rare instance in which simultaneous delivery of different speeches (by Dol Common, Face, and Mammon) is required and so set out in F1 by being printed in parallel columns. The passage is preceded by the SD '*They speak together.*'

All at once cry out and wring their hands

ALL And all our joy and all our hope is dead,
           Dead, lost, undone, absented, wholly fled.

CAPULET Cruel, unjust, impartial destinies,   85
           Why to this day have you preserved my life?
           To see my hope, my stay, my joy, my life,
           Deprived of sense, of life, of all by death?
           Cruel, unjust, impartial destinies!

[PARIS] O sad-faced sorrow, map of misery,   90
           Why this sad time have I desired to see,
           This day, this unjust, this impartial day,
           Wherein I hoped to see my comfort full,
           To be deprived by sudden destiny?

CAPULET'S WIFE O woe, alack, distressed, why should I live   95
           To see this day, this miserable day?
           Alack the time that ever I was born
           To be partaker of this destiny.
           Alack the day, alack and well-a-day.

FRIAR LAURENCE O peace, for shame, if not for charity.   100
           Your daughter lives in peace and happiness,
           And it is vain to wish it otherwise.
           Come, stick your rosemary in this dead corpse,
           And, as the custom of our country is,

---

83 SH] Q1 *(All cry:)*   90 SH] *Eichhoff; Cap:* Q1   100 O peace] Q1*;* Peace ho Q2   100 if not for charity] Q1*;* confusions
care liues not Q2   103 in] Q1*;* On Q2   103 dead corpse] Q1 *(coarse);* faire Coarse Q2   104 custom . . . is] Q1 *(subst.);*
custome is Q2

84 **absented** withdrawn, absent.

85 **impartial** Misused for 'partial' (*OED*
Impartial *a*. 3).

85–99 These three speeches are not only of
identical length but also have a similar structure,
beginning with an exclamation before raising self-
indulgent rhetorical questions about the speakers
themselves (e.g. lines 86, 91, 95–6) in a way Q2's
do not.

87 **stay** support (cf. 'what hope, what stay',
John 5.7.68).

90 SH This and the preceding speech are
assigned to Capulet, though the content makes
clear that the second is to be spoken by Paris.

90 This alliterative line consists of two expres-
sions not otherwise in Shakespeare. For 'sad-
faced', see *Tit.* 5.3.66. In the same play, Titus calls
the mutilated Lavinia a 'map of woe' (3.2.12).

99 **well-a-day** An exclamation of sorrow – cf.
'alas' – of which Q2's Nurse uses a dialectal form,
'weraday' (3.2.37, 4.5.15).

100 The line parallels 'Peace, peace! For shame,
if not for charity' (*R3* 1.3.271), whereas the corresponding Q2 line ('Peace ho for shame, confusions
care liues not') does not. It seems possible that
memorial agency accounts for the parallel with
R3.

100–6 Friar Laurence's Q1 speech is shorter by
twelve lines than its equivalent in Q2, and omits
his extended exhortation against excessive grief.

104–6 Brooke at the equivalent point also
refers to this 'custom' (calling it 'use', line 2523).
According to it, the dead are 'Borne to their
church' (line 2524), which corresponds closely to
Q2's 'beare her to Church' (4.5.81). See Introduction, pp. 12–13.

In all her best and sumptuous ornaments   105
Convey her where her ancestors lie tombed.
CAPULET Let it be so. Come, woeful sorrow-mates,
Let us together taste this bitter fate.

They all but the Nurse go forth,
casting rosemary on her and shutting the curtains[, and exeunt].

Enter [three] MUSICIANS

NURSE Put up, put up, this is a woeful case.   *Exit*
FIRST MUSICIAN Ay, by my troth, mistress, is it. It had need be   110
mended.

Enter SERVING-MAN

SERVING-MAN Alack, alack, what shall I do? Come, fiddlers, play
me some merry dump.
FIRST MUSICIAN Ah sir, this is no time to play.
SERVING-MAN You will not then?   115
FIRST MUSICIAN No, marry, will we.
SERVING-MAN Then will I give it you, and soundly too.
FIRST MUSICIAN What will you give us?
SERVING-MAN The fiddler. I'll re you, I'll fa you, I'll sol you.
FIRST MUSICIAN If you re us and fa us, we will note you.   120

105–6] Q1 *(subst.);* And in her best array beare her to Church: Q2   105 In all] Q1; And in Q2   108 SH] Q1 *(1.)*
(throughout scene)   108 SD.1–2] Q1 *(subst.);* F*xeunt manet.* Q2   108 SD.2 *and exeunt*] *This edn; not in* Q1   108 SD.3
three] *This edn; not in* Q1   109 woeful] Q1 *(wofull);* pitifull Q2   110–11 It . . . mended] Q1 *(it);* the case may be
amended Q2   114] Q1 *(subst.);* Not a dump we, tis no time to play now. Q2   116] Q1 *(subst.);* No. Q2   117] Q1
(subst.); I will then giue it you soundly. Q2   119 The fiddler] Q1 *(fidler);* No money on my faith, but the gleeke Q2
120] Q1 *(subst.);* And you re vs, and fa vs, you note vs. Q2

106 **tombed** entombed, buried ('Thy unused
beauty must be tombed with thee', *Son.* 4.13).
107 **sorrow-mates** See 'masquing mates' (*MV*
2.6.59) and 'skains-mates' (*Rom.* 2.4.128) for similar compound words.
107–8 Almost a rhyming couplet, with which
Shakespeare often ends his scenes or scenic movements, but the rhyme here, unusually, is imperfect.
Q2's equivalent speech is seven lines long and parallels a passage in Brooke (lines 2511–14) which
antithetically opposes the wedding they had anticipated to the funeral they now have to prepare (see
Introduction, pp. 12–13). It is followed by a five-
line speech by Friar Laurence, of which Q1 shows
no trace, in which he urges the Capulets and Paris
to prepare for the funeral. Q1 does not provide an

exit for the Capulets and Paris, nor does it indicate the number of musicians, though the ensuing
SHS mention three of them. Editors are divided
in following Q1, where the musicians enter at this
point, or Q4, where they enter earlier on with Paris
and Friar Laurence. The shutting of the curtains
may suggest that Juliet remains onstage until the
final scene, by which time her bed would thus have
become her tomb. See Introduction, pp. 27–8.
108 SD Q1's SD 'is appropriated in various ways
by most editors' (Oxford).
110 SD Q2's SD reads '*Enter Will Kemp*', indicating that the famous comedian of the Lord
Chamberlain's Men seems to have been the first
impersonator of this serving-man. Note Capulet's
mention of 'Will' earlier in this scene (41 above).

SERVING-MAN I will put up my iron dagger and beat you with my
    wooden wit. Come on, Simon Soundpost, I'll pose you.
FIRST MUSICIAN Let's hear.
SERVING-MAN [*sings*] When griping grief the heart doth wound,
                 And doleful dumps the mind oppress,   125
                 Then music with her silver sound –
    Why 'silver sound'? Why 'silver sound'?
FIRST MUSICIAN I think because music hath a sweet sound.
SERVING-MAN Pretty. What say you, Mathew Minikin?
SECOND MUSICIAN I think because musicians sound for silver.   130
SERVING-MAN Pretty too. Come, what say you?
THIRD MUSICIAN I say nothing.
SERVING-MAN I think so. I'll speak for you because you are the
    singer. I say 'silver sound' because such fellows as you have
    seldom gold for sounding. Farewell, fiddlers, farewell.   135

                                                Exit

FIRST MUSICIAN Farewell and be hanged. Come, let's go.

                                        Exeunt

---

121 beat] Q1 *(beate); dry-beate* Q2   121–2 my wooden wit] Q1 *(wodden);* an yron wit Q2   122 Soundpost] *Levenson;*
found Pot Q1; sound post Q2; sound Pot *Furness (Q1);* Sound-pot *Hubbard*   124 SD] *Jowett; not in* Q, F   124 grief]
Q1 *(griefe);* griefes Q2   128 music] Q1 *(musicke);* siluer Q2   129 Pretty] Q1 *(Pretie);* Prates Q2   129 Mathew
Minikin] Q1 *(minikine);* Hugh Rebick Q2   130 SH] Q1 *(2.)*   132 SH] Q1 *(3.)*   134 such fellows as you] Q1 *(Fellowes);*
Musitions Q2   135 seldom] Q1 *(sildome);* no Q2

122 **Soundpost** In Q2, the first musician is
called 'Simon Catling', the second 'Hugh Rebick',
and the third 'James Soundpost' (4.5.124–9). In
Q1, the second is called 'Mathew Minikin', the
third is given no name, whereas the first is called
'Simon Soundpost', which blends the other two
names in Q2. Levenson's emendation (Q1 reads
'found Pot') is convincing not only because of
the name's presence in Q2 but also because of
the serving-man's pun on '-post' and 'pose'.

125 This line is not in Q2, perhaps because
Shakespeare only recorded the first and last lines
of the stanza or, as Levenson argues, because the
serving-man is shown to muddle the song before
he interrupts it. Many modern editors (including NCS, Gibbons, and Jowett) follow Capell in
incorporating the Q1 line into their edition.

129 **Pretty** Clever, ingenious (*OED* Pretty *a.*
2.b).

129 **Minikin** The name has several connota-
tions: a minion or favourite (*OED n.*[1] 1); a kind
of small pin (*OED n.*[1] 2); 'A thin strand of catgut
used for the treble strings of a lute or viol' (*OED
n.* 2.a).

133–5 This speech is printed as prose in Q1 but
as verse in Q2, though the metrical irregularity in
the latter has led most editors since Pope to set it
as prose.

135 In Q2, Peter, as the Serving-man is called,
continues the song before exiting: 'Then Musique
with her siluer sound with speedy help doth lend
redresse' (4.5.134–5).

135 **fiddlers** 'Fiddler' could also mean 'trifler'
(*OED* 2.a).

[18]   *Enter* ROMEO

ROMEO If I may trust the flattering eye of sleep,
         My dream presaged some good event to come.
         My bosom-lord sits cheerful in his throne,
         And I am comforted with pleasing dreams.
         Methought I was this night already dead –   5
         Strange dreams that give a dead man leave to think –
         And that my lady Juliet came to me
         And breathed such life with kisses in my lips
         That I revived and was an emperor.

                Enter BALTHASAR, *his man, booted*

         News from Verona! How now, Balthasar,   10
         How doth my lady? Is my father well?
         How fares my Juliet? That I ask again.
         If she be well, then nothing can be ill.
BALTHASAR Then nothing can be ill, for she is well.
         Her body sleeps in Capels' monument,   15
         And her immortal parts with angels dwell.
         Pardon me, sir, that am the messenger
         Of such bad tidings.

---

1 eye] Q1 (Eye); truth Q2   2 dream] Q1 (Dreame); dreames Q2   2 good event to come] Q1 (euent); ioyfull newes at hand Q2   3 cheerful] Q1 (chearfull); lightly Q2   4] Q1 (subst.); And all this day an vnaccustomd spirit, / Lifts me aboue the ground with chearfull thoughts, Q2   5–7] Q1 (subst.); I dreamt my Lady came and found me dead, / Strange dreame that giues a deadman leaue to thinke, Q2   9 SD] Q1 (subst.); Enter Romeos man. Q2   12 fares my Juliet] Q1 (Juliet); doth my Lady Iuliet Q2; doth my Juliet Pope   13] Q1; For nothing can be ill if she be well. Q2   14] Q1 (subst.); Then she is well and nothing can be ill, Q2   16 parts] Q1; part Q2   16 dwell] Q1; liues Q2   17] Q1 (subst.); O pardon me for bringing these ill newes, / Since you did leaue it for my office sir. Q2   17–18] *Arranged as in Hubbard; printed as one line* Q1

Scene 18
Act 5, Scene 1 in the NCS edition.
In its general outline, this scene corresponds closely to its Q2 counterpart. In terms of its specific linguistic composition, however, it regularly differs from the longer text. Most lines have their identifiable counterpart in Q2, but there are numerous substitutions and rearrangements both within and between lines, and a mere ten lines show no substantive variant. Q1's scene is sixty-four lines long, as opposed to eighty-six in Q2. The difference in length is accounted for by a series of short omissions (none longer than three lines) and condensations. Q1 indicates a break by a row of printer's ornaments above the beginning of the scene.

1 **eye of sleep** Nineteenth-century editors, fol-

lowing Malone, often preferred this reading to Q2's 'truth of sleep'.

9 Following this line, Q2 adds Romeo's exclamation, 'Ah me, how sweete is loue it selfe possesst, / When but loues shadowes are so rich in ioy!' (5.1.10–11).

9 SD *booted* Only Q1 adds this detail, suggesting that Balthasar comes from riding.

10 Following this line and further below, Q2 has short passages (5.1.13, 31–3) absent from Q1 in which Romeo enquires for news from Friar Laurence. In Q1 and Q2 Friar Laurence promised to send news regularly through Romeo's man (12.135–7 and 3.3.169–71), so the differences in this scene do not seem part of a larger pattern of revision or abridgement.

ROMEO Is it even so? Then I defy my stars.
   Go, get me ink and paper, hire post-horse,   20
   I will not stay in Mantua tonight.
BALTHASAR Pardon me, sir, I will not leave you thus;
   Your looks are dangerous and full of fear.
   I dare not, nor I will not leave you yet.
ROMEO Do as I bid thee: get me ink and paper,   25
   And hire those horse. Stay not, I say.

           Exit Balthasar

   Well, Juliet, I will lie with thee tonight.
   Let's see for means. As I do remember,
   Here dwells a 'pothecary whom oft I noted
   As I passed by, whose needy shop is stuffed   30
   With beggarly accounts of empty boxes;
   And in the same an alligator hangs,
   Old ends of packthread, and cakes of roses
   Are thinly strewèd to make up a show.
   Him as I noted, thus with myself I thought: 35
   'And if a man should need a poison now,
   Whose present sale is death in Mantua,
   Here he might buy it.' This thought of mine did but
   Forerun my need. And hereabout he dwells.
   Being holiday, the beggar's shop is shut.   40
   What ho! Apothecary, come forth, I say.

---

19 defy my] Q1 *(defie); denie you Q2   20 post-horse] Q1 *(post horse); post horses Q2   21 not stay in Mantua] Q1 *(Mantua); hence Q2   22] Q1 *(subst.); I do beseech you sir, haue patience: Q2   23 dangerous . . . fear] Q1 *(subst.);* pale and wilde Q2   26 horse] Q1; horses Q2   28–9 As . . . oft] Q1 *(subst.);* I do remember an Appothacarie, / And here abouts a dwells which late Q2   32 alligator] Q1 *(Aligarta); allegater Q2   33 Old ends] Q1 *(Olde endes); Remnants Q2   33 cakes] Q1; old cakes Q2   34 Are] Q1; Were Q2   34 strewèd] Q1 *(strewed);* scattered Q2   35 Him . . . with] Q1; Noting this penury, to Q2   35 thought] Q1; said Q2   36 should] Q1; did Q2   37 present . . . death] Q1; sale is present death Q2   38 he . . . it] Q1; liues a Caitiffe wretch would sell it him Q2   38 This . . . mine] Q1; O this same thought Q2   38–9] *Arranged as in Hubbard;* Here . . . mine / . . . dwels. Q1   39 And . . . dwells.] Q1 *(subst.);* As I remember this should be the house, Q2   41 come . . . say] Q1 *(subst.); not in Q2

19 **defy** Most editors since Pope have preferred this to Q2's 'deny', though the latter has recently been supported by Williams and Levenson (Oxford).

20 **post-horse** 'horse' as a plural form was still in general use in Shakespeare's time (*OED n.* 1b).

25 Only Q1 repeats 'get me ink and paper' (see line 20). Q2 at this point reads: 'do the thing I bid thee do' (5.1.30).

26 **those horse** See line 20 above, and note.

28 **for means** Following these words, Q2 has a line and a half absent from Q1: 'O mischiefe, thou are swift, / To enter in the thoughts of desperate men' (5.1.35–6). It seems significant that here as elsewhere (e.g. above 9), passages absent from the short but present in the long text are of a general, proverbial nature.

29 **'pothecary** Aphetic form of 'apothecary'.

30 Following this line, Q2 adds a three-line description of the apothecary's 'meager . . . lookes' (5.1.39–41).

30–2 **whose . . . hangs** In Q2 the shop is described more extensively and somewhat differently, with a hanging tortoise and a stuffed alligator, not a hanging alligator in a stuffed shop.

36 **And if** See note at 1.124.

39 **my need** Following which Q2 adds: 'And this same needie man must sell it me' (5.1.54).

Enter APOTHECARY

APOTHECARY Who calls? What would you, sir?
ROMEO   Here's twenty ducats.
         Give me a dram of some such speeding gear
         As will dispatch the weary taker's life
         As suddenly as powder being fired   45
         From forth a cannon's mouth.
APOTHECARY Such drugs I have, I must of force confess,
         But yet the law is death to those that sell them.
ROMEO Art thou so bare and full of poverty,
         And dost thou fear to violate the law?   50
         The law is not thy friend, nor the law's friend,
         And therefore make no conscience of the law.
         Upon thy back hangs ragged misery,
         And starvèd famine dwelleth in thy cheeks.
APOTHECARY My poverty, but not my will, consents.   55
ROMEO I pay thy poverty, but not thy will.
APOTHECARY [*Handing Romeo poison*] Hold, take you this,
         And put it in any liquid thing you will,
         And it will serve, had you the lives of twenty men.
ROMEO Hold, take this gold, worse poison to men's souls   60
         Than this which thou hast given me. Go, hie thee hence,
         Go, buy thee clothes, and get thee into flesh.
                                              [*Exit Apothecary*]

---

42 Who . . . sir?] Q1 *(subst.)*; Who calls so lowd? Q2   42 Here's twenty] Q1 *(subst.)*; there is fortie Q2   43 Give me]
Q1 *(Giue)*; let me haue Q2   43 some such] Q1; poison, such soone Q2   44] Q1 *(subst.)*; As will dispearse it selfe
through all the veines, / That the life-wearie-taker may fall dead, Q2   45 suddenly] Q1; violently Q2   45 powder
being] Q1; hastie powder Q2   46 a cannon's mouth] Q1 *(Cannons)*; the fatall Canons wombe Q2   47 drugs . . .
confess] Q1 *(subst.)*; mortall drugs I haue Q2   48 yet the] Q1; *Mantuas* Q2   48 those . . . sell] Q1; any he that vtters
Q2   49 poverty] Q1 *(pouertie)*; wretchednesse Q2   51 law] Q1 *(Law)*; world Q2   51 law's friend] Q1 *(Lawes frend)*;
worlds law Q2   53] Q1 *(subst.)*; Contempt and beggerie hangs vpon thy backe: Q2   54 starvèd . . . dwelleth] Q1 *(subst.)*;
famine is Q2   56 pay] Q1; pray Q2; pay Q4   56 but] Q1; and Q2   57 SD] *Jowett; not in* Q, F   57] *Arranged as in*
Hubbard; as prose Q1   57–8 Hold . . . it] Q1 *(subst.)*; Put this Q2   59 lives] Q1 *(liues)*; strength Q2   60 Hold, take
this] Q1; There is thy Q2   62 buy thee] *Eichhoff*; buy the Q1   62 clothes] Q1 *(cloathes)*; foode Q2   62 thee into]
Q1; thy selfe in Q2   62 SD] *Wilson-Duthie; not in* Q1

47 of force perforce, necessarily.

49–54 As elsewhere in this scene, Romeo's
speech is shorter than and considerably rearranges
the corresponding material in Q2.

49–50 This question arguably makes better
sense than that in Q2, where Romeo asks the
Apothecary why, considering his poverty, he
should fear 'to die' (5.1.69).

51 nor the As Levenson points out, 'thou' may
be elliptically omitted between these words (see
Abbott 399).

52 make no conscience have no scruples
about (*OED* Conscience 11).

56 pay Most editors here prefer Q1 to Q2's
'pray', though Levenson (Oxford) has recently
returned to the latter.

59 serve be enough.

61 Preceding this line, Q2's Romeo speaks the
parenthetical 'Doing more murther in this loath-
some world', and following this line, he reinforces
his point by adding: 'I sell thee poison, thou hast
sold me none' (5.1.81, 83).

Come, cordial, and not poison, go with me
To Juliet's grave. For there must I use thee.   *Ex[it]*

[19]   *Enter* FRIAR JOHN

FRIAR JOHN   What, Friar Laurence, brother, ho!

           [*Enter* FRIAR LAURENCE]

FRIAR LAURENCE   This same should be the voice of Friar John.
       What news from Mantua? What, will Romeo come?
FRIAR JOHN   Going to seek a barefoot brother out,
       One of our order, to associate me,   5
       Here in this city visiting the sick,
       Whereas the infectious pestilence remained,
       And being by the searchers of the town
       Found and examined, we were both shut up.
FRIAR LAURENCE   Who bare my letters then to Romeo?   10
FRIAR JOHN   I have them still, and here they are.
FRIAR LAURENCE   Now by my holy order,
       The letters were not nice but of great weight.
       Go, get thee hence, and get me presently
       A spade and mattock.   15
FRIAR JOHN   Well, I will presently go fetch thee them.   *Exit*
FRIAR LAURENCE   Now must I to the monument alone,
       Lest that the lady should, before I come,

---

64 SD] *Wilson-Duthie; Exeunt.* Q1   0 SD] Q1 *(subst.); Enter Frier* Iohn *to Frier* Lawrence. Q2   1 SH] Q1 *(Iohn:)*
(throughout scene)   1 SD] Q2 *(Enter* Lawrence.*); not in* Q1   1 What . . . Laurence] Q1 *(subst.);* Holy *Franciscan* Frier
Q2   3 What news] Q1 *(newes);* Welcome Q2   3 will . . . come] Q1 *(subst.);* sayes *Romeo* Q2   4 seek] Q1 *(seeke);*
find Q2   7 remained] Q1 *(remaind);* did raigne Q2   10 letters] Q1*;* Letter Q2   11] Q1 *(subst.);* I could not send it,
here it is againe, Q2   12 holy order] Q1 *(Order);* Brotherhood Q2   13 letters were] Q1*;* Letter was Q2   13 of great
weight] Q1*;* full of charge Q2   15 spade and mattock] Q1 *(mattocke);* Iron Crow Q2

Scene 19
Act 5, Scene 2 in the NCS edition.
With the exception of its final three lines, this short
scene corresponds quite closely to its corresponding lines in Q2, though Q1's scene amounts to only
twenty lines whereas Q2 totals thirty. Q1 indicates
a break by a row of printer's ornaments above the
beginning of the scene.
   1 SD Q2 provides two entrances for Friar
Laurence (at the beginning and after the first line),
whereas Q1 provides none. In the light of Friar
John's opening words, this seems the appropriate
moment for Laurence's appearance.
   7 Duncan-Jones points out that 'Q1 presents
Verona's outbreak of "infectious pestilence" as a

narrative fact', whereas 'in Q2 we are given no more
than suspicion of plague' (447). See also note at
20.177.
   7 **remained** continued to exist (*OED* Remain
v. 6.a).
   13 **weight** importance.
   17–20 The first line of Friar Laurence's final
speech in this scene is identical with that in Q2,
but the rest is entirely different as well as shorter,
three lines as opposed to six. Q1's Friar does not
mention the specific time span within which Juliet
is to awake ('three houres', 5.2.25), nor does he
think of writing again to Romeo to call him back
to Verona.

                    Be waked from sleep. I will hie
                    To free her from that tomb of misery.   20

                                                                    Exit

[**20**]   *Enter County* PARIS *and his* PAGE *with flowers and sweet water*
           [*and a torch*]

PARIS Put out the torch, and lie thee all along
                    Under this yew tree,
                    Keeping thine ear close to the hollow ground.
                         [*His Page puts out the torch.*]
                    And if thou hear one tread within this churchyard,
                    Straight give me notice.   5
PAGE   I will, my lord.
                         [*He retires*]
                    Paris strews the tomb with flowers
PARIS Sweet flower, with flowers I strew thy bridal bed,
                    Sweet tomb that in thy circuit dost contain
                    The perfect model of eternity.
                    Fair Juliet, that with angels dost remain,   10
                    Accept this latest favour at my hands,
                    That living honoured thee, and being dead,

---

0 SD *and a torch*] *Capell, after Rowe; not in* Q1   1 lie] Q1 *(lye);* lay Q2   2 this yew tree] Q1 *(this Ew-tree);* yond young
Trees Q2; yond yew trees *Pope*   2–3] *Arranged as in Hubbard; as one line* Q1   3 Keeping] Q1 *(keeping);* Holding Q2
3 thine] Q1; thy Q2   3 SD] *Jowett; not in* Q, F   5 Straight] *Eichhoff;* Staight Q1; *not in* Q2   6, 14 SHS] Q2; *Boy:* Q1
6 SD .1] *Capell; not in* Q, F1; *Exit* F2   7 I . . . bed] Q1 *(subst.);* thy Bridall bed I strew Q2

Scene 20
Act 5, Scene 3 in the NCS edition.
The final scene is the longest in both substantive early editions, 223 lines in Q1 and 310 in Q2. With the exception of Romeo's dying speech (which preserves less than half of its forty-seven Q2 lines and from which a ten-line passage disappears in its entirety), the differences between Q1 and Q2 are usually not a matter of lengthy cuts but rather of condensations and local omissions. While Q1 dramatises the same events as Q2 and usually (though not always: see notes at 123–7 and 129–36) in the same order, the wording differs considerably, and only thirty of the lines are substantively the same, with another sixteen containing only one substantive variant. In other words, only about 20 per cent of Q1's lines are (almost) identical with those in Q2. Q1 indicates a break by a row of printer's ornaments above the beginning of the scene.

0 SD It is possible that Juliet has remained onstage since the curtains of her bed were drawn (see note at 17.107–8), a bed that would thus serve to represent her tomb in this scene.

4–5 This sentence condenses a corresponding five-line passage in Q2 (5.3.5–9).

7 **bridal bed** The resonance of these words may be reinforced if Juliet's bed remains onstage after Scene 17 and here becomes the tomb in which she lies. See note at 17.107–8 and 0 SD above.

7–13 Except for its first line, Paris's monologue constitutes a substantially different version from that in Q2 which forms a sestet rhyming ababcc (5.3.12–17).

12–13 An extremely elliptical passage: *while you were living, I honoured thee, and you now being dead, I do adorn thy tomb.* See note at 166 below and Abbott 382, 399–402.

With funeral praises do adorn thy tomb.

[Page] whistles and calls

[PAGE] My lord!

Enter ROMEO *and* BALTHASAR, *with a torch, a mattock,
and a crow of iron*

PARIS The boy gives warning, something doth approach.   15
What cursèd foot wanders this way tonight,
To stay my obsequies and true love's rites?
What, with a torch? Muffle me, night, a while.

[He retires]

ROMEO Give me this mattock and this wrenching iron.
And take these letters. Early in the morning   20
See thou deliver them to my lord and father.
So get thee gone and trouble me no more.
Why I descend into this bed of death
Is partly to behold my lady's face,
But chiefly to take from her dead finger   25
A precious ring which I must use
In dear employment. But if thou wilt stay,
Further to pry in what I undertake,
By heaven, I'll tear thee joint by joint
And strew this hungry churchyard with thy limbs.   30
The time and my intents are savage, wild.

BALTHASAR Well, I'll be gone and not trouble you.

ROMEO So shalt thou win my favour. Take thou this.

[He gives money.]

Commend me to my father. Farewell, good fellow.

---

13 SD *Page*] *This edn; Boy* Q1   14 SH] *This edn; not in* Q1   14 SD] Q1 *(subst.); Enter* Romeo *and* Peter Q2 *(after 18)*   14 SD *a mattock*] Q1 *(a a mattocke)*   16 way] Q2; was Q1   17 stay] Q1; crosse Q2   17 rites] Q1; right Q2   18 SD] *Capell; not in* Q, F; Steps aside. *Douai MS.*   19 this . . . this] Q1; that . . . the Q2   20 And] Q1; Hold Q2   20 these letters] Q1; this Letter Q2   21 them] Q1; it Q2   22 get thee gone] Q1; stand all aloofe Q2   25 from] Q1; thence from Q2   26 ring which] Q1; Ring: a Ring that Q2   27 wilt stay] Q1; iealous dost returne Q2   28 undertake] Q1 *(vndertake); farther shall intend to doo* Q2   29 I'll] Q1 *(Ile);* I will Q2   31 savage, wild] Q1 *(sauage, wilde);* sauage wilde Q2; savage-wild *Steevens (1778)*   32 Well, I'll] Q1 *(Ile);* I will Q2   32 gone] Q1; gone sir Q2   32 you] Q1; ye Q2   33 win my favour] Q1 *(fauour);* shew me friendshid Q2 *(friendship Q3)*   33 this] Q1; that Q2   33 SD] *Jowett; not in* Q, F   34 Commend . . . father] Q1 *(Father);* Liue and be prosperous Q2

20 **these letters** Q1 consistently has 'letters' where Q2 mentions a single 'letter'.

25–9 Q1's speech contains three extrametrical lines (25, 26, and 29) which all slightly depart from their metrically regular equivalents in Q2.

32 Another metrical infelicity owing to slight departures from the equivalent Q2 line.

BALTHASAR [*Aside*] Yet, for all this will I not part from hence.   35

[*He retires*]
Romeo opens the tomb
ROMEO Thou detestable maw, thou womb of death,
Gored with the dearest morsel of the earth,
Thus I enforce thy rotten jaws to ope.
PARIS [*Aside*] This is that banished haughty Montague
That murdered my love's cousin. I will apprehend him.   40
[*Comes forward*]
Stop thy unhallowed toil, vile Montague.
Can vengeance be pursued further than death?
I do attach thee as a felon here.
The law condemns thee, therefore thou must die.
ROMEO I must indeed, and therefore came I hither.   45
Good youth, be gone, tempt not a desperate man.
Heap not another sin upon my head
By shedding of thy blood. I do protest
I love thee better than I love myself,
For I come hither armed against myself.   50
PARIS I do defy thy conjurations
And do attach thee as a felon here.
ROMEO What dost thou tempt me? Then have at thee, boy!

---

35 SD.1] *Capell; not in* Q, F   35 SD.2] *Hanmer (Balthasar retires); not in* Q, F1; *Exit.* F2   35 SD.3] Q1; *not in* Q2   37
Gored] Q1 *(Gorde);* Gorg'd Q2   38 ope] Q1; open Q2   39 SD] *Jowett; not in* Q, F   41 SD] *Cam.; not in* Q, F   43
attach] Q1; apprehend Q2   44 The . . . therefore] Q1 *(subst.);* Obey and go with me, for Q2   46 youth, be gone] Q1
(youth be); gentle youth Q2   47 Heap] Q1 *(Heape);* Put Q2   48 shedding . . . blood] Q1 *(subst.);* vrging me to furie
Q2   49] Q1 *(subst.);* By heauen I loue thee better then my selfe, Q2   51 conjurations] Q1 *(coniurations);* commiration
Q2; commisseration Q3; commiseration Q4   52 do . . . as] Q1 *(doe);* apprehend thee for Q2   53 What . . . tempt] Q1;
Wilt thou prouoke Q2

35 SD.3 As Williams has pointed out, this stage direction should be understood as meaning 'Romeo busies himself with opening the tomb' as the tomb is still not open (or not fully open) when Paris asks Romeo to open it in line 56.
37 Gored Hubbard and Levenson emend Q1's 'Gorde' to 'Gorg'd'/'Gorged' by reference to Q2, but Q1 makes good sense and is in keeping with the 'gory weapons' (97 below) later in the scene.
40 cousin Q2 here inserts a three-line passage into Paris's speech which leaves no trace in Q1, while the words before and after these lines are closely parallel in the two texts.
50 Q1 omits two lines at the end of Romeo's speech.
51 conjurations Modern editors usually fol-

low Capell in emending Q2's 'commiration' to 'conjuration' (solemn entreaty) by reference to Q1. A simple minim misreading ('coniuration', 'commiration') can account for the word in Q2.
52 Except for the first word, this is identical with 43 above, while the corresponding Q2 lines significantly differ not only from Q1's but also from each other.
53 Jowett has Romeo draw his sword at the outset of the fight, but Alan C. Dessen has considered the alternative possibility that he kills Paris 'more savagely, by means of his prying tools' (*Recovering Shakespeare's Theatrical Vocabulary* (Cambridge, 1995), p. 195). Note though that Friar Laurence later discovers 'gory weapons' (97 below) which are 'goarie swords' (5.3.142) in Q2.

They fight

PAGE O Lord, they fight. I will go call the watch.   [*Exit*]

PARIS Ah, I am slain. If thou be merciful,   55
       Open the tomb, lay me with Juliet. [*Dies*]

ROMEO I'faith, I will. Let me peruse this face.
       Mercutio's kinsman, noble County Paris!
       What said my man when my betossèd soul
       Did not regard him as we passed along?   60
       Did he not say Paris should have married Juliet?
       Either he said so, or I dreamed it so.
       But I will satisfy thy last request,
       For thou hast prized thy love above thy life.
       [*Laying Paris in the tomb*]
       Death, lie thou there, by a dead man interred.   65
       How oft have many at the hour of death
       Been blithe and pleasant, which their keepers call
       A lightning before death. But how may I
       Call this a lightning? Ah, dear Juliet,
       How well thy beauty doth become this grave.   70
       O, I believe that unsubstantial death
       Is amorous and doth court my love.

---

54 SH] Q4; *Boy:* Q1; *line unassigned* Q2   54 SD] *Capell; not in* Q, F   55 Ah] Q1; O Q2   56 SD] *Theobald (*Dyes.*); not in* Q, F   60 regard] Q1; attend Q2   60 passed along] Q1 *(past);* rode Q2   61–2] *Arranged as in Hubbard;* Did . . . married / *Iuliet* . . . so Q1   61 Did he not say] Q1; I thinke / He told me Q2   62] Q1 *(subst.);* Said he not so? Or did I dreame it so? Q2   64 SD] *Theobald (subst.); not in* Q, F   66–7 have . . . pleasant] Q1 *(subst.);* when men are at the point of death / Haue they bene merie Q2   68 But] Q1; Oh Q2   70] Q1 *(subst.);* Why art thou yet so faire? Q2   71 O, I believe] Q1 *(subst.);* I will beleeue, / Shall I beleeue Q2; I will believe *Pope;* Shall I believe *Theobald*

57–79 Romeo's speech in Q1 (23 lines) is less than half as long as that in Q2 (47 lines).

58 John C. Meagher points out that 'Paris and Mercutio have never been linked before' and argues that the most plausible reason why they are here 'is that Paris and Mercutio were roles borne by the same actor' (*Shakespeare's Shakespeare: How the Plays Were Made* (New York, 1997), p. 106). See Appendix B, p. 163.

61 Another extrametrical line in Q1 with a corresponding regular line in Q2.

63–4 These two lines are a substitute for a seven-line passage in Q2 (5.3.80–6) in which Romeo describes in lyrically beautiful terms how the dead Juliet transforms the vault into a 'feasting presence full of light'. Romeo's insistence on Paris's merit is unique to Q1.

70–5 How . . . chambermaids. These six lines are all that remains of a twenty-four line passage in Q2 (5.3.92–115) which is strongly indebted to contemporary poetry, notably to Samuel Daniel's *Rosamond*. In particular, Q1 omits a ten-line passage in which Romeo describes the dead Juliet in Petrarchan terms and sees and addresses the dead Tybalt. Q1's omission of Tybalt may well be a result of casting exigencies (see Appendix B).

72 Another extrametrical line at a point where Q1 departs from Q2. Romeo's belief that death 'doth court my love' condenses Q2's formulation, 'the leane abhorred monster keepes / Thee here in darke to be his parramour' (5.3.104–5). Following this line, Q1 omits a six-line passage present in Q2.

Therefore will I, O here, O ever here,
Set up my everlasting rest with worms
That are thy chambermaids. Come, desperate pilot,   75
Now at once run on the dashing rocks
Thy sea-sick weary barge. Here's to my love!
                              [*Drinks the poison*]
O, true apothecary, thy drugs are swift.
Thus with a kiss I die.
                              Falls [*and dies*].

Enter FRIAR [LAURENCE] *with a lantern*[*, a mattock, and a spade*].

[FRIAR LAURENCE] How oft tonight have these my aged feet   80
    Stumbled at graves as I did pass along.
    Who's there?
BALTHASAR   A friend and one that knows you well.
FRIAR LAURENCE Who is it that consorts so late the dead?
    What light is yon? If I be not deceived,
    Methinks it burns in Capels' monument.   85
BALTHASAR It doth so, holy sir, and there is one
    That loves you dearly.
FRIAR LAURENCE   Who is it?
BALTHASAR   Romeo.
FRIAR LAURENCE How long hath he been there?
BALTHASAR Full half an hour and more.
FRIAR LAURENCE Go with me thither.   90

74–9] *This edn;* Set . . . rest / . . . chamber mayds. / . . . on /. . . . barge. / . . . Apothecary: / . . . dye. Q1   77
barge] Q1; barke Q2   77 SD] *Theobald; not in* Q, F   78 swift] Q1; quicke Q2   79 SD.1] *This edn; Falls.* Q1; Dies.
Theobald   79 SD.2 LAURENCE] *This edn; not in* Q1   79 SD.2 *a mattock and a spade*] *This edn; not in* Q1; *Crowe, and*
Spade Q2   80 SH] Q2 *(Frier); no* SH Q1   80 these my aged] Q1; my old Q2   81 graves . . . along] Q1 *(subst.);*
graues Q2   82 SH] Q4 *(Balt.); Man.* Q1, Q2   82 A friend] Q1 *(frend);* Heeres one, a friend Q2   84 light] Q1; torch
Q2   84 yon] Q1; yond Q2   85 Methinks] Q1 *(Me thinkes);* as I discerne Q2   85 burns] Q1 *(burnes);* burneth
Q2   85 Capels'] Q1 *(Capels);* the Capels Q2   86 SH] Q4 *(Balt.); Man* Q1; *Man.* Q2   86–7 there . . . dearly] Q1
(subst.); theres my maister, one that you loue Q2   87, 89 SHS BALTHASAR] Q4 *(Balt.); Man.* Q1, Q2   89 hour and
more] Q1; houre Q2   90 thither] Q1; to the Vault Q2

73–5 Q1 rearranges the corresponding passage
in Q2: 'here, here will I remaine / With wormes
that are thy Chamber-maides; O here / Will I set
vp my euerlasting rest' (5.3.108–10).

75 **chambermaids** Q2 here inserts lines
which 'specify the actor's gestures as he pre-
pares to drink the poison' (Oxford): 'take your last
embrace . . . lips . . . seale with a righteous kisse'
(5.3.113–14).

77 **barge** bark.

79 SD.1 Following this SD, Q1 has another row

of printer's ornaments, although the action is continuous.

79 SD.2 **mattock . . . spade** Later in the scene,
the Friar is arrested 'with tools' (123), and in the
preceding scene, he asks Friar John to 'get me
presently / A spade and mattock' (19.14–15). In
Q2, Friar Laurence asks for an 'Iron Crow' (5.2.21)
rather than a mattock, and enters with 'Crowe, and
Spade' according to the corresponding Folio SD.

83 **consorts** See note at 10.27.

BALTHASAR I dare not, sir, he knows not I am here.
         On pain of death he charged me to be gone
         And not for to disturb him in his enterprise.
FRIAR LAURENCE Then must I go. My mind presageth ill.
      Friar [Laurence] stoops and looks on the blood and weapons
     What blood is this that stains the entrance   95
         Of this marble stony monument?
         What means these masterless and gory weapons?
         Ah me, I doubt. Who's here? What, Romeo dead?
         Who – And Paris too? What unlucky hour
         Is accessory to so foul a sin?   100
                    JULIET *rises*
     The lady stirs.
[JULIET]   Ah, comfortable Friar,
         I do remember well where I should be
         And what we talked of. But yet I cannot see
         Him for whose sake I undertook this hazard.
FRIAR LAURENCE Lady, come forth, I hear some noise at hand;   105
         We shall be taken. Paris, he is slain,
         And Romeo dead. And if we here be ta'en,

---

91 SH] Q4 *(Balt.); Man:* Q1*; Man.* Q2   91 he] Q1*; My Master* Q2   91 I am here] Q1 *(heere);* but I am gone
hence Q2   94 SD *Laurence] This edn; not in* Q1   97 means] Q1 *(meanes);* meane Q2   97 weapons] Q1*;* swords
Q2   98–9 What . . . too] Q1 *(subst.); Romeo,* oh pale! Who else, what *Paris* too? Q2   99 unlucky] Q1 *(vnluckie);* vnkind
Q2   100] Q1 *(subst.);* Is guiltie of this lamentable chance? Q2   101 SH] Q2 *(Iuli.); no SH* Q1 *(Iul: catchword on preceding
page)*   101 Ah] Q1*;* O Q2   103–4] Q1 *(subst.);* And there I am, where is my *Romeo?* Q2   105 noise at hand] Q1*;*
noyse Q2

---

93 A hexameter that is unique to Q1.

93 **for to** to (Abbott 152).

94 SD Q1 is alone in printing this SD. Q2, in the
equivalent place, prints a suggestive short speech
by Balthasar: 'As I did sleepe vnder this yong tree
heere, / I dreampt my maister and another fought,
/ And that my maister slew him' (5.3.137–9).
The theatrical Q1 thus builds up suspense through
stage action – Friar Laurence approaches, stoops,
looks, and realises – while Q2 does so by momentarily suspending the action through the insertion
of a speech. See Erne, pp. 223–4.

95 **entrance** Trisyllabic (see Wright, 153–4).

96 A headless iambic pentameter (see Wright,
175).

97 **means** For the third person plural in –s, see
Abbott 333.

98 **doubt** anticipate with apprehension, fear
(*OED* Doubt *v.*6).

104 **hazard** risk, danger.

105–9 Q1 condenses Friar Laurence's speech
from nine to five lines and almost entirely
rephrases it.

107 **And Romeo dead** Q1 disposes of the odd-
ity that Juliet, looking for Romeo, is told by Friar
Laurence that he 'in thy bosome there lies dead'
(5.3.155), which may have been awkward onstage.

107–8 **And if . . . accessory.** Only Q1's Friar
spells out the reason why he wants to escape.

> We shall be thought to be as accessory.
> I will provide for you in some close nunnery.
> JULIET Ah, leave me, leave me, I will not from hence.   110
> FRIAR LAURENCE I hear some noise. I dare not stay, come, come.
>> *[Exeunt Friar Laurence and Balthasar]*
> JULIET Go, get thee gone.
> What's here? A cup closed in my lover's hands?
> Ah churl, drink all and leave no drop for me?
> CAPTAIN OF THE WATCH *[Within]* This way, this way.   115
> JULIET Ay, noise? Then must I be resolute.
>> *[Taking Romeo's dagger]*
> O happy dagger, thou shalt end my fear.
> Rest in my bosom. Thus I come to thee.
>> *She stabs herself and falls. [Dies.]*

---

109 provide for you] Q1 *(prouide); dispose of thee Q2   **109** some . . . nunnery] Q1 *(Nunery);* a Sisterhood of holy Nunnes Q2   **111** SD] *This edn; not in Q1; Exit.* Q2   **112** gone] Q1; hence Q2   **113** lover's] Q1 *(louers);* true loues Q2   **113** hands] Q1; hand Q2   **114** Ah] Q1; O Q2   **114** drink . . . leave] Q1 *(subst.);* drunke . . . left Q2   **114** drop for me] Q1; friendly drop Q2   **115** SH] *NCS; Watch.* Q1   **115** SD] *Capell; Enter watch.* Q1 *(following 114)*   **116** Ay] Q1 *(I);* Yea Q2   **116** must. . resolute] Q1; ile be briefe Q2   **116** SD] *Douai MS.; not in* Q, F   **117–18** thou . . . thee.] Q1 *(subst.);* This is thy sheath, there rust and let me dye. Q2   **118** Rest] Q1; rust Q2

109 you Like Juliet's parents (see notes at 14.89 and 118), Friar Laurence addresses Juliet with 'you' at a point where Q2 has 'thee'.

109 close secluded.

110–12 In Q2, Juliet's first line following Friar Laurence's exit ('Go get thee hence, for I will not away, 5.3.160) is made up of elements which in Q1 are transposed to two lines in different speeches.

111 In Q2, Friar Laurence's final appeal to Juliet comes at the end of his preceding speech, 'Come go, good Iuliet, I dare no longer stay' (5.3.159), immediately followed by his exit.

111 SD Editors often follow the early quartos in failing to provide an exit for Balthasar despite the fact that he re-enters, led by a watchman, later in the scene. He may of course leave the stage earlier, at the end of the dialogue with Friar Laurence (as in Garrick's version), but since he decided 'not [to] part from hence' (35 above), it seems perhaps more plausible that the noise of the approaching watchmen causes him to depart at the same time as Friar Laurence.

114 Following this line, Q2's Juliet utters her wish to die through a poisoned kiss and, having kissed Romeo, realises that his lips are still warm. The passage makes for powerful theatre, and Q1's omission of it is surprising.

115 SD Q1 prints '*Enter watch*' twice, following lines 114 and 118, a duplication which 'may perhaps be interpreted to indicate that [115] was spoken within' (NCS).

118 Rest Many nineteenth-century editors preferred Q1's 'Rest' to Q2's 'rust', though the latter has been defended by recent editors.

118 thee Juliet's dying words are powerfully ambiguous as 'thee' can refer both to Romeo – whom she wants to join in death – and to the dagger she has been addressing, a dagger which is of course Romeo's and metonymically related to him.

118 SD.1 Following this SD, Q1 has another row of ornaments, although the action is continuous.

118 SD.2 Q1 disposes of Paris's Boy who, in Q2, enters with the watch and leads it to 'the place there where the torch doth burne' (5.3.171). The SD does not specify the number of watchmen, but it may be assumed that the Captain of the Watch enters with two other watchmen: he addresses 'friends' in line 120, and two watchmen exit and re-enter in the following lines. Additional, mute watchmen seem unlikely in a scene where casting demands are particularly high. Note that Q2 requires a greater number of watchmen, a total of at least six: the Captain and two groups of watchmen who leave the stage, the second consisting of at least three men ('Go some of you' (5.3.173); 'Go tell the Prince, runne to the *Capulets,* / Raise vp the *Mountagues,* some others search' (5.3.177–8)). See Appendix B, pp. 163–5.

Enter watch

CAPTAIN OF THE WATCH Come, look about. What weapons have
          we here?
          See, friends, where Juliet, two days burièd,   120
          New bleeding, wounded – Search and see who's near.
          Attach and bring them to us presently.
                                        [*Exeunt watchmen*]

Enter [SECOND WATCHMAN] *with the* FRIAR [*with a mattock
          and a spade*]

SECOND WATCHMAN Captain, here's a friar with tools about him
          Fit to ope a tomb.
CAPTAIN OF THE WATCH A great suspicion, keep him safe.   125

Enter [THIRD WATCHMAN] *with* [BALTHASAR]

THIRD WATCHMAN Here's Romeo's man.
CAPTAIN OF THE WATCH Keep him to be examined.

Enter PRINCE *with others*

PRINCE What early mischief calls us up so soon?
CAPTAIN OF THE WATCH O, noble Prince, see here
          Where Juliet, that hath lain entombed two days,   130

---

118 SD] *Douai MS.; not in* Q; *Kils herselfe* F   119 SH] *NCS; Cap* Q1; *Watch.* Q2   121 New . . . wounded] Q1; bleeding,
warme, and newlie dead Q2   122 SD.1] *This edn; not in* Q1   122 SD.2 SECOND WATCHMAN] *This edn; one* Q1   122
SD.2 *with . . .spade*] *This edn; not in* Q1   123 SH] *Levenson; 1.* Q1   124] Q1 *(subst.); fit to open / These dead mens
Tombes.* Q2 *(in the chief watchman's speech following 20.133)*.   125 SH] *NCS; Cap:* Q1   125 SD] Q1 *(Enter one with
Romets Man.)*   125 SD THIRD WATCHMAN] *This edn; one* Q1   126 SH] LEVENSON; *1.* Q1   127, 129 SHS] *NCS;
Capt:* Q1   127 SD] Q1; *Enter the Prince.* Q2   128 mischief] Q1 *(mischiefe); misaduenture* Q2   128 us . . . soon] Q1
(subst.); our person from our morning rest Q2   130 lain] Q1 *(lyen)*

119–33 This sequence, characterised by hectic
stage action, contains fewer close parallels to the
equivalent passage in Q2 than usual and considerably rearranges its order.
119–22 Q1 compresses the equivalent Q2 speech
from ten to four lines and entirely rephrases it,
thereby reducing the number of watchmen.
122 SD.1 One of the watchmen thus seems to
exit only to re-enter immediately with Friar Laurence.
122 SD.2 For the tools, which the Second
Watchman goes on to mention, see 79 SD.2 above
and note.
123–7 Q1 reverses the order of Q2 where
Balthasar is brought onstage before Friar Laurence.

123–4 Q2 has two speeches reporting Friar Laurence's arrest: by the Third Watchman addressing the Captain (5.3.184–6) and by the Captain
addressing the Prince (5.3.199–201). Even though
Q1's speech, in terms of dramatic action and
sequence, is a version of the former, it is linguistically closer to the latter.
128–34 This rearranges the order of Q2 where
the Capulets enter before the Captain informs the
Prince of what has happened.
129–32 Ellipsis of forms of 'to be', of which
there seem to be one or two instances in these
lines, is quite common in Shakespeare (see Abbott
403).

> Warm and fresh bleeding, Romeo and County Paris
> Likewise newly slain.

PRINCE Search, seek about to find the murderers.

Enter old CAPULET *and his* WIFE

CAPULET What rumour's this that is so early up?

CAPULET'S WIFE The people in the streets cry 'Romeo'   135
> And some on Juliet, as if they alone
> Had been the cause of such a mutiny.

CAPULET See, wife, this dagger hath mistook. For, lo,
> The back is empty of young Montague,
> And it is sheathèd in our daughter's breast.   140

Enter old MONTAGUE

PRINCE Come, Montague, for thou art early up
> To see thy son and heir more early down.

MONTAGUE Dread sovereign, my wife is dead tonight,
> And young Benvolio is deceasèd too.
> What further mischief can there yet be found?   145

PRINCE First come and see, then speak.

MONTAGUE [*Seeing Romeo's body*] O thou untaught! What manners
> is in this
> To press before thy father to a grave?

---

133 SD] Q1 *(subst.)*; *Enter Capels.* Q2   135 The] Q1; O the Q2   135 streets] Q1 *(streetes)*; street Q2   136 And . . .
Juliet] Q1 *(Iuliet)*; Some *Iuliet*, and some *Paris* Q2   138 mistook] Q1 *(mistooke)*; mistane Q2   138–9] *This edn;* . . .
mistooke. / For . . . Q1   139 The . . . empty] Q1 *(subst.)*; his house / Is emptie on the back Q2   140 sheathèd]
Q1 *(sheathed)*; missheathd Q2   140 our] Q1; my Q2   140 breast] Q1; bosome Q2   140 SD] Q1 *(subst.)*; *Enter
Mountague.* Q2   142 more early down] Q1 *(downe)*; now earling downe Q2; now early downe Q3   143 Dread
sovereign] Q1 *(subst.)*; Alas my liege Q2   144] Q1 *(subst.)*; Griefe of my sonnes exile hath stopt her breath. Q2   145
mischief . . . found] Q1 *(subst.)*; woe conspires against mine age Q2   146] Q1 *(subst.)*; Looke and thou shalt see.
Q2   147 SD] *Jowett; not in* Q, F

---

134 Compare the similar passage in Q2 as the
Prince enters: 'What misaduenture is so early vp'
(5.3.188). The parallel is noteworthy as the collocation 'so early up' does not exist elsewhere in
Shakespeare.

135–6 cry . . . on call out about (cf. 'What noise
is this that cries on murder', *Oth.* 5.1.49).

136–7 as . . . mutiny This Q1 substitution for
Q2's 'and all runne / With open outcry toward our
Monument' (5.3.192–3) conveniently forestalls
the question of why it is that no one else appears
at the monument if 'all' are running towards it.

139 back sheath. 'The dagger was anciently
worn behind the back' (Furness, p. 290).

140 Following this line, Q1 omits Q2's two-line

speech by Lady Capulet in which she refers to
'my old age'. Q1 thus cuts both of Q2's (arguably
contradictory) indications regarding the age of
Lady Capulet, the present one and the earlier one
according to which she gave birth to Juliet around
the age of fourteen, thus making her approxi-
mately twenty-eight (1.3.73–4).

142 more early down Editors from Steevens
to Jowett have occasionally preferred Q1's 'more'
to Q2's 'now'.

143–4 The necessities of doubling may best
account for the sudden death of Montague's Wife
(shared by Q2) and Benvolio (which is unique to
Q1). See Appendix B, pp. 164–5.

PRINCE Come, seal your mouths of outrage for a while,
    And let us seek to find the authors out   150
    Of such a heinous and seldseen mischance.
    Bring forth the parties in suspicion.
FRIAR LAURENCE I am the greatest, able to do least.
    Most worthy Prince, hear me but speak the truth,
    And I'll inform you how these things fell out.   155
    Juliet, here slain, was married to that Romeo
    Without her father's or her mother's grant.
    The Nurse was privy to the marriage.
    The baleful day of this unhappy marriage
    Was Tybalt's doomsday; for which Romeo   160
    Was banishèd from hence to Mantua.
    He gone, her father sought by foul constraint
    To marry her to Paris. But her soul,
    Loathing a second contract, did refuse
    To give consent. And therefore did she urge me   165
    Either to find a means she might avoid
    What so her father sought to force her to,
    Or else all desperately she threatened

---

149 Come, . . . mouths] Q1 *(subst.)*; Seale vp the mouth Q2   **152** in] Q1; of Q2   **156**] Q1 *(subst.)*; *Romeo* there dead, was husband to that *Iuliet*, Q2   **159–60** The . . . doomsday] Q1 *(subst.)*; their stolne marriage day / Was *Tibalts* doomesday Q2   **160–1** for . . . Mantua.] Q1 *(subst.)*; whose vntimely death / Banisht the new-made Bridegroome from this Citie. Q2   **166** means] Q1 *(meanes)*; meane Q2; means Q3   **168–9**] Q1 *(subst.)*; Or in my Cell there would she kill her selfe. Q2

151 heinous grievous (*OED*, 2).

151 seldseen seldom to be seen (*OED*).

152 in suspicion under suspicion. The collocation is not used elsewhere by Shakespeare.

153–93 The Friar's speech totals forty-one lines, making it the longest speech in Q1. In Q2, he is interrupted by the prince after five lines, before continuing for another forty-one lines. The first line in the Q1 speech is substantively identical with and the last four lines are close to Q2. Yet the rest of the speech, even though Friar Laurence relates the same events and arranges them in roughly the same order, is largely independent with only occasional echoes of Q2.

155 fell out happened, came to pass.

157 grant permission (*OED* Grant *n.*1, 1.a).

158 marriage Trisyllabic.

158 Q2's Friar does not provide this information until shortly before the end of his long speech: '& to the marriage her Nurse is priuie' (5.3.265–6).

159 baleful miserable, sorrowful (*OED* 2).

162–3 her . . . Paris The difference of Q1 from Q2 is particularly noteworthy here: in Q2, Friar Laurence explains and excuses the Capulets' behaviour and addresses them – 'You to remoue that siege of griefe from her' (5.3.237) – while in Q1 he does not address them and harshly accuses Juliet's father.

163–7 This further contributes to making this a rather different speech from its Q2 equivalent, more sympathetic towards Juliet and more critical of her father: Friar Laurence reiterates his stress on Capulet's coercion of his daughter. Moreover, Juliet's motif in refusing to marry Paris is irreproachable, and her appeal to the Friar thus seems reasonable – contrary to that in Q2 where she urges him with 'wild lookes' (5.3.240).

166 a means . . . avoid Another ellipsis (a means *by which* she might avoid). 'The Elizabethan authors objected to scarcely any ellipsis, provided the deficiency could be easily supplied from the context' (Abbott, 382).

Even in my presence to dispatch herself.
Then did I give her, tutored by mine art,   170
A potion that should make her seem as dead,
And told her that I would with all post-speed
Send hence to Mantua for her Romeo,
That he might come and take her from the tomb.
But he that had my letters, Friar John,   175
Seeking a brother to associate him,
Whereas the sick infection remained,
Was stayèd by the searchers of the town.
But Romeo, understanding by his man
That Juliet was deceased, returned in post   180
Unto Verona for to see his love.
What after happened touching Paris' death
Or Romeo's is to me unknown at all.
But when I came to take the lady hence,
I found them dead, and she awaked from sleep,   185
Whom fain I would have taken from the tomb,
Which she refusèd seeing Romeo dead.
Anon I heard the watch, and then I fled.
What after happened I am ignorant of.

170] Q1 *(subst.)*; Then gaue I her *(*so tuterd by my art*)* Q2   171] Q1 *(subst.)*; A sleeping potion, which so tooke effect / As I intended, for it wrought on her / The forme of death, Q2   172–4] Q1 *(subst.)*; meane time I writ to *Romeo* / That he should hither come as this dire night / To help to take her from her borrowed graue, / Being the time the potions force should cease. Q2   175] Q1 *(subst.)*; But he which bore my letter, Frier *Iohn*, Q2   176–8] Q1 *(subst.)*; Was stayed by accident, and yesternight / Returnd my letter back, Q2   182–5 What . . . dead,] Q1 *(subst.)*; But when I came, some minute ere the time / Of her awakening, here vntimely lay, / The Noble *Paris*, and true *Romeo* dead. Q2   184 to . . . hence] Q1 *(subst.)*; to take her from her kindreds Vault Q2   185 and . . . sleep] Q1 *(subst.)*; She wakes, Q2   186–9] Q1 *(subst.)*; I entreated her come forth / And beare this worke of heauen with patience: / But then a noyse did scare me from the Tombe, / And she too desperate would not go with me: / But as it seemes, did violence on her selfe. Q2

---

172 post-speed Characterised by haste or speed like that of a post or courier (*OED* Post *n.2* 12.f).

176 associate accompany (*OED* Associate *v.*5). In Q1 (but not in Q2), Friar Laurence uses the very word Friar John employed in the preceding scene (19.5; 5.2.6). The word is very rare in Shakespeare as a verb, the only other occurrence outside *Rom.* being in *Tit.* in a short passage added in Q2 (1600) to Lucius' speech at 5.3.159.

177 Whereas Q1 makes clear that the plague is the reason why Romeo's letter was not delivered, Q2's Friar John was simply 'stayed by accident' (5.3.251). In Q1 there is thus a sense, whereas in Q2 there is not, 'that Mercutio's invocation of "a plague on both thy houses" (or, as Q1 more brutally

has it, "pox") has been actualized' (Duncan-Jones, 447). London's severe plague outbreak of 1593–4 preceded the composition of *Romeo and Juliet* only by a year or so. See also note at 19.7.

177 infection Pronounced as four syllables.

179–81 Q2's speech contains no equivalent passage. Instead, Friar Laurence reveals his plan to release Juliet from the vault and 'to keepe her closely at my Cell, / Till I conueniently could send to Romeo' (5.3.254–5). Q2's Friar thus reports from his own perspective, whereas Q1's infers what Romeo intended and did.

180 in post in haste (*OED* Post *n.2* 8.d).

183 unknown at all entirely unknown. Modern English requires a negation: not known at all.

And if in this ought have miscarrièd   190
By me or by my means, let my old life
Be sacrificed some hour before his time
To the most strictest rigour of the law.
PRINCE We still have known thee for a holy man.
      Where's Romeo's man? What can he say in this?   195
BALTHASAR I brought my master word that she was dead,
      And then he posted straight from Mantua
      Unto this tomb. These letters he delivered me,
      Charging me early give them to his father.
PRINCE Let's see the letters; I will read them over.   200
                [*He takes the letters*]
      Where is the County's boy that called the watch?
PAGE I brought my master unto Juliet's grave,
      But one approaching, straight I called my master.
      At last they fought, I ran to call the watch,
      And this is all that I can say or know.   205
PRINCE These letters do make good the Friar's words.
      Come, Capulet, and come, old Montague.
      Where are these enemies? See what hate hath done.
CAPULET Come, brother Montague, give me thy hand.
      There is my daughter's dowry.   210
      For now no more can I bestow on her.
      That's all I have.

190–1 And . . . means] Q1 *(subst.)*; And if ought in this miscaried by my fault, Q2   192 sacrificed] Q1 *(sacrificd)*; sacrified *Furness* (Q1), *Hubbard*   193] Q1 *(subst.)*; Vnto the rigour of seuerest law. Q2   193 strictest] Q1 *(strickest)*   195 in] Q1; to Q2   196 word . . . dead] Q1 *(subst.)*; newes of *Iuliets* death Q2   197 he posted straight] Q1 *(poasted)*; in poste he came Q2   198 These letters] Q1 *(Letters)*; This Letter Q2   200 Let's see] Q1 *(Lets)*; Giue me Q2   200 letters] Q1 *(Letters)*; Letter Q2   200 read them over] Q1 *(ouer)*; looke on it Q2   200 SD] *This edn (after Jowett); not in* Q, F   201 boy] Q1 *(Boy)*; Page Q2   201 called] Q1 *(calld)*; raisd Q2   202 SH] F1; *Boy*. Q   206 These . . . do] Q1 *(doe)*; This Letter doth Q2   207–8] Q1 *(subst.)*; Where be these enemies? *Capulet, Mountague?* / See what a scourge is laide vpon your hate? Q2   207 Come] Q1; O Q2   210 There] Q1; This Q2   210 dowry] Q1; ioynture Q2   210–13] *This edn;* There . . . more / . . . haue. / . . . erect / . . . golde: Q1   211 now no] Q1; no Q2   211 bestow on her] Q1 *(bestowe)*; demaund Q2

---

193 **most strictest** The double superlative, still possible in early modern English, served 'the purpose of greater emphasis' (Abbott 11).

195–206 Unlike Q2, Q1 presents the questioning of Romeo's and Paris's servants as a strictly symmetrical sequence: the Prince asks a one-line question starting 'Where is'/'Where's'; Balthasar and the Page each give a four-line answer starting 'I brought my master'; and the Prince ends with an additional line concerning the letters.

199 **early** in good time, before it is too late

(*OED* Early *adv.* 5.a).

206 Following this line, Q1 omits the Prince's four-line summary of the letter in Q2.

208 Q2's Prince goes on to include himself in the pattern of misdeeds and their consequences: 'And I for winking at your discords too / Haue lost a brace of kinsmen, all are punish't' (5.3.294–5).

211 **bestow on her** Q1's Capulet says that the only 'dowry' he can 'bestow on' Juliet is a handshake with Montague; for Q2's Capulet, by contrast, the handshake is all he can 'demaund' as

MONTAGUE   But I will give them more.
  I will erect her statue of pure gold,
  That while Verona by that name is known,
  There shall no statue of such price be set   215
  As that of Romeo's lovèd Juliet.
CAPULET As rich shall Romeo by his lady lie,
  Poor sacrifices to our enmity.
PRINCE A gloomy peace this day doth with it bring.
  Come, let us hence to have more talk of these sad things.   220
  Some shall be pardoned and some punishèd.
  For ne'er was heard a story of more woe
  Than this of Juliet and her Romeo.

                                                              [*Exeunt*]

---

212 will give them] Q1 *(giue)*; can giue thee Q2   **213** erect] Q1; raie Q2; rayse Q4, F1   **213** of] Q1; in Q2   **214** while] Q1; whiles Q2   **215** statue of such price] Q1; figure at such rate Q2   **216** Romeo's lovèd] Q1 *(subst.)*; true and faithfull Q2   **217** Romeo . . . lady] Q1 *(subst.)*; Romeos . . . Ladies Q2; *Romeo . . . Lady* F1   **218** to] Q1; of Q2   **219** gloomy] Q1 *(gloomie)*; glooming Q2; gloomy F4   **219** day . . . bring] Q1; morning . . . brings Q2   **220**] *Arranged as in Hubbard;* . . . hence, / . . . things. Q1   **220** Come, let us] Q1 *(vs)*; Go Q2   **222** ne'er was heard] Q1 *(nere)*; neuer was Q2   **223** SD] F *(Exeunt omnes.)*; not in Q1, Q2 *(both print 'FINIS.' after last line of dialogue)*

Juliet's 'ioynture' (5.3.296–7). The jointure is thus the marriage settlement made by the bridegroom's father. In other words, Q1's Capulet *makes* whereas Q2's Capulet *accepts* a gesture of reconciliation.

212 In Q2, Shakespeare's verse enacts the reconciliation of Capulet and Montague by having them share a line; the relineation of Q1 produces the same result and avoids a short line in 213 (though it also creates one in line 210).

215–23 Q1 ends with couplets by Montague and Capulet and three unrhymed lines and a final couplet by the Prince. Q2 also has a couplet each by Montague and Capulet but followed by a sestet (with a cross-rhymed quatrain and a couplet) by the Prince.

216 lovèd beloved. For dropped prefixes in Shakespeare, see Abbott 460.

220 A last extrametrical line in Q1 with a corresponding regular line in Q2.

APPENDIX A. SCENE DIVISION

No sixteenth- or seventeenth-century edition of *Romeo and Juliet* divides the play into acts and scenes. The Folios have an initial 'Actus Primus. Scœna Prima', but no act or scene breaks thereafter.[1] Rowe introduced act and scene division in 1709, his act division being adopted till this day, even though his scene division differs from modern conventions in several ways, most importantly in Act 1, which Rowe divided into two scenes only. The first quarto omits the only feature of Q2 that might be taken to suggest an act break (the Chorus, at the beginning of what most modern editions call Act 2), and I therefore follow the convention adopted in most other editions in the 'Early Quartos' series by dividing the play exclusively into scenes.

But how many scenes are there? Modern editors disagree. Gibbons and Evans have five scenes in Acts 1, 3, and 4, six scenes in Act 2, and three scenes in Act 5. Jowett, in the Oxford Shakespeare, reduces the number of scenes in Act 2 to five and in Act 4 to four. Levenson's Oxford Shakespeare edition follows Jowett in Acts 2 and 4, but, in addition, reduces Act 1 to four scenes. In other words, the play has twenty-four scenes in Gibbons and Evans's, twenty-two scenes in Jowett's, and twenty-one scenes in Levenson's edition. This edition follows Levenson's scene division except that it prints as continuous what corresponds to 4.3 and 4.4 in her Oxford Shakespeare text, thus reducing the total number of scenes to twenty.

What is the rationale for this scene division? A preliminary observation first: for a modern editor, an important consideration in adopting a certain scene division is the weight of tradition. Most nineteenth- and twentieth-century editions had done what Gibbons and Evans did in the 1980s, and the convenience and ease of reference that follow from adopting the conventions Shakespeareans are used to is considerable. As I divide the play into scenes, not acts and scenes, this consideration has no weight in the context of this edition. I therefore suggest looking at the evidence afresh, taking as my starting point William Ringler's observation that 'a scene is marked by a momentary clearing of the stage'.[2]

The scene divisions in what corresponds to the first two acts need not detain us long. Editorial tradition going back to Pope inserts a scene break between the episode with the masquers (Romeo, Mercutio, Benvolio), including the Queen Mab speech (1.4), and the beginning of the Capulet's dance (1.5). Yet in fact, the masquers do not leave the stage, and the action is continuous (Scene 4 in this edition). This is especially clear in the first quarto where the festive scene begins ('*Enter old* CAPULET *with the Ladies*') with Romeo, Mercutio, and Benvolio already onstage. In Act 2, most editors since Pope editorially separate the opening sequence, in which Mercutio and Benvolio make fun of Romeo (2.1), and the 'Balcony Scene' (2.2), but here, too, Romeo remains onstage and the action is continuous (Scene 5 in this edition).

In Act 4, the situation is more complex. In 4.3, Juliet drinks the potion, then '*falls upon her bed within the curtains*'. In 4.4, the wedding preparations in the Capulet household are fully under way. In 4.5, the Nurse wants to wake up Juliet but discovers her to be 'dead'.

---

[1] Note that continuous staging without any pauses between scenes and acts seems to have been standard practice of Shakespeare's company up to 1609 when they started performing at their indoor theatre, the Blackfriars.

[2] Ringler, p. 114.

As for the transition from 4.3 to 4.4 (where all modern editors seem to begin a new scene), McKerrow opined that no scene break occurs, an opinion I share.[3] Juliet remains onstage where she will be discovered by the Nurse later on. It is important to recall how this moment may have been staged (see above, pp. 27–8): Juliet's bed may well have been thrust out from the tiring house and would thus still be onstage at the end of 4.3, with Juliet hidden from view behind the curtains of the canopied bed. Such a staging keeps Juliet very much onstage, invisible but a conspicuous presence of which spectators would have been well aware. This adds to the dramatic irony for which *Romeo and Juliet* has rightly been praised, the general business in the Capulet household ('Make haste, make haste') contrasting with the immobile Juliet on her bed. The continuation of the scene also provides a sense that Juliet's soliloquy, like Faustus's final soliloquy, telescopes time: she withdraws around midnight and the Nurse re-enters around four o'clock (three o'clock in Q2), her soliloquy thus providing no more than a summary of her nightly agony. That the traditional scene break is no more than a matter of convention is suggested by Evans who starts a new scene but writes in a note: 'Location: Scene continues'. It is true that Q1 has a row of printer's ornaments below the stage direction indicating that Juliet falls on her bed, but Q1's ornaments repeatedly occur at the end of scenic movements rather than the end of scenes.

As for 4.4 and 4.5, the continuity of the action is again particularly clear in Q1 where the Nurse, who is already onstage, is asked by Capulet to wake up Juliet and straight away goes on to try to do so. Gibbons points out that 'It is convenient to mark a new scene for ease of reference, but the Nurse has not in fact left the stage' and Evans similarly notes that the 'scene continues'. In the introduction, Evans states that 'In Elizabethan terms these three scenes [4.3, 4.4, and 4.5] represent one continuous scene.'[4] In fact, the action spanning 4.3 to 4.5 constitutes one of Shakespeare's grand scenic constructions which Emrys Jones has so astutely analysed.[5] The famous director and critic Harley Granville-Barker was acutely aware of the nature of Shakespeare's dramatic construction and fiercely objected to an editorial convention that obscures it:

Her nurse and her mother leave her; she drinks the potion, and . . . *She falls upon the bed within the curtains* . . . What Shakespeare aims at in the episodes that follow is to keep us conscious of the bed and its burden . . . till the bridal music is playing, till, to the very sound of this, the Nurse bustles up to draw back the curtains and disclose the girl there stark and still. . . . It is one scene, one integral stretch of action; and its common mutilation by *Scene iv. Hall in Capulet's house . . . Scene v. Juliet's chamber. Enter Nurse . . .* is sheer editorial murder.[6]

This edition avoids this murder by presenting – for the first time in the play's editorial history, as far as I am aware – the long dramatic sequence as a carefully constructed continuous scenic movement (Scene 17).

---

[3] McKerrow's view is reported in Oxford, p. 316.
[4] NCS p. 33.
[5] See Emrys Jones, *Scenic Form in Shakespeare* (Oxford, 1971).
[6] Harley Granville-Barker, *Prefaces to Shakespeare* [1930], vol. 4 (London, 1963), pp. 62–3.

APPENDIX B. CASTING AND DOUBLING

Doubling was standard practice on the early modern stage since plays regularly had more parts than the company actors. Shakespeare must have known in advance how many adult and boy actors he could count on to perform a play, and this knowledge contributed to shaping his methods of dramatic construction. Students of Shakespeare's plays have much to gain from an awareness of this practice, and casting charts are becoming an increasingly common part of modern scholarly editions. Providing a casting chart for Q1 *Romeo and Juliet* seems all the more appropriate as I have argued in the Introduction that the text is the closest we can get to the play as it was performed by Shakespeare's company. The information the text can provide about casting may therefore be particularly valuable.

Different scholars arrive at different casting charts with different numbers of actors. This does not mean that some get it right and others don't; more likely, the reason for the differences resides in different conventions underlying their casting charts, conventions which are not always spelled out in sufficient detail. As has been pointed out, 'variations include whether actors double both male and female roles, whether speaking actors double non-speaking roles, whether actors double parts where there are few or even no intervening lines to cover a costume-change, and so forth'.[1] The conventions I accept here are adopted from a recent essay by Ann Thompson and Neil Taylor about doubling in the three substantive texts of *Hamlet*. My chart (see pp. 160-1) thus follows the six following rules:

(1) every line in the relevant text is performed; (2) no role is played by more than one actor, but (3) one actor can play any number of roles – so long as (4) he or 'she' has time to leave the stage for at least a few minutes before returning in a new role; (5) female roles are played by boys; (6) boys can nevertheless also occasionally play adult male roles.[2]

As a result of (6), 'Juliet' can double as a serving-man in the first scene and 'the Nurse' can double not only as Montague's Wife in Scene 1 but also as Paris's Page and the Captain of the Watch in Scene 20. As for rule (4), I believe that little time is needed to effect a costume change. David Bradley holds that the minimum number of lines between exit and re-entrance in a doubled role was twenty-five, but I assume that in special cases (of which I discuss one below), fewer lines may have been sufficient.[3]

In order to calculate the minimum number of actors, I further need to adopt a rule concerning the small (and often mute) parts, parts of characters whose exact numbers may not even be specified in stage directions. As William Ringler pointed out, 'In calculating the size of the cast the speaking parts are easy to identify; the main problem is to ascertain the number of mute attendants and others who are supposed to be on stage in each particular

[1] Ann Thompson and Neil Taylor, '"Your sum of parts": doubling in *Hamlet*', in Erne and Kidnie, pp. 111–26, 115.

[2] Thompson and Taylor, '"Your sum of parts"', p. 117. As Thompson and Taylor point out, 'there is no reason to believe that boys could never have played adult male roles. Of course, they played both women and adult males in the plays put on by the children's companies' (p. 117). For another analysis of casting practices, see David Bradley, *From Text to Performance in the Elizabethan Theatre: Preparing the Play for the Stage* (Cambridge, 1992), pp. 40–57, 229–43.

[3] Bradley, *From Text to Performance*, pp. 43–4. Ringler similarly believes that 'on the Elizabethan stage [costume] changes were apparently executed with considerable celerity' (p. 120).

Table 1: *Casting chart for Q1 Romeo and Juliet*

Actor	Prol.+1	2	3	4	5	6	7	8	9	10	11	12	13	14	15	16	17	18	19	20
1	-1MSer-**Rom**	-Rom		Rom-	Rom	-Rom	-Rom		**Rom**	-Rom-		-Rom		Rom-				Rom		-Rom
2	-Ca-	Ca-		-Ca-									Ca	-Ca-		Ca	-Ca-	-Apo-		-Ca
3	-Ben	-Ben		Ben-	-Ben-	-Ben-	Ben-			**Ben**								-Bal-		-Bal
4	-2MSer-	Par-		Mer-	-Mer-	Mer-	Mer-			**Mer-**			Par		Par-		-Par-			Par
5	-Tyb-			-Tyb-		*FrL*			*FrL*	-Tyb-		*FrL*			*FrL*		-FrL-	-FrL	-FrL	-FrL
6	Prol-Pri-			-C'sC-						-Pri									FrJ-	-Pri
7	1CSer-	-Ser-	-Ser	-1CSer-			-Pet									Ser-	-Ser-			
8+	2CSer-	-Ser-	-Ser	-*Jul*	-*Jul*-			*Jul*-	-*Jul*		*Jul*			*Jul*	-*Jul*-	-*Jul*-	*Jul*			-*Jul*
9+	-*CaW*-		*CaW*-	*CaW*-	-*CaW*-					-*CaW*			*CaW*-	*CaW*-		*CaW*-	*CaW*-			-*CaW*
10+	-*MoW*-	*Nur*	-*Nur*	-*Nur*	-*Nur*		-*Nur*	-*Nur*	-*Nur*		-*Nur*	-*Nur*-		-*Nur*-		*Nur*-	*Nur*-			PP-CW
11(+)	-**Mo**-			-CSer-						-**W**							-1Mus	-**Mo**		-**Mo**
12(+)	-1Cit-			-T'sP-						**MerP-**							-2Mus			-3W
13(+)	-2Cit-			Page-						-**Cit**							-3Mus			-2oth
14(+)																				-1oth

Key

-	enters after beginning of scene	
-	exits before the end of scene	
Italic	female	
	bold	male
	underline	mute
	+	boy actor

Roles in order of entry:

Prol	Prologue	1Cit	First Citizen	Cit	Citizen
1CSer	First Capulet Serving-man	2Cit	Second Citizen	1Mus	First Musician
2CSer	Second Capulet Serving-man	Rom	Romeo	2Mus	Second Musician
1MSer	First Montague Serving-man	Par	Paris	3Mus	Third Musician
2MSer	Second Montague Serving-man	Ser	Serving-man	Bal	Balthasar
Ben	Benvolio	Nur	Nurse	Apo	Apothecary
Tyb	Tybalt	Page	Page	FrJ	Friar John
Pri	Prince	C'sC	Capulet's Cousin	PP	Paris's Page
Mo	Montague	T'sP	Tybalt's Page	CW	Captain of the Watch
MoW	Montague's Wife	FrL	Friar Laurence	2W	Second Watchman
Ca	Capulet	Pet	Peter	3W	Third Watchman
CaW	Capulet's Wife	MerP	Mercutio's Page	1oth	First 'other'
		W	Watchman	2oth	Second 'other'

scene.'[4] Ringler proposes a sensible solution which I have adopted in my chart: 'a plural for mute "attendants," "soldiers," etc., should usually be interpreted as no more than two, unless there is evidence in the text to the contrary, for on the Shakespearean stage two is a crowd, and "four or five most vile and ragged foils" are enough to represent the opposing armies at Agincourt'.[5] In order to apply the rule consistently, I have thus taken any unspecified plural to refer to two: two citizens in Scene 1, two Capulet servants in Scene 4, and two 'others' in Scene 20.

Even once rules are established and adhered to, problems remain: the presence of characters may be suggested in various ways, but not on all occasions do we therefore assume that these characters are present onstage. In Scene 2, the Serving-man's letter with Capulet's invitations to the feast refers to at least twenty people for whom the play provides neither exits nor dialogues. We do not have to imagine that they all decline Capulet's invitation to believe that no actors need to be assigned to these characters in Scene 4. In the absence of stage directions, a useful distinction seems to be whether characters are directly addressed (in which case they need to be onstage) or only talked about (in which case they may or may not be onstage). So when Capulet orders 'More lights, you knaves, and turn these tables up' (4.99), I assume that there are two Capulet servants present. By contrast, when Juliet, later in the same scene, enquires about gentlemen whom the Nurse identifies as 'The son and heir of old Tiberio' and 'young Petruchio' (4.194–7), I do not assume that actors playing these two gentlemen need to be onstage.

A last preliminary point: like Thompson and Taylor, I assume that 'acting companies in Shakespeare's day wished to restrict the number of actors they employed' and that small or 'non-speaking parts might be played by people who were not necessarily regular members of the company'.[6] As far as observance of my stated rules allows it, I thus try to cast the play for as few actors as possible. I also attempt to limit the number of principal actors performing the principal parts. It is true that the endeavour to be 'as economical of the company's workforce as is logically possible produces results which may rarely if ever have been put into practice'.[7] Yet the aim of the chart is not in the first place to try to guess what Shakespeare's company did but to try to work out what they could have done or what any other company could do, if the aim was to reduce the cast as much as possible. In my comments below, I shall also keep in mind what further economies in personnel are possible if my rules were not strictly observed.

To sum up the results presented in my chart, Q1 *Romeo and Juliet* could be performed by a cast of fourteen, seven principal male actors, three boys performing the four female parts, and four 'extras' (who could be boys or adults) performing very small and often mute parts.[8]

In order to explain how I arrive at these figures, I first need to comment on the three scenes that require the greatest number of actors: Scenes 1, 4, and 20. In Scene 1, thirteen characters are onstage simultaneously, two Capulet and two Montague Serving-men, Benvolio, Tybalt, the Prince, Montague, Capulet and their wives, and (two) mute 'citizens'. Most characters exit at line 62, after which Romeo does not enter for another twenty lines. Juliet does not appear in this scene at all, so both 'Romeo' and 'Juliet' can double in minor parts. In cases of emergency, the minimum number could easily have been reduced by one or two by disposing of the mute citizens. In Scene 4, thirteen characters are onstage during the dance: Romeo, Benvolio, Mercutio, Capulet, Capulet's cousin, Tybalt, Tybalt's page, Capulet's Wife, Juliet,

---

[4] Ringler, p. 115.
[5] Ibid.
[6] Thompson and Taylor, '"Your sum of parts"', p. 117.
[7] Ibid.
[8] For the presentational features of my chart, I am indebted to Thompson and Taylor, '"Your sum of parts"'.

the Nurse, and two mute servant 'knaves' (4.99), whom Capulet asks for more light, plus the equally mute page mentioned in the scene's opening stage direction. In cases of emergency, the minimum number could have been reduced by disposing of the mute page and one of the mute 'knaves'. In Scene 20, finally, fifteen characters are onstage: Paris and his Page, Romeo, Balthasar, Juliet, Friar Laurence, three watchmen, the Prince with (two) mute 'others', Capulet, Capulet's Wife, and Montague. Paris's Page exits early and can easily double as a watchman or a mute 'other' later in the scene, so the minimum number of actors is fourteen, all onstage at the end of the play. In cases of emergency, the minimum number could easily have been reduced by one or two by disposing of the mute 'others'.

The boy playing Capulet's Wife is the only figure among the principal actors who does not double, though 'Capulet', 'Romeo', and 'Juliet' only do so in one scene in small speaking parts. 'Capulet' doubles as the Apothecary, though 'Mercutio'/'Paris' could do so equally well. It might be tempting to have Friar Laurence and the Apothecary double for reasons which are spelled out by Meagher:

On his first falling in love with [Juliet], [Romeo] had visited Friar Laurence, whom we first meet in 2.3, just before Romeo's entry, as he gathers herbs from the monastic garden and philosophizes on the divers properties of various plants, including how the medicinal can be poisonous if misapplied, and how human willfulness can choose death over grace. This characterization of the Friar establishes his credentials for concocting the potion by which Juliet later attempts to feign death in order to get out of her otherwise impossible position . . . Surely it would occur to Shakespeare to make [the] apothecary of last resort, the purveyor of poison to end Romeo's life, reminiscent of the druggist-friar with whom this whole episode began. It would make splendid dramatic sense for Shakespeare to give his audience the jolt of making the apothecary visibly parallel to the friar.[9]

Thematic doubling of this kind may be attractive, but it would leave Friar Laurence only three lines between the end of Scene 18 and the beginning of 19 to change costumes. In any case, the number of actors needed to perform the play is not affected.

Having 'Romeo' double as a Montague servant and 'Juliet' as a Capulet servant produces the interesting result of having 'them' meet as early as the violent clash in Scene 1, an ironic effect of which a first-time audience would of course not be aware. 'Benvolio' doubles as Balthazar, and Melchiori has argued that it makes good sense for him to do so.[10] It explains Benvolio's absence in the last scene, an absence Q1 (contrary to Q2) explains by having Montague announce Benvolio's death (20.144). Their age is similar, as is their relationship to Romeo, though it is probably fallacious to assume that actors regularly doubled in roles that are similar.

The doubling of Mercutio and Paris also deserves a comment. We do not find out until the last scene that the two characters are kinsmen – after killing Paris in a sword-fight, Romeo exclaims: 'Mercutio's kinsman, noble County Paris!' (20.58). It has been suggested that the reason why this information is provided at such a late stage is that the two characters were doubled:

If so, we as audience have seen this all along, and have been denied the direct dramatic linkage only so that Shakespeare can here, at a decisive point in Romeo's life, make the connection between the friend who he thought had died for him and the innocent bridegroom of Juliet whom he has just ironically killed through a terrible misunderstanding.[11]

[9] John C. Meagher, *Shakespeare's Shakespeare: How the Plays Were Made* (New York, 1997), pp. 103–4.
[10] Giorgio Melchiori, 'Peter, Balthasar, and Shakespeare's art of doubling', *Modern Language Review* 78 (1983), 778–92, 788.
[11] Meagher, *Shakespeare's Shakespeare*, p. 106. See also Irace, pp. 126–31.

An implication of this is that Paris would necessarily be absent during Capulet's feast in Scene 4. He is invited by Capulet in Scene 2 and certainly has good reasons, psychologically speaking, to attend. In many modern productions (including the Zeffirelli and Luhrman films), much is made of Romeo's rival during this scene. However, no stage direction expressly mentions his presence, and casting exigencies make it seem possible that he sometimes was not present onstage in early modern productions.

The doubling of Tybalt and Friar Laurence works well enough in case of need, a typical instance of deficiency doubling as opposed to thematic or conceptual doubling.[12] The swiftest costume change would have to occur at the beginning of Scene 10. Friar Laurence exits at the end of the previous scene, and Tybalt does not enter until line 20, which may leave enough time for a costume change, all the more so as Friar Laurence might simply have thrown off his monk's gown before re-entering in Tybalt's gallant costume, which the actor was wearing under the gown. Actor number 7 can be called the 'clown servant': the first of the two Capulet Serving-men ('Sampson' in Q2), who starts the bawdy talk and bites his thumb at the Montague Serving-men (Scene 1); the illiterate Capulet Serving-man with the list of guests (Scene 2; note that Q2 calls this character '*Clowne*' in a stage direction); the Serving-man, called clown in a Q1 stage direction and speech heading, who urges Capulet's Wife to hurry (Scene 3); one of the servant 'knaves' whom Capulet asks for more light (Scene 4); the punning Capulet Serving-man in Scene 16; the Capulet Serving-man who enters with 'logs and coals' (Scene 17) and the Serving-man who, at the end of the same scene, enters with the three musicians. The Q2 stage direction at this point reads '*Enter Will Kemp*', which, unusually, allows us to identify the actor who played this part, Will Kemp having been the Lord Chamberlain's Men's clown from 1594 to 1599. Since no Capulet servant is onstage between Scenes 4 and 16, it seems likely, as suggested by Melchiori,[13] that Kemp would have doubled as Peter, the Nurse's man, in Scene 7.[14]

As for the remaining actors, the boy playing the Nurse could easily have doubled as Montague's Wife, who only appears in Scene 1. Actors 11 to 14 in my chart could be 'extras' with small and often mute parts. Actor 11 speaks twenty-nine lines, actor 12 a mere four lines, and actor 13 a single line. Indeed, his only words are 'I say nothing' (17.132), a nice in-joke if it was indeed intended as such. Actor 14 has only one mute part in the last scene and would thus be easy to do without. Montague is the most important part performed by one of these actors. He is onstage in the first and the last scenes, and since all major characters are onstage with him in at least one of these scenes, he can only be performed by an extra. If this is what happened, it might explain why Montague's part seems to have been reduced more than any other between Q2 and Q1. In the opening scene, Montague has twenty-eight lines in Q2 but only five in Q1, with all the others having been cut or reassigned to his wife.

As we have seen, Scenes 4 and 20, along with Scene 1, put the highest demands on the company's resources, so it seems significant that both show differences from Q2 which may have been caused by casting requirements. In particular, no stage direction in Scene 4 provides for music at the Capulets' dance,[15] and in Scene 20, Tybalt's corpse is not visibly

---

[12] I owe the expression 'deficiency doubling' to A. C. Sprague, *The Doubling of Parts in Shakespeare's Plays* (London, 1966). For an analysis of thematic or conceptual doubling, see Thomas L. Berger, 'Casting *Henry V*', *S.St.* 20 (1988), 89–104.

[13] Melchiori, 'Shakespeare's art of doubling', 789.

[14] The only other actor whose role we may infer with some confidence is Richard Burbage who 'is known to have taken almost all the leading roles till 1619' (Gurr, *Shakespeare Company*, p. 15) and thus seems likely to have played Romeo. Note that Burbage would have been aged 26 in 1595 (Gurr, *Shakespeare Company*, p. 17), younger than most of his fellow players.

[15] For the argument that the absence of music is related to the reduction in acting parts, see Hoppe, pp. 95–7.

present in the Capulets' tomb, nor even referred to, likely instances of revision prompted by casting requirements. Benvolio and Montague's Wife die offstage more or less gratuitously (see 20.143–4), meaning that they as well as the Nurse are not present in the last scene either, the actors thus becoming available to play other parts.

How do my figures relate to scholarly assumptions about the size of Shakespeare's company around the time of *Romeo and Juliet*? Gurr tells us that 'At the outset the Chamberlain's seems to have been led by eight sharers, the standard number for the time': George Bryan, Richard Burbage, John Heminges, Will Kemp, Augustine Phillips, Thomas Pope, Shakespeare, and probably Will Sly.[16] We also know of hired men – Gurr mentions John Sincler and John Holland[17] – plus there must have been a small number of boy actors. A very tight casting arrangement with seven principal adult and three boy actors plus four supernumeraries corresponds well to these figures. Ringler tried to show by means of doubling patterns that no more than sixteen actors are required for any of Shakespeare's plays written up to 1599 and that 'when Shakespeare sat down to write a play he usually had in mind a cast of 16 to produce it'.[18] Relying on somewhat different assumptions, Meagher – writing about a group of plays that includes *Romeo and Juliet* – claims that 'in a pinch, all seven of our plays *can* be delivered by thirteen speakers, and that there is reason to think that Shakespeare designed a large number of his plays with this minimum in mind'.[19] These figures also square well enough with my assessment.

On the other hand, what we know about the size of Shakespeare's company in the mid-1590s seems impossible to reconcile with the casting demands of the second quarto. For instance, at the beginning of 1.4, Q2 has Romeo, Mercutio, Benvolio, and 'fiue or sixe other Maskers, torchbearers' (a total of at least eight actors). At the point where some editors start a new scene, this group is said to 'march about the Stage' as four 'Seruingmen come forth', which brings the total up to twelve. With all these characters still onstage, we get to the actual beginning of the Capulets' feast, for which not only the hosts, Capulet and his wife, and their daughter (and, presumably the Nurse) but also 'all the guests and gentlewomen' enter. The scene requires a minimal cast of twenty, without taking into account the 'Musick' required by a stage direction. As Jowett indicates, the scene is excessive in its demands for extras.[20] The evidence from casting analyses corroborates what I argue in the Introduction: the text of the second quarto was not intended to be acted prior to abridgement and revisions with a view to the practicalities of performance; the first quarto, by contrast, is the closest we get to the play as it would have been performed on the early modern stage.

To sum up, my analysis shows that, by rigidly applying the conventions I have adopted above, a cast of a minimum of fourteen actors is needed to perform Q1, including at least three boy actors. The more flexible summary goes like this though: it would have been difficult though not impossible to perform the play with twelve, thirteen, or fourteen actors, a performance with fifteen actors would still have been tight, but the company could have performed the play comfortably with sixteen actors.[21]

---

[16] Gurr, *Shakespeare Company*, p. 13. Henry Condell probably replaced Bryan by 1597.

[17] Ibid., p. 18.

[18] Ringler, p. 123n. Ringler points out that 'there are never more than 16 characters in any one scene, and never more than 14 on stage at any one time' (p. 117), which also corresponds to my figures for Q1 *Romeo and Juliet*, where the maximal number of characters in one scene is fifteen with fourteen of them present at the same time (Scene 20).

[19] Meagher, *Shakespeare's Shakespeare*, p. 99.

[20] Jowett, p. 291.

[21] Alfred Hart thought that 'eight sharers, together with their apprentices' could have performed Q1, while Hoppe believed that 'the Q1 version could have been handled by about 12', hypotheses which are not incompatible with my present examination (Hart, p. 131; Hoppe, p. 95).

APPENDIX C. 'BEL-VEDÉRE' (1600)

In 1600, the year after the second quarto had superseded the first, the first quarto of *Romeo and Juliet* was repeatedly quoted from in the anthology *Bel-vedére or the Garden of the Muses*. *Bel-vedére* consists of a great number of unattributed snippets excerpted from literary texts (including Shakespeare's), probably by John Bodenham.[1] The quotations are thematically grouped ('Of Paine', 'Of Loue', 'Of Vertue', 'Of Women', etc.), and I indicate below under which heading the lines from *Romeo and Juliet* appear. Twelve passages totalling eighteen lines can be assigned to the play, often to the first quarto, as can be seen from the following list (I highlight significant differences):

1. Of Paine: 'One paine is lessened **by** anothers anguish.' (O7r, p. 205)
   Q1: 'One paine is lessned **with** anothers anguish:' (2.37)
   Q2: 'On paine is lesned **by** an others anguish,'

2. Of Loue: 'No stonie limits can hold out true loue.' (C7v, p. 30)
   Q1: 'For stonie limits cannot hold loue out,' (5.105)
   Q2: 'For stonie limits cannot hold loue out,'

3. Of Loue: 'What loue can doe, that dare it still attempt.' (C7v, p. 30)
   Q1: 'And what loue can doo, that dares loue attempt,' (5.106)
   Q2: 'And what loue can do, that dares loue attempt:'

4. Of Loue: 'Loue goes toward loue **like** schoole-boyes from their bookes: / But loue from loue, **to** schoole with heauie lookes.' (C7v, p. 30)
   Q1: 'Loue goes toward loue **like** schoole boyes from their bookes, / But loue from loue, **to** schoole with heauie lookes.' (5.171–2)
   Q2: 'Loue goes toward loue **as** schooleboyes from their bookes, / But loue from loue, **toward** schoole with heauie lookes.'

5. Of good Deeds: 'There's nought so vile that **on the earth** doth liue, / But to the earth some speciall good doth giue.' (N1v, p. 178)
   Q1: 'For nought so vile, that **vile on earth** doth liue, / But to the earth some speciall good doth giue:' (6.11–12)
   Q2: 'For nought so vile, that **on the earth** doth liue, / But to the earth some speciall good doth giue:'

6. Of good Deeds: 'There's nought so good, but strain'd from that faire vse: / Reuolts **to vice, and stumbles** on abuse.' (N2r, p. 179)
   Q1: 'Nor nought so good, but straind from that faire vse, / Reuolts **to vice and stumbles** on abuse:' (6.13–14)
   Q2: 'Nor ought so good but straind from that faire vse, / Reuolts **from true birth, stumbling** on abuse.'

7. Of Vertue: 'Vertue it selfe turnes vice, being misapplyed: / And vice **sometimes** by action dignified.' (C1r, p. 17)
   Q1: 'Vertue it selfe turnes vice being misapplied, / And vice **sometimes** by action dignified.' (6.15–16)

---

[1] See Charles Crawford, '*Belvedere, or The Garden of the Muses*', *Englische Studien* 43 (1910–11), 198–228. The Shakespeare passages are printed in Charles Crawford, 'Appendix D: J. Bodenham's *Belvedere*', in *The Shakspere Allusion-Book*, ed. C. M. Ingleby, 2 vols. (London, 1909), vol. 2, pp. 489–518.

Q2: 'Vertue it selfe turnes vice being misapplied, / And vice **sometime** by action dignified.'

8. Of Age: 'Care keepes his watch in euery old man eye, / And where care **lodgeth**, sleepe **can** neuer lie.' (P8v, p. 224)

Q1: 'Care keepes his watch in euerie old mans eye, / And where care **lodgeth**, sleep **can** neuer lie:' (6.30–1)

Q2: 'Care keepes his watch in euery old mans eye, / And where care **lodges**, sleepe **will** neuer lye:'

9. Of Youth: 'Looke where vnbruised youth, with vnstuft **braines** / Doth couch his limbes, there golden sleepe **remaines**.' (P6v, p. 220)

Q1: 'But where vnbrused youth with vnstuft **braines** / Doth couch his limmes, there golden sleepe **remaines**:' (6.32–3)

Q2: 'But where vnbrused youth with vnstuft **braine** / Doth couch his lims, there golden sleepe **doth raigne**.'

10. Of Women: 'Women may fall, when there's no strength in men.' (H5v, p. 106)

Q1: 'Women may fal, when ther's no strength in men.' (6.75)

Q2: 'Women may fall, when theres no strength in men.'

11. Of Youth: Youths loue is quicke, swifter than swiftest speed.' (P6v, p. 220)

Q1: 'Youths loue is quicke, swifter than swiftest speed.' (9.9)

Q2 no equivalent

12. Of Teares, Mourning: '*Venus* smiles seldome in a house of teares.' (N7r, p. 189)

Q1: 'For *Venus* smiles not in a house of teares,' (15.8)

Q2: 'For *Venus* smiles not in a house of teares.'

Bodenham did not slavishly copy the lines but felt free to transform them, turning them into self-contained sententiae or aphorisms. Unsurprisingly, Bodenham's favourite character is Friar Laurence (quoted seven times), especially his opening speech in Scene 6 (2.3). Passages 4, 6 to 9, and 11 establish beyond doubt that Q1 was used. The first passage follows Q2 rather than Q1, though it may do so accidentally, as 'by' may have been the more natural word to use than Q1's 'with'. Passage 5 seems indebted to Q2, but since the following lines in Friar Laurence's speech are also quoted from, and this time from Q1, it seems difficult to determine whether Bodenham consulted Q2 or agreed with it accidentally. In any case, the use of the first quarto in many passages can be clearly established, and Bodenham, like the editor of Q4 (see p. 43), clearly did not consider Q1 *Romeo and Juliet* as bad.

APPENDIX D. Q1 IN EIGHTEENTH-CENTURY EDITIONS OF 'ROMEO AND JULIET'

Modern editors of *Romeo and Juliet* adopt few readings from the dialogue of the first quarto. By contrast, eighteenth-century editors incorporated a considerable number of them. It is well known that Alexander Pope (1723–5) thought highly of Q1 and often preferred it to the longer text, but it is less well known that later eighteenth-century editors did the same. As I show in this Appendix, the eighteenth-century editor with the greatest number of Q1 readings is, surprisingly, not Pope but Edmond Malone (1790).

The textual theories available to eighteenth-century editors were different from those informing modern editorial practice. Eighteenth-century editors failed to recognise that Q1 derives from a version close to Q2, a failure that clearly shaped eighteenth-century editorial practice. Notoriously, Pope disparaged the Folio, which he thought contained 'additions of trifling and bombast' added by the actors (vol. 1, p. xvi). Pope singles out *Romeo and Juliet* as evidence for such practice: 'as proof that [Shakespeare] could not escape it, in the old editions of *Romeo* and *Juliet* there is no hint of a great number of mean conceits and ribaldries now to be found there' (vol. 1, p. xvi). Consequently, he often adopted readings from Q1, noting in footnotes 'from the first edition' (e.g., vol. 6, p. 284). At other times, he abridges in conformity with Q1: 'The verses left out here are not in the old edition' (vol. 6, p. 285); 'Here follows . . . a great deal of nonsense, not one word of which is to be found in the first edition' (vol. 6, p. 304); 'Some few unnecessary verses omitted in this scene [Scene 12/3.3] according to the oldest editions [sic]' (vol. 6, p. 305). Pope announces further omissions at the beginning of Juliet's encounter with her parents in Scene 14 (3.5), which 'is printed more agreeably to the first edition' (vol. 6, p. 308).

The limitations of Pope's approach to the two substantive versions of *Romeo and Juliet* thus seem obvious enough. Nevertheless, Pope's error of judgement is not devoid of interest. What seems remarkable about it is that it contrasts with his view of the other early quartos which twentieth-century bibliographers labelled 'bad'. About *The Merry Wives of Windsor* Pope writes that the quarto edition 'was alter'd and improved by the Author almost in every speech' (vol. 1, p. 233). Similarly, *Henry V* has been 'very much enlarged and improved by the author since the editions of 1600, and 1608' (vol. 3, p. 429), and *The Second and Third Parts of Henry VI*; have been 'vastly improved by the Author' (vol. 4, p. 101) since the quarto editions.[1] The intrinsic quality of what used to be called the 'bad quartos' of *The Merry Wives of Windsor*, *Henry V*, and *2* and *3 Henry VI* seems to have prevented Pope from thinking of the shorter versions as in some ways superior to the longer versions. Not so with *Romeo and Juliet*. This corroborates a point I make in the Introduction, namely that Q1 *Romeo and Juliet* is a remarkably good text among what used to be called Shakespeare's 'bad quartos'.

Pope's practice of omitting or confining to footnotes passages from the long version of *Romeo and Juliet* found no favour among his successors. Lewis Theobald (1733) wrote that Pope 'has attack'd [Shakespeare] like an unhandy *Slaughterman*; and not lopp'd off the *Errors*, but the *Poet*' (vol. 1, p. xxxv). Edward Capell (1768) and Malone shared Theobald's objection.[2] What these successors of Pope did not object to, however, is his practice of

---

[1] Pope was of course not aware of Q1 *Hamlet*, which was not rediscovered until 1823.
[2] Capell calls 'an abuse' Pope's and Thomas Hanmer's practice 'of putting out of the text passages that they did not like' (vol. 1, p. 9); for Malone's objection to Pope's omissions, see vol. 10, p. 115.

liberally adopting readings from Q1 and substituting them for those in the longer version. As tables 2.1 and 3 show, Pope did so on more than 120 occasions. Theobald vociferously protested against a few such adoptions by Pope,[3] but he silently followed some 80 per cent of them. Capell resisted more of Pope's Q1 adoptions but still preserved over a third of them. In addition, as table 4 demonstrates, he independently drew on Q1 no fewer than 36 times in passages where no earlier editor had done so. Malone, finally, adhered to almost two thirds of Pope's Q1 adoptions, he accepted 34 of Capell's 36 additional Q1 readings, and he introduced another 20 words or phrases from Q1 (see table 5).

As tables 2.1 and 2.2 show, only a very small fraction of these Q1-based readings make it into modern editions. All in all, 199 Q1 readings were first adopted by eighteenth-century editors. Of these, 14 survive in modern editions. One inference to be drawn from the great number of Q1 readings in eighteenth-century editions is that, long before the New Bibliography started operating with the 'bad quarto' label, Q1 *Romeo and Juliet* was often found to provide good readings, readings which editors preferred to those in the longer version. The difference in treatment of Q1 between modern and eighteenth-century editions further allows instructive insights into how the practice of modern editors departs from that of, say, Pope or Malone. Copy-text editing with rigorously applied bibliographical principles is a product of the twentieth century. Pope's editorial practices, as has been pointed out, were still 'extremely various and in some ways self-contradictory',[4] often built on the assumption 'that Shakespeare shared the dominant aesthetic principles of the eighteenth century' and therefore resulting from 'a misunderstanding of the pronunciation, metrical principles, and stylistic decorums of Shakespeare's period'.[5] This explains some of Pope's Q1 adoptions. For instance, Pope is alone in adopting Q1's metrically smooth 'Revolts to vice and stumbles on abuse' (6.14), where the line in the longer version appropriately stumbles: 'Revolts from true birth, stumbling on abuse' (2.3.20). Likewise, later editors do not follow Pope's Q1 adoption of 'displease' for 'dislike' in 'Neither, fair maid, if either thee dislike' (2.2.61). The line in Q2 must have started to sound archaic by the time of Pope – Malone explains that it corresponds to 'the phraseology of Shakespeare's age' (vol. 10, p. 61) – a valid reason for Pope to prefer Q1. As Marcus Walsh explains, Pope 'set out to "correct" Shakespeare by standards of taste of [his] own time',[6] and he repeatedly drew on Q1 when it could help in this endeavour. As Walsh puts it, 'It is clear that many of Pope's text-editorial decisions were made for essentially aesthetic reasons, rather than to reconstruct an original authorial text. He used Quarto readings not as a matter of course, but where it seemed to him to make better poetry or better drama.'[7]

Theobald has been highly praised by recent scholars as 'perhaps the first great Shakespeare editor' and as 'one of the finest editors of the last three centuries'.[8] Yet his highly derivative treatment of Q1 highlights a limitation of his editorial practice of which scholars have long been aware. As Malone pointed out as early as 1790, Theobald's 'edition being printed from

[3] For instance, Theobald ridicules Pope's Q1 adoption of 'from company' instead of 'to walk abroad' in Benvolio's 'A troubled mind drive me to walk abroad' (1.71; 1.1.111; Theobald, vol. 7, p. 131).

[4] Simon Jarvis, *Scholars and Gentlemen: Shakespearian Textual Criticism and Representations of Scholarly Labour, 1725–1765* (Oxford, 1995), p. 61.

[5] Gary Taylor, 'General Introduction', in Stanley Wells and Gary Taylor, with John Jowett and William Montgomery, *William Shakespeare: A Textual Companion*, (Oxford, 1987) p. 54.

[6] Marcus Walsh, *Shakespeare, Milton, and Eighteenth-Century Literary Editing: The Beginnings of Interpretative Scholarship* (Cambridge, 1997), p. 119.

[7] Ibid., p. 130.

[8] Barbara Mowat, 'The reproduction of Shakespeare's texts', in *The Cambridge Companion to Shakespeare*, ed. Margreta de Grazia and Stanley Wells (Cambridge, 2001), p. 15; and Wells and Taylor, *Textual Companion*, p. 54.

that of his immediate predecessor, while a few arbitrary changes made by Pope were detected, innumerable sophistications were silently adopted' (vol. 1, p. lxvii). Not that Theobald, by producing 'a modified reprint'[9] of Pope, was unusual for his time. On the contrary: the text of eighteenth-century Shakespeare editions from Nicholas Rowe (1709) to Samuel Johnson (1765) was 'traditionary': Rowe is based on the fourth Folio, Pope on Rowe (the 1714 text), Theobald on Pope, Warburton on Pope and Theobald, and Johnson on William Warburton (1747) and Theobald.[10] So Theobald's Q1 readings show that he largely followed Pope even where we might have thought Pope's practice particularly vulnerable and open to criticism.

Capell's 1768 text is the first edition that was not a modified reprint of a recent predecessor and 'was the first collected edition ever published based upon the earliest authoritative documents'.[11] For these reasons alone, it 'constitutes a decisive step forward in textual method',[12] a step towards an attempted recovery of 'Shakespeare's original intention'. Q1 *Romeo and Juliet* did not therefore lose its importance. Capell mentions Q1 *Romeo and Juliet* among a list of texts that are 'either first draughts, or mutilated and perhaps surreptitious impressions' (vol. 1, p. 2). However, these texts, Capell adds, 'are not wholly useless': 'in some particular passages of them, where there happens to be a greater conformity than usual between them and the more perfect editions, there is here and there a various reading that does honour to the Poet's judgment, and should upon that account be presum'd the true one' (vol. 1, p. 3). Capell's subjective reason for the inclusion of Q1 readings exemplifies what Walsh has called the 'lingering tendency to an aesthetic approach'[13] in eighteenth-century editing, even long after Pope: the 'true' reading is that which according to Capell does greater honour to Shakespeare's judgement. Examples of this are not difficult to find. For example, when Q1 reads 'eyes' instead of Q2's 'sight' in 'I have night's cloak to hide me from their eyes' (2.2.75), Capell's reason for preferring Q1 seems purely aesthetic.

The last important Shakespeare edition of the eighteenth century, Malone's of 1790, is said to have 'synthesized, climaxed, and canonized the eighteenth-century tradition'.[14] Malone decidedly turned away from what he called 'the era of conjectural criticism and capricious innovation' (vol. 1, p.lv). For Pope and the editors following him, Malone writes, 'to alter Shakespeare's text and to restore it, were considered synonymous terms', but Malone strives 'to *restore*, in the true sense of the word' which means that he proposes 'to eject the arbitrary and capricious innovations made by our predecessors from ignorance of the phraseology and customs of the age in which Shakespeare lived' (vol. 1, p. xi). As Malone established a paradigm which remained dominant into the twentieth century, we might expect Malone's edition to show an editorial devaluation of Q1, but the opposite is in fact the case. Similarly to Capell, Malone considered Q1 'an imperfect sketch' which 'cannot be entirely relied on' but nevertheless 'furnishes many valuable corrections of the more perfect copy . . . printed in 1599' (vol. 1, p. xviii). As he puts it in a footnote, 'the original copy in 1597 . . . in my opinion is preferable in this and various other places, to the subsequent copies' (vol. 10, p. 153). Elsewhere, he adds that 'in almost every speech of this play', Q1 offers readings which are 'much preferable to those of the succeeding ancient copies' (vol. 10, p. 98). Even though Pope wanted to 'improve' whereas Malone endeavoured to 'restore', eighteenth-century editors remained surprisingly constant in finding in Q1 a rich source for the pursuit of their editorial aims.

---

[9] Wells and Taylor, *Textual Companion*, p. 55.
[10] See Walsh, *Shakespeare*, p. 178.
[11] Wells and Taylor, *Textual Companion*, p. 55.
[12] Walsh, *Shakespeare*, p. 184.
[13] Ibid., p. 132.
[14] Wells and Taylor, *Textual Companion*, p. 55.

By focussing in this Appendix on the editions of Pope, Theobald, Capell, and Malone, I have tried to include the chief witnesses for the editorial treatment of Q1 in the eighteenth century. Pope, Capell, and Malone introduced the vast majority of Q1-based readings. The point of the inclusion of Theobald is a different one: it illustrates the mixture of reaction against and dependence upon his immediate predecessor. Together, the tables aim at providing as full a summary as the limited space allows of Q1 in eighteenth-century editions.

Tables 2.1 and 2.2 list Q1 readings first adopted by eighteenth-century editors which survive in at least one of the following modern scholarly editions of *Romeo and Juliet*: Gibbons, Evans (NCS), Jowett, and Levenson (Oxford). Where modern editors disagree, I signal this parenthetically in the right-hand column. The number of Q1 readings first adopted by eighteenth-century editors that subsist in modern editions is low: a mere fourteen, of which nine were first adopted by Pope (table 2.1) and five by other editors (table 2.2), three by Capell and two by George Steevens (1773). The tables show that eighteenth-century editors usually took over the Q1 readings adopted by earlier editors, though Capell on four occasions and Malone on one occasion did not.

Table 3 lists Q1 readings first adopted by Pope which do not survive in modern editions. The number of such Q1 adoptions by Pope is 112. Of these Theobald adopts 89 but rejects 23; Capell adopts 38 and rejects 74; and Malone adopts 69 and rejects 43.

Table 4 lists Q1 readings first adopted by Capell which do not survive in modern editions. The number of such Q1 adoptions by Capell is 36. Of these Malone adopts 34 and rejects 2.

Table 5 lists Q1 readings first adopted by Malone which do not survive in modern editions. The number of such Q1 adoptions by Malone is 20.

Table 6 lists Q1 readings first adopted by eighteenth-century editors other than Pope, Capell, and Malone, readings which do not survive in modern editions. The total number of such Q1 adoptions is 17: two by Rowe, one by Theobald, one by Hanmer, one by Warburton, ten by Steevens (1773), and one each by Steevens (1778) and Steevens (1793).[15] As Table 6 shows, Pope (2), Theobald (2), Capell (3), and Malone (13) all follow a number of these Q1 adoptions by earlier editors.

In summary, the total number of Q1 readings first adopted in the eighteenth-century thus is:

Pope	123
Theobald	100
Capell	85
Malone	149

Of these are adopted in at least one modern edition (Gibbons, NCS Jowett, Oxford):

Pope	9
Theobald	9
Capell	8
Malone	13

All in all, the number of Q1-based readings first adopted by eighteenth-century editors is 199. Of these, 14 are adopted in at least one of the above-cited modern scholarly editions.

---

[15] It seems unlikely that Rowe, Theobald, or Hanmer were using Q1 when preparing their editions, and it seems likely that their adoptions of Q1 were accidental.

Table 2.1 *Q1 readings first adopted by Pope and accepted in modern editions*

	Q1	Q2	Pope	Theobald	Capell	Malone	NCS
3.59; 1.3.67	honor	houre	honour	honour	hour	honour	It is an honour that I dream not of.
4.7–8; 1.4.7–8	Nor no without booke Prologue faintly spoke / After the Prompter, for our entrance.	(*not in* Q2–5, F, *Rome*)	Nor a without-book prologue faintly spoke / After the prompter, for our enterance.	Nor a without-book prologue faintly spoke / After the prompter, for our entrance.	(*not in Capell*)	Nor no without-book prologue, faintly spoke / After the prompter, for our entrance:	Nor no without-book prologue, faintly spoke / After the prompter, for our entrance; (*not in Oxford*)
4.51; 1.4.69	maide	man (woman F2–4, *Rome*)	maid	maid	maid	maid	Pricked from the lazy finger of a maid.
5.11; 2.1.10	Pronounce but Loue and Doue,	prouaunt, (pronounce Q4; Couply F2–4, couple *Rome*) but loue and day,	couple but *love* and *dove*,	couple but *love* and *dove*,	couple but love and dove;	pronounce but love and dove;	pronounce but 'love' and 'dove',
5.60; 2.2.20	eyes	eye	eyes	eyes	eye	eye	her eyes (eye *Jowett, Oxford*) in heaven

10.91; 3.1.115	fier eyed	fier end (fier and Q3; fire and Q4–5, F1–2; fire, and F3–4; Fire and *Rome*)	fire-ey'd	fire-ey'd	fire-ey'd	fire-ey'd	And fire-eyed fury be my conduct now!
18.12; 5.1.15	How fares my *Juliet?*	How doth my Lady *Iuliet?*	How doth my *Iuliet?*	How doth my *Iuliet?*	How doth my *Iuliet?*	How fares my Juliet?	How doth my Juliet? (How doth my lady Juliet? *Oxford*)
18.19; 5.1.24	defie my	denie you	defy you	defy you	deny you	defy my	then I defy you, stars! (deny *Oxford*)
20.2; 5.3.3	this Ew-tree	yond young Trees	yond yew-trees	yond yew-trees	yond yew-trees	yond yew-trees	Under yond yew trees

Table 2.2 *Q1 readings first adopted by eighteenth-century editors other than Pope and accepted in modern editions*

	Q1	Q2	Capell	Steevens	Malone	NCS
5.14; 2.1.13	**trim**	true	true	**trim**	**trim**	**trim** (true *Oxford*)
10.138; 3.1.179	**hates**	hearts	**hates'**	**hates'**	**hates'**	I have an interest in your hearts' (**hate's** *Jowett*) proceeding;
17.125; 4.5.121	**And dolefull dumps the minde oppresse:**	(*not in* Q2)	*and dolefull dumps the mind oppress,*	*and dolefull dumps the mind oppress,*	*and dolefull dumps the mind oppress,*	**And dolefull dumps the mind oppress,** (*not in Oxford*)
18.12; 5.1.15	**How fares my Juliet?**	How doth my Lady *Iuliet?* (my *Juliet Pope, Theobald*)	How doth my *Juliet?*	**How fares my Juliet?**	**How fares my Juliet?**	How doth (**fares** *Jowett*) my Juliet?
20.51; 5.3.68	**conjurations**	commiration	**conjuration**	**conjuration**	**conjurations**	I do defy thy **conjuration,**

Table 3 *Q1 readings first adopted by Pope and not accepted in modern editions*

NCS line ref	Q1	Q2	Pope	Theobald	Capell	Malone	NCS
1.70; 1.1.110	**Peept through**	Peerde forth	**Peep'd through**	**Peer'd through**	Peer'd forth	Peer'd forth	the worshipped sun / Peered forth
1.71; 1.1.111	**drew me from companie**	driue (drave Q3–5, F, *Rome*) me to walke abroad	**drew me from company**	**drew me** to walk abroad	drave me to walk abroad	drave me to walk abroad	A troubled mind drive me to walk abroad
1.78; 1.1.118	**That most are busied when th'are most alone,**	Which then most sought, where most might not be found:	**That most are busied when they're most alone,**	**(That most are busied when they're most alone,)**	Which then most sought where most might not be found,	**That most are busied when they're most alone,**	Which then most sought where most might not be found,
1.115; 1.1.178	**them**	it	**them**	**them**	it	it	Griefs . . . / Which thou wilt propagate to have it pressed
1.118; 1.1.181	**raisde**	made	**rais'd**	**rais'd**	made	**rais'd**	Love is a smoke made with the fume of sighs,
1.127; 1.1.190	**whome she is**	who is that	**who she is**	**who she is**	who is that	**who she is**	Tell me in sadness, who is that you love?
1.136; 1.1.199	**But**	Well,	**But**	**But**	Well,	Well,	Well, in that hit you miss:
1.139; 1.1.202	**vnharm'd**	vncharmd	**unharm'd**	**unharm'd**	**unharm'd**	**unharm'd**	From Love's weak childish bow she lives uncharmed.

(cont.)

Table 3 (cont.)

NCS line ref	Q1	Q2	Pope	Theobald	Capell	Malone	NCS
3·56; 1.3.64	And that same marriage Nurce, is the	Marrie, that marrie is the very	And that same marriage is the very	And that same marriage is the very	Marry, that marry is the very	Marry, that marry is the very	Marry, that 'marry' is the very theme
3·69; 1.3.99	engage	endart	ingage	indart	endart	endart	But no more deep will I endart mind eye
4·44; 1.4.58	Athwart mens noses when	ouer mens noses as	Athwart mens noses as	Athwart mens noses as	Over men's noses as	Athwart men's noses as	Over men's noses as they lie asleep.
4·47–8; 1.4.64–5	The . . . The	her . . . her	The . . . The	The . . . The	Her . . . Her	The . . . The	Her traces of the smallest spider web, / Her collars
4·58; 1.4.77	Lawers lap	Courtiers nose	lawyer's nose	lawyer's nose	courtier's nose	courtier's nose	Sometime she gallops o'er a courtier's nose,
4·59; 1.4.81	And then dreames he	then he dreames	Then dreams he	Then dreams he	Then he dreams	Then dreams he	Then he dreams of another benefice.
4·82; 1.4.103	face	side	face	face	face	face	Turning his side to the dew-dropping south.
4·95; 1.5.16	Will haue about	will walke about	we'll have a bout	we'll have a bout	will have a bout	will have a bout	Unplagued with corns will walk a bout with you.
4·123; 1.5.50	happie	blessed	happy	happy	blessed	happy	And touching hers, make blessed my rude hand.

4.161; 1.5.92	If I prophane with my vnworthie hand,	If I prophane with my vnworthiest hand,	If I prophane with my vnworthy hand,	If I profane with my unworthy hand	If I prophane with my unworthy hand	If I profane with my unworthy hand	If I profane with my unworthiest hand
4.197; 1.5.130	*That as I thinke is yong* Petruchio.	Marrie that I thinke be young Petruchio.	That as I think is young Petruchio.	That, as I think, is young *Petruchio.*	Marry, that, I think, be young *Petruchio.*	Marry, that, I think, be young Petruchio.	Marry, that I think be young Petruchio.
5.3; 2.1.3	*Romeo.*	Romeo, Romeo.	*Romeo.*	Romeo.	*Romeo!*	Romeo!	Romeo! my cousin Romeo! Romeo!
5.71; 2.2.31	lasie pacing	lazie puffing	lazy-pacing	lazy-pacing	lazy-pacing	lazy-pacing	the lazy puffing clouds (lazy-passing *Jowett*)
5.82; 2.2.44	name	word	name	name	name	name	By any other word would smell as sweet;
5.97; 2.2.59	that tongues vtterance	thy tongus vttering	that tongue's uttering	that tongue's uttering	that tongue's uttering	that tongue's utterance	My ears have yet not drunk a hundred words / Of thy tongue's uttering,
5.99; 2.2.61	Saint	maide	saint	Saint	saint	saint	Neither, fair maid, if either thee dislike

(cont.)

Table 3 (cont.)

NCS line ref	Q1	Q2	Pope	Theobald	Capell	Malone	NCS
5.99; 2.2.61	displease	dislike	displease	dislike	dislike	dislike	Neither, fair maid, if either thee dislike
5.122; 2.2.84	would	should	would	would	would	would	I should adventure for such merchandise.
5.133; 2.2.95	thou thinke	thou thinkest (thou think'st Q5)	thou think	you think	thou think'st	thou think'st	Or if thou think'st I am too quickly won
5.139; 2.2.101	more cunning	coying (more coying Q4–5; more coyning F2–4, Rome)	more cunning	more cunning	more cunning	more cunning	Than those that have more coying to be strange.
5.153; 2.2.115	true harts	hearts deare	true heart's	true heart's	heart's dear	heart's dear	If my heart's dear love –
5.184; 2.2.167	At what	What	At what	At what	At what	At what	What a'clock tomorrow / Shall I send to thee?
5.196; 2.2.178	her	his	her	her	her	her	a wanton's bird / That lets it hop a little from his hand,
5.198; 2.2.180	silke	silken	silk	silk	silk	silk	And with a silken thread plucks it back again,
6.14; 2.3.20	to vice and stumbles	from true birth, stumbling	to vice, and stumbles	from true Birth, stumbling	from true birth, stumbling	from true birth, stumbling	Revolts from true birth, stumbling on abuse

6.17 2.3.23	small	small	small	small	weake	this weak flower
6.21; 2.3.27	foes	foes	foes	kings	Kings (Kinds *Rowe*)	Two such opposèd kings
6.35; 2.3.40	by	by	by	by	with	Thou art uproused with some distemp'rature;
6.61; 2.3.66	whome	whom	whom	whom	that	Is Rosaline, that thou didst love so dear,
6.69; 2.3.74	ring yet	ring yet	ring yet	yet ring	yet ringing (yet ring Q4-4, F2-4, *Rowe*)	Thy old groans yet ringing in mine ancient ears;
6.80; 2.3.85	not	not	not	not	me not	I pray thee chide me not.
6.83; 2.3.88	and	and	and	and	that	Thy love did read by rote, that could not spell.
7.18; 2.4.20	rests me his minum rest	rests his minum	rests his minum	he rests his minum	he rests, his minum rests, (he rests his minum F, *Rowe*)	he rests his minim rests
7.25; 2.4.26	accents	accents	accents	accents	accent	these new tuners of accent
7.31; 2.4.32	**Heere comes Romeo.**	**Here comes Romeo.**	Here comes Romeo, here comes Romeo.	Here comes Romeo, here comes Romeo.	Here Comes Romeo, here comes Romeo.	Here comes Romeo, here comes Romeo.

(cont.)

Table 3 (cont.)

NCS line ref	Q1	Q2	Pope	Theobald	Capell	Malone	NCS
7.34; 2.4.35	**but a**	a	**but a**	**but a**	a	**but a**	Laura to his lady was a kitchen wench
7.86; 2.4.88	**of the two**	face	**of the two**	of the two	of the two	**of the two**	her fan's the fairer face
7.96; 2.4.97	**yong**	the yong	**young**	the young	the young	the young	where I may find the young Romeo
7.134; 2.4.136	**into**	in	**into**	**into**	**into**	**into**	if ye should lead her in a fool's paradise
8.9; 2.5.25	**let me rest**	giue me leaue	**let me rest**	let me rest	give me leave	give me leave	give me leave a while
10.6; 3.1.8	**it**	him	**it**	**it**	**it**	**it**	draws him [his sword] on the drawer
10.35; 3.1.53	**hate**	loue	**hate**	love	**hate**	**hate**	Romeo, the love I bear thee
10.89; 3.1.113	**A liue**	He gan (gon Q3–4, F1–2; gone Q5, F3–4, Rowe)	**Alive?**	**Alive?**	Again?	**Alive?**	Again, in triumph, and Mercutio slain?
10.96; 3.1.120	**Or**	Either	**Or**	**Or**	Either	Either	Either thou or I, or both, must go with him.
10.108; 3.1.138	**Vnhappie sight? Ah**	O Prince, O Cozen, husband, O	**Unhappy sight! alas**	**Unhappy sight! alas,**	O prince! O husband! O,	**Unhappy sight! ah,**	O prince! O husband! O, the blood is spilled
11.2; 3.2.2	**To . . . mansion**	Towards . . . lodging	**To . . . mansion**	Tow'rds . . . mansion	Towards . . . lodging	Towards . . . mansion	Towards Phoebus' lodging

11.2; 3.2.2	**To ... mansion**	Towards ... lodging	**To ... mansion**	**Tow'rds ... mansion**	Towards ... lodging	Towards ... mansion	Towards Phoebus' lodging
11.27; 3.2.66	**deare loude**	dearest	**dear-lov'd**	**dear-lov'd**	dearest	dear-lov'd	My dearest cousin
11.28; 3.2.67	**let the**	dreadfull	**let the**	**let the**	dreadful	dreadful	Then, dreadful trumpet, sound the general doom,
11.30; 3.2.69	**dead**	gone	**dead**	**dead**	gone	gone	Tybalt is gone
12.14; 3.3.14	**Than death it selfe**	Much more then death	**Than death it self**	**Much more than death**	Much more than death	Much more than death	Much more than death
12.20; 3.3.20	**world exiled**	worlds exile	**world-exil'd**	**world-exil'd**	world's-exile	world's exile	And world's exile is death
12.20; 3.3.21	**banishment**	banished	**banishment**	**banishment**	banishment	banishment	Calling death 'banished'
12.27; 3.3.28	**mere**	deare	**meer**	**dear**	dear	dear	This is dear mercy
12.47; 3.3.51	**Banishment**	banished	**banishment**	**banishment**	banishment	banishment	that word 'banished'
12.50; 3.3.54	**beare off**	keepe off	**bear off**	**keep off**	keep off	keep off	I'll give thee armour to keep off that word:
12.60; 3.3.64	**what**	that	**what**	**what**	what	what	Thou canst not speak of that thou dost not feel.
12.70; 3.3.77	**wilfulness**	simplenes	**wilfulness**	**wilfulness**	simpleness	wilfulness	What simpleness is this?
12.95; 3.3.101	**cryes... calles**	calls... cries	**cries... calls**	**cries... calls**	calls... cries	calls... cries	And Tybalt calls, and then on Romeo cries,

(cont.)

Table 3 (cont.)

NCS line ref	Q1	Q2	Pope	Theobald	Capell	Malone	NCS
12.111; 3.3.117	too, that liues in thee	that in thy life lies (lives F4, Rome)	too, that lives in thee	that in thy Life lives	that in thy life lives	too that lives in thee	And slay thy lady that in thy life lives,
14.16; 3.5.16	Then stay awhile, thou shalt not goe soone.	Therefore stay yet, thou needst not to be gone.	Then stay a while, thou shalt not go so soon.	Then stay a while, thou shalt not go so soon.	Therefore stay yet, thou need'st not to be gone.	Therefore stay yet, thou need'st not to be gone.	Therefore stay yet, thou need'st not to be gone.
14.17–18; 3.5.17–18	Let me stay here, let me be tane, and dye: / If thou wilt haue it so, I am content.	Let me be tane, let me be put to death, / I am content, so thou wilt haue it so.	Let me then stay, let me be ta'en and dye; / If thou wilt haue it so, I am content.	Let me be ta'en, let me be put to death, / I am content, if thou wilt haue it so.	Q2 subst.	Q2 subst.	Let me be tane, let me be put to death, / I am content, so thou wilt have it so.
14.21; 3.5.21–3	Ile say it is the Nightingale that beates / The vaultie heauen so high aboue our heads, / And not the Larke the Messenger of Morne.	Nor that is not the Larke whose noates do beate / The vaultie heauen (Heav'ns F3–4, Rome) so high aboue our heads, / I haue more care to stay then will to go:	as in Q1 (subst., except heav'ns)	as in Q2 (subst., except heav'ns)	as in Q2 (subst.)	as in Q2 (subst.)	Nor that is not the lark whose notes do beat / The vaulty heaven so high above our heads. / I have more care to stay than will to go:
14.25; 3.5.25	What sayes my Loue?	How ist my soule?	What says my love?	How is't, my Soul?	How is't, my soul?	How is't, my soul?	How is't, my soul?

Line							
14.51; 3.5.55	below	so lowe	below	below	so low	below	Methinks I see thee now, thou art so low,
14.71; 3.5.81	are	be	are	are	are	are	Villain and he be many miles asunder. —
14.73; 3.5.88	I soone would send to	Ile send to one in	I soon would send to	I'll send to one in	I'll send to one in	I'll send to one in	I'll send to one in Mantua
14.75; 3.5.91	should	shall	should	shall	shall	shall	That he shall soon keep Tybalt company;
14.79; 3.5.95	Thus	so	Thus	so	so	so	so for a kinsman vexed
14.76; 3.5.103	you	thou	you	thou	thou	thou	Find thou the means
14.81; 3.5.104	needful	needie	needful	needful	needful	needful	in such a needy time
14.94; 3.5.121	doo,	do, I sweare	do,	do,	do, I swear,	do, I swear,	I will not marry yet, and when I do, I swear
14.126; 3.5.165	sent	lent	sent	sent	lent	sent	That God had lent us but this only child,
14.176; 3.5.222	you	you are	you	you	you are	you are	I think you are happy in this second match,
15.18; 4.1.18	Welcome my loue,	Happily met	Welcome my love,	Welcome, my love,	Happily met,	Happily met,	Happily met,
15.23; 4.1.23	were to	I should	were to	were to	were to	were to	were to	To answer that, I should confess to you.

(cont.)

Table 3 (*cont.*)

NCS line ref	Q1	Q2	Pope	Theobald	Capell	Malone	NCS
15.43; 4.1.44	**Goe**	O	**Go**	**Go**	O,	O,	O shut the door,
15.55; 4.1.66	**Speake not, be briefe: for I desire**	Be not so long to speake, I long	**Speak not, be brief; for I desire**	Be not so long to speak; I long	Be not so long to speak; I long	Be not so long to speak; I long	Be not so long to speak, I long to die,
15.61; 4.1.72	**or**	of	**or**	of	of	of	Thou hast the strength of will to slay thyself,
15.67; 4.1.78	**yonder**	any	**yonder**	**yonder**	any	**yonder**	From off the battlements of any tower,
15.70; 4.1.81	**shut**	hide	**shut**	**shut**	hide	**shut**	Or hide me nightly in a charnel-house
15.73; 4.1.86	**named**	told	**nam'd**	**nam'd**	told	told	Things that to hear them told have made me tremble –
15.76–83; 4.1.89–97	*as in this edn (subst.)*	*as in NCS (subst.)*	*as in Q1 (subst., except for Q2's cold and drowsie humour where Q1 has dull and heauie slumber)*	*mostly based on Q2*	*based on Q2*	*mostly based on Q2*	*based on Q2*
15.80; 4.1.94	**distilled**	distilling	**distilled**	**distilled**	**distilled**	**distilled**	And this distilling liquor

15.82–3; 4.1.96	slumber, which shall seaze / vitall spirit: for no Pulse naturall	humour: for no pulse	**humour, which shall seize / Each vital spirit; for no pulse nat'ral**	**humour, which shall seize / Each vital spirit; for no Pulse nat'ral**	humour, which shall **seize / Each** vital spirit; for no pulse nat'ral	humour; for no pulse	**humour, which shall seize / Each vital spirit; for no pulse natural**	humour; for no pulse
1.84; 4.1.97	**naturall**	natiue			native	**natural**	no pulse / Shall keep his native progress
15.84; 4.1.97	**surcease to beate**	surcease	**surcease to beat**	**surcease to beat**	surcease	**surcease to beat**	pulse / Shall [. . .] surcease
16.14; 4.2.14	commeth from **Confession**	comes from shrift with merie looke	comes from her **confession**	comes from Shrift with merry Look	comes from shrift with merry look	comes from shrift with merry look	comes from shrift with merry look
16.20–1; 4.2.20	to fall prostrate here, / **And** craue	to fall prostrate here, / To beg	to fall prostrate here, / **And** beg	to fall prostrate here, / **And** beg	to fall prostrate here, / To beg	to fall prostrate here, / **And** beg	to fall prostrate here / To beg
17.5; 4.3.6	doo you need	need you	**do you need**	**do you need**	need you	**do you need**	need you my help?
17.13; 4.3.22	Must I of force be married to the Countie?	Shall I be married then to morrow morning?	**Shall I of force be marry'd to the Count.**	**Shall I of force be marry'd to the Count?**	Shall I be marry'd then to-morrow morning?	Must I of **force be married to the County?**	Shall I be married then tomorrow morning?
17.27; 4.3.58	*Romeo* I come, this doe I drinke to thee.	*Romeo, Romeo, Romeo,* heeres drinke; I drinke to thee.	*Romeo, I* come! this do I drink to thee.	*Romeo, I* come! this do I drink to thee.	*Romeo, I* come! this do I drink to thee.	*Romeo, I* come! this do I drink to thee.	Romeo, Romeo, Romeo! Here's drink – I drink to thee.

(*cont.*)

Table 3 *(cont.)*

NCS line ref	Q1	Q2	Pope	Theobald	Capell	Malone	NCS
17.66; 4.5.29	wan.	field.	field. /	field. /	field.	field. /	field.
	Accursed time, vnfortunate olde man.		Accursed time! unfortunate old man!	Accursed time! unfortunate old man!		Accursed time! unfortunate old man!	
17.71; 4.5.36	see, where	there	see, there	see, there	see, there	See, there	There she lies
17.129; 4.5.126	Pretie,	Prates,	Pretty!	Pretty!	Pratee.	Pretty!	Prates!
17.131; 4.5.129	Pretie too:	Prates to,	Pretty too!	Pretty too!	Pratee too.	Pretty too!	Prates too!
17.134; 4.5.132	because such Fellowes as you haue	Because Musitions haue	because such fellows as you have	because such fellows, as you, have	because such fellows as you have	because such fellows as you have	because musicians have
18.22; 5.1.27	Pardon me Sir, I will not leaue you thus,	I do beseech you sir, haue patience:	Pardon me, Sir, I dare not leave you thus.	Pardon me, Sir, I dare not leave you thus.	I do beseech you, sir, have patience:	Pardon me, sir, I will not leave you thus:	I do beseech you, sir, have patience:
18.29; 5.1.37	whom	which	whom	whom	whom	whom	an apothecary, / ... which late I noted
18.62; 5.1.84	thee into rites	thy selfe in right	thee into rites	thee into rite	thyself in rites	thyself in rites	get thyself in flesh my obsequies and true love's rite
20.17; 5.3.20							
20.33; 5.3.41	win my fauour	shew me friendshid (friendship Q3)	win my favour	shew me Friendship	shew me friendship	shew me friendship	So shalt thou show me friendship.
20.114; 5.3.163	drinke...leaue	drunke...left	drink...leave	drink...leave	drink...leave	drink...leave	O churl, drunk all, and left no friendly drop
20.135; 5.3.191	The	O the	The	The	The	The	O, the people in the street

Table 4 *Q1 readings first adopted by Capell and not accepted in modern editions*

	Q1	Q2	Capell	Malone	NCS
4.95; 1.5.17	**ah ha my Mistresses,**	Ah my mistresses (Ah me, mistresses F2–4)	**Ah ha, my mistresses!**	**Ah ha, my mistresses!**	Ah, my mistresses
4.175; 1.5.106	**yours**	thine	**yours**	**yours**	Thus from my lips, by thine, my sin is purged.
4.198; 1.5.131	**there**	here	**there**	**there**	What's he that follows here,
5.30; 2.1.30	**those**	these	**those**	**those**	he hath hid himself among these trees
5.37; 2.1.37	**Ah . . . ah**	O . . . ô	**Ah, . . . ah,**	**Ah, . . . ah,**	O . . . O
5.96; 2.2.58	**not yet**	yet not	**not yet**	**not yet**	My ears have yet not drunk a hundred words
5.107; 2.2.69	**let**	stop	**let**	**let**	thy kinsmen are no stop to me
5.113; 2.2.75	**sight**	eies	**sight**	**sight**	I have night's cloak to hide me from their eyes,
5.118; 2.2.80	**who**	that	**who**	**who**	By Love, that first did prompt me to enquire:
5.185; 2.2.168	**At**	By	**At**	**At**	By the hour of nine.
5.196; 2.2.178	**Who**	That	**Who**	**Who**	a wanton's bird / That lets it hop
5.206; 2.2.188	**fathers**	Friers close	**father's**	**father's**	Hence will I to my ghostly sire's (Friar's *Oxford*) close cell,
6.10; 2.3.16	**hearbes, plants,**	Plants, hearbes,	**herbs, plants,**	**herbs, plants,**	In plants, herbs, stones, and
7.5; 2.4.6	**of**	to	**of**	**of**	Tybalt, the kinsman to old Capulet
7.12; 2.4.14	**shot thorough**	runne through	**shot thorough**	**shot thorough**	run through the ear with a love-song
7.16; 2.4.18	**cattes I can tell you**	Cats	**cats, I can tell you**	**cats, I can tell you**	More than Prince of Cats
7.16; 2.4.18	**he is**	hees	**he is**	**he is**	O, he's the courageous captain

(cont.)

Table 4 (cont.)

	Q1	Q2	Capell	Malone	NCS
7.24; 2.4.25	fantasticoes	phantacies	fantasticoes	fantasticoes	such antic, lisping, affecting phantasimes
7.51; 2.4.53	Well said	Sure wit	Well said	Well said	Sure wit!
7.57; 2.4.59	thy	our	thy	thy	if our wits run the wild-goose chase
7.57; 2.4.59	haue	am	have	have	I am done
7.82–3; 2.4.83	Mer. A saile, a saile, a saile. / Ben. Two, two	Ro. [. . .] A sayle, a sayle. / Mer. Two two	MER. A sail, a sail, a sail! / BEN. Two, two	Mer. A sail, a sail, a sail! / Ben. Two, two	ROMEO [. . .] A sail, a sail! / MERCUTIO Two, two
7.104; 2.4.106	supper	some supper	supper	some supper	She will indite him to some supper.
7.132–3; 2.4.135	bad . . . bad	bid . . . bid	bad . . . bad	bade . . . bade	my young lady bid me enquire you out; what she bid me say
10.80; 3.1.104	kinsman	Cozen	kinsman	kinsman	Tybalt, that an hour / Hath been my cousin
12.88; 3.3.94	she not	not she	she not	she not	Doth not she think me an old murderer
14.143; 3.5.179	Princely	noble	princely	princely	A gentleman of noble parentage,
14.143; 3.5.180	trainde	liand	train'd	train'd	Of fair demesnes, youthful and nobly ligned, (lined Jopett)
14.145; 3.5.182	heart coulde	thought would	heart could	heart could	Proportioned as one's thought would wish a man,
15.45; 4.1.46	Ah	O	Ah	Ah	O Juliet,
16.23; 4.2.30	holy reuerent	reuerend holy	holy reverend	reverend holy	reverend holy Friar
17.105; 4.5.81	In all	And in	In all	In all	And in her best array
17.124; 4.5.121	griefe	griefes	grief	grief	'When griping griefs the heart doth wound,
17.135; 4.5.132	sildome	no	seldom	seldom	because musicians have no gold
20.3; 5.3.4	thine	thy	thine	thine	Holding thy ear
20.105; 5.3.271	in	to	in	in	what can he say to this?

Table 5 *Q1 readings first adopted by Malone and not accepted in modern editions*

	Q1	Q2	Malone	NCS
1.30; 1.1.28	two of	of	two of	comes of
1.73; 1.1.113	the Citties side	this Citie side	the city's side	this city side
1.131; 1.1.194	Ah	A	Ah	A word ill urged to one that is so ill:
5.97; 2.2.59	that tongues vtterance	thy tongus vttering	that tongue's utterance	My ears have yet not drunk a hundred words / Of thy tongue's uttering,
5.145; 2.2.107	sweare	vow	swear	Lady, by yonder blessed moon I vow,
5.183; 2.2.167	Madame	My neece (deere Q4–5, sweete F2; sweet F3; Sweet F4)	Madam	My niesse? (nyas Gibbons, Jowett, Oxford)
6.4; 2.3.4	Titans fierie wheeles	Titans burning wheeles	Titan's firy wheels	Titan's burning wheels
7.3; 2.4.4	Ah	Why	Ah	Why, that same pale hard-hearted wench
7.18–19; 2.4.20	rests me his minum rest	he rests, his minum rests, (he rests his minum F)	rests me his minim rest	he rests his minim rests
7.118; 2.4.121	Marry farewell. Pray	I pray you sir,	Marry, farewell! I pray you, sir	I pray you, sir,
12.48; 3.3.52	but speake a word	a little speake (speak F)	but speak a word	hear me a little speak
12.86; 3.3.92	sir. Wel death's	sir, deaths	sir! Well, death's	Ah, sir, as sir, death's the end of all.
14.38; 3.5.43	my Lord, my Loue, my Frend	loue, Lord, ay (ah F2–4) husband, friend	my love! my lord! my friend!	Art thou gone so, love, lord, ay husband, friend?
14.186; 3.5.227	I and from my soule	And from my soule too,	Ay, and from my soul;	And from my soul too,
17.13; 4.3.22	Must I of force be married to the Countie?	Shall I be married then to morrow morning?	Must I of force be married to the County?	Shall I be married then tomorrow morning?
18.1; 5.1.1	flattering Eye	flattering truth	flattering eye	the flattering truth of sleep
18.19; 5.1.24	defie my	denie you	defy my	then I defy you, stars!
20.43; 5.3.69	doe attach	apprehend	do attach	apprehend thee for a felon here
20.47; 5.3.62	Heape	Put	Heap	Put not another sin upon my head,
20.142; 5.3.209	more early downe	now earling (now early Q3) downe	more early down	thy son and heir now early down

Table 6 *Q1 readings first adopted by eighteenth-century editors other than Pope, Capell, or Malone and not accepted in modern editions*

Rowe

	Q1	Q2	Rowe	Pope	Theobald	Capell	Malone	NCS
5.86; 2.2.48	that	thy	that	that	thy	that	that	And for thy name
13.7; 3.4.8	time to	times to	time to	time to	time to	time to	time to	These times of woe afford no times to woo

Theobald

	Q1	Q2	Pope	Theobald	Capell	Malone	NCS
14.114; 3.5.149	**chop logicke**	chopt lodgick	*line omitted*	**Chop Logick**	chop logick	**chop logick**	chopt-logic

Hanmer

	Q1	Q2	Hanmer	Capell	Malone	NCS
12.15; 3.3.15	**Hence**	**Hence**	**Hence**	Here	**Hence**	Here from Verona art thou banished.

Warburton

	Q1	Q2	Warburton	Capell	Malone	NCS
1.27; 1.1.22	**the**	their	**the**	their	their	the heads of the maids, or their maidenheads

Steevens

Reference	Q1	Q2	as in Q1 (subst.)	as in Q2 (subst.)	NCS
2.25; 1.2.32	Such amongst view of many myne being one,	Which one more view, of many, mine being one,			Which on more view of many, mine, being one,
5.178; 2.2.163	*Romeos* name	*Romeo*	Romeo's name	Romeo's name	With repetition of my Romeo's name
7.55; 2.4.57	wits faile	wits faints (wits faint Q5; wit faints F2–4)	wits fail	wits fail	my wits faints
7.157; 2.4.181	*Peter*, take my fanne, and goe before.	Before and apace.	*Peter*, Take my fan, and go before.	*Peter*, Take my fan, and go before.	Before and apace.
12.107; 3.3.113	Or	And	Or	Or	And ill-beseeming beast
14.74; 3.5.90	That should bestow on him so sure a draught,	Shall giue him such an vnaccustomd dram,	That shall bestow on him so sure a draught,	That shall bestow on him so sure a draught,	Shall give him such an unaccustomed dram
16.24; 4.2.31	vnto	to him	unto	to him	is much bound to him
17.19; 4.3.29	Man: / I will not entertaine so bad a thought.	man.	man: / I will not entertain so bad a thought.	man: / I will not entertain so bad a thought.	man.
18.22; 5.1.27	Pardon me Sir, I will not leaue you thus,	I do beseech you sir, haue patience:	Pardon me, sir, I will not leave you thus:	Pardon me, sir, I will not leave you thus:	I do beseech you, sir, have patience:
18.53; 5.1.71	Vpon thy backe hangs ragged Miserie,	Contempt and beggerie hangs ypon thy backe:	Upon thy back hangs ragged misery,	Upon thy back hangs ragged misery,	Contempt and beggary hangs upon thy back;

Steevens (1778)

Reference	Q1	Q2	Steevens (1778)	Malone	NCS
17.70; 4.5.36	bride	wife	bride	bride	Hath Death lain with thy wife.

Steevens (1793)

Reference	Q1	Q2	Steevens (1793)	Malone	NCS
5.121; 2.2.83	furthest	farthest	furthest	farthest	As that vast shore washed with the farthest sea,

READING LIST

Dessen, Alan C., 'Q1 *Romeo and Juliet* and Elizabethan theatrical vocabulary', in *Shakespeare's 'Romeo and Juliet': Texts, Contexts, and Interpretation*, ed. Jay L. Halio, Newark, 1995, pp. 107–22.

Erne, Lukas, *Shakespeare as Literary Dramatist*, Cambridge, 2003.

Farley-Hills, David, 'The "bad" quarto of *Romeo and Juliet*', *S.Sur.* 49 (1996), 27–44.

Goldberg, Jonathan, '"What? in a names that which we call a rose": the desired texts of *Romeo and Juliet*', in *Crisis in Editing: Texts of the English Renaissance*, ed. Randall McLeod, New York, 1994, pp. 173–202.

Gurr, Andrew, 'Maximal and minimal texts: Shakespeare v. the Globe', *S.Sur.* 52 (1999), 68–87.

Halio, Jay L., 'Handy-dandy: Q1/Q2 *Romeo and Juliet*', in *Shakespeare's 'Romeo and Juliet': Texts, Contexts, and Interpretation*, ed. Jay L. Halio, Newark, 1995, pp. 125–50.

Hoppe, Harry R., *The Bad Quarto of 'Romeo and Juliet': A Bibliographical and Textual Study*, Ithaca, NY, 1948.

Hosley, Richard, 'The use of the upper stage in *Romeo and Juliet*', *SQ* 5 (1954), 371–9.

Irace, Kathleen O., *Reforming the 'Bad' Quartos: Performance and Provenance of Six Shakespearean First Editions*, Newark, NJ, 1994.

Jowett, John, 'Henry Chettle and the first quarto of *Romeo and Juliet*', *PBSA* 92 (1998), 53–74.

Levenson, Jill L. and Barry Gaines, eds., *Romeo and Juliet, 1597*, Malone Society Reprints, Oxford, 2000.

Maguire, Laurie E., *Shakespearean Suspect Texts: The 'Bad' Quartos and Their Contexts*, Cambridge, 1996.

Melchiori, Giorgio, 'The music of words: from madrigal to drama and beyond: Shakespeare foreshadowing an operatic technique', in *Italian Culture in Early Modern English Drama: Rewriting, Remaking, Refashioning*, ed. Michele Marrapodi, Aldershot, 2007, forthcoming.

Thomson, Leslie, '"With patient ears attend": *Romeo and Juliet* on the Elizabethan stage', *Studies in Philology* 92 (1995), 230–47.

Urkowitz, Steven, 'Two versions of *Romeo and Juliet* 2.6 and *Merry Wives of Windsor* 5.5.215–45: an invitation to the pleasures of textual/sexual di(per)versity', in *Elizabethan Theater: Essays in Honor of S. Schoenbaum*, ed. R. B. Parker and S. P. Zitner, Newark, 1996, 222–38.

Werstine, Paul, 'A century of "bad" Shakespeare quartos', *SQ* 50 (1999), 310–33.
  'Narratives about printed Shakespeare texts: "foul papers" and "bad" quartos', *SQ* 41 (1990), 65–86.

Printed in Great Britain
by Amazon.co.uk, Ltd.,
Marston Gate.